Retirement Heist

ELLEN E. SCHULTZ

Retirement Heist

**HOW COMPANIES
PLUNDER AND PROFIT
FROM THE NEST EGGS
OF AMERICAN WORKERS**

PORTFOLIO / PENGUIN

PORTFOLIO / PENGUIN
Published by the Penguin Group
Penguin Group (USA) Inc., 375 Hudson Street,
New York, New York 10014, U.S.A.
Penguin Group (Canada), 90 Eglinton Avenue East, Suite 700, Toronto,
Ontario, Canada M4P 2Y3 (a division of Pearson Penguin Canada Inc.)
Penguin Books Ltd, 80 Strand, London WC2R 0RL, England
Penguin Ireland, 25 St. Stephen's Green, Dublin 2, Ireland
(a division of Penguin Books Ltd)
Penguin Books Australia Ltd, 250 Camberwell Road, Camberwell,
Victoria 3124, Australia (a division of Pearson Australia Group Pty Ltd)
Penguin Books India Pvt Ltd, 11 Community Centre,
Panchsheel Park, New Delhi—110 017, India
Penguin Group (NZ), 67 Apollo Drive, Rosedale, Auckland 0632,
New Zealand (a division of Pearson New Zealand Ltd)
Penguin Books (South Africa) (Pty) Ltd, 24 Sturdee Avenue,
Rosebank, Johannesburg 2196, South Africa

Penguin Books Ltd, Registered Offices: 80 Strand, London WC2R 0RL, England

First published in 2011 by Portfolio / Penguin, a member of Penguin Group (USA) Inc.

10 9 8 7 6 5 4 3 2 1

LIBRARY OF CONGRESS CATALOGING-IN-PUBLICATION DATA
Schultz, Ellen.
Retirement heist : how companies plunder and profit from the nest eggs
of American workers / Ellen E. Schultz.
p. cm.
Includes bibliographical references and index.
ISBN 978-1-59184-333-7 (hardback)
1. Pensions—United States. 2. Corporations—Moral and ethical aspects—
United States. 3. Life insurance policies—United States. I. Title.
HD7125.S38 2011
331.25'20973—dc22
2011015064

Printed in the United States of America
Set in Granjon LT Std
Designed by BTD / NYC

CONTENTS

Retirement Heist

Introduction

I N DECEMBER 2010, General Electric held its Annual Outlook Investor Meeting at Rockefeller Center in New York City. At the meeting, chief executive Jeffrey Immelt stood on the *Saturday Night Live* stage and gave the gathered analysts and shareholders a rundown on the global conglomerate's health. But in contrast to the iconic comedy show that is filmed at Rock Center each week, Immelt's tone was solemn. Like many other CEOs at large companies, Immelt pointed out that his firm's pension plan was an ongoing problem. The "pension has been a drag for a decade," he said, and it would cause the company to lose thirteen cents per share the next year. Regretfully, to rein in costs, GE was going to close the pension plan to new employees.

The audience had every reason to believe him. An escalating chorus of bloggers, pundits, talk show hosts, and media stories bemoan the burgeoning pension-and-retirement crisis in America, and GE was just the latest of hundreds of companies, from IBM to Verizon, that have slashed pensions and medical benefits for millions of American retirees. To justify these cuts, companies complain that they're victims of a "perfect storm" of uncontrollable economic forces—an aging workforce, entitled retirees, a stock market debacle, and an outmoded pension system that cripples their chances of competing against pensionless competitors and companies overseas.

What Immelt didn't mention was that, far from being a burden, GE's pension and retiree plans had contributed billions of dollars to the company's bottom line over the past decade and a half, and were responsible for a chunk of the earnings that the executives had taken credit for. Nor were these retirement programs—even with GE's 230,000 retirees—bleeding the company of cash. In fact, GE hadn't contributed a cent to the workers' pension plans since 1987 but still had enough money to cover all the current and future retirees.

And yet, despite all this, Immelt's assessment wasn't entirely inaccurate. The company did indeed have another pension plan that really was a burden: the one for GE executives. And unlike the pension plans for a quarter of a million workers and retirees, the executive pensions, with a $4.4 billion obligation, have always been a drag on earnings and have always drained cash from company coffers: more than $573 million over the past three years alone.

So a question remains: With its fully funded pension plan, why was GE closing its pensions?

That is one of the questions this book seeks to answer. *Retirement Heist* explains what really happened to GE's pensions as well as to the retirement benefits of millions of Americans at thousands of companies. No one disputes that there's a retirement crisis, but the crisis was no demographic accident. It was manufactured by an alliance of two groups: top executives and their facilitators in the retirement industry—benefits consultants, insurance companies, and banks—all of whom played a huge and hidden role in the death spiral of American pensions and benefits.

Yet, unlike the banking industry, which was rightly blamed for the subprime mortgage crisis, the masterminds responsible for the retirement crisis have walked away blame-free. And, unlike the pension raiders of the 1980s, who killed pensions to extract the surplus assets, they face no censure. If anything they are viewed as beleaguered captains valiantly trying to keep their overloaded ships from being sunk in a perfect storm. In reality, they're the silent pirates who looted the ships and left them to sink, along with the retirees, as they sailed away safely in their lifeboats.

The roots of this crisis took hold two decades ago, when corporate pension plans, by and large, were well funded, thanks in large part to rules enacted in the 1970s that required employers to fund the plans adequately and laws adopted in the 1980s that made it tougher for companies to raid the plans or use the assets for their own benefit. Thanks to these rules, and to the long-running bull market that pumped up assets, by the end of the 1990s pension plans at many large companies had such massive surpluses that the companies could have fully paid their current and future retirees' pensions, even if all of them lived to be ninety-nine and the companies never contributed another dime.

But despite the rules protecting pension funds, U.S. companies siphoned billions of dollars in assets from their pension plans. Many, like Verizon, used the assets to finance downsizings, offering departing employees additional pension payouts in lieu of cash severance. Others, like GE, sold pension surpluses in restructuring deals, indirectly converting pension assets into cash.

To replenish the surplus assets in their pension piggy banks, companies cut benefits. Initially, employees didn't question why companies with multi-billion-dollar pension surpluses were cutting pensions that weren't costing them anything, because no one noticed their pensions were being cut. Employers used actuarial sleight of hand to disguise the cuts, typically by changing the traditional pensions to seemingly simple account-style plans.

Cutting benefits provided a secondary windfall: It boosted earnings, thanks to new accounting rules that required employers to put their pension obligations on their books. Cutting pensions reduced the obligations, which generated gains that are added to income. These accounting rules are the Rosetta Stone that explains why companies with massively overfunded pension plans went on a pension-cutting spree and began slashing retiree health benefits even when their costs were falling. By giving companies an incentive to reduce the liability on their books, the accounting rules turned retiree benefits plans into cookie jars of potential earnings enhancements and provided employers with the means to convert the trillion dollars in pensions and retiree benefits into an immediate, dollar-for-dollar benefit for the company.

With perfectly legal loopholes that enabled companies to tap pension plans like piggy banks, and accounting rules that rewarded employers for cutting benefits, retiree benefits plans soon morphed into profit centers, and populations of retirees essentially became portfolios of assets and debts, which passed from company to company in swirls of mergers, spin-offs, and acquisitions. And with each of these restructuring deals, the subsequent owner aimed to squeeze a profit from the portfolio, always at the expense of the retirees.

The flexibility in the accounting rules, which gave employers enormous latitude to raise or lower their obligations by billions of dollars, also turned retiree plans into handy earnings-management tools.

Unfortunately for employees and retirees, these newfound tricks coincided with the trend of tying executive pay to performance. Thus, deliberately or not, the executives who green-lighted massive retiree cuts were indirectly boosting their own pay.

As their pay grew, managers and officers began diverting growing amounts into deferred-compensation plans, which are unfunded and therefore create a liability. Meanwhile, their supplemental executive pensions, which are based on pay, ballooned along with their compensation. Today, it's common for a large company to owe its executives several *billion* dollars in pensions and deferred compensation.

These growing "executive legacy liabilities" are included in the pension obligations employers report to shareholders, and account for many of the "growing pension costs" companies are complaining about. Analysts, shareholders, and others don't understand that executive obligations are no different from pension obligations for rank-and-file workers and retirees—they are governed by the same accounting rules, and they represent IOUs that a company has on its books. In some ways, executive liabilities are like public pensions: large, growing, and under-funded (or, as in the case of the executives, unfunded).

Unlike regular pensions, the growing executive liabilities are largely hidden, buried within the figures for regular pensions. So even as employers bemoaned their pension burdens, the executive pensions and deferred comp were becoming in some companies a bigger drag on profits.

To offset the impact of their growing executive liabilities on profits, many companies take out billions of dollars of life insurance on their employees, using the policies as informal executive pension funds and collecting death benefits when workers, former employees, and retirees die.

With the help of well-connected Washington lobbyists and leading law firms, over the past two decades employers have steadily used legislation and the courts to undermine protections under federal law, making it almost impossible for employees and retirees to challenge their employers' maneuvers. With no punitive damages under pension law, employers face little risk when they unilaterally slash benefits, even when promised in writing, since they can pay their lawyers with pension assets and drag out the cases until the retirees give up or die.

As employers curtail traditional pensions, employees are increasingly relying on 401(k) plans, which have already proven to be a failure. Employees save too little, too late, spend the money before retiring, and can see their savings erased when the market nosedives.

But 401(k)s have other features that ensure that the plans, as they exist, will never benefit the majority of employees. The plans are supposed to provide a level playing field, the do-it-yourself retirement vehicle so perfect for an "ownership" society. But the game has been rigged from the beginning. Many companies use these plans as part of a strategy to borrow money cheaply, or in schemes to siphon assets from pension funds.

And just as the new accounting rules led to such mischief, so too did new anti-discrimination rules. Implemented in the 1990s, the rules were intended to ensure that employers didn't use taxpayer-subsidized 401(k) plans for the favored few, but would make them available to a broad swath of workers. But thanks to the creativity of benefits consultants, employers have used the discrimination rules to shut millions of low-paid employees out of their plans and to provide them with less generous benefits, while enacting other restrictions that make the plans more valuable to managers and executives, at the expense of everyone else.

Today, pension plans are collectively underfunded, hundreds are frozen, and retiree health benefits are an endangered species. And as executive pay and executive pensions spiral, these executive liabilities are slowly replacing pension obligations on many corporate balance sheets.

Meanwhile, the same crowd that created this mess—employers, consultants, and financial firms—are now the primary architects of the "reforms" that will supposedly clean it up. Under the guise of improving retirement security, their "solutions" will enable employers to continue to manipulate retirement plans to generate profit and enrich executives at the expense of employees and retirees. Shareholders pay a price, too.

Their tactics haven't served as case studies at Harvard Business School, and aren't mentioned in the copious surveys and studies consultants produce for a gullible public. But the masterminds of this heist should take a bow: They managed to take hundreds of billions of dollars in retirement benefits that were intended for millions of workers and divert them to corporate coffers, shareholders, and their own pockets. And they're still at it. It might not be possible to resuscitate pension plans, but it isn't too late to expose the machinations of the retirement industry, which has its tentacles into every type of retirement benefit: profit-sharing plans, 401(k)s, employee stock ownership plans (ESOPs), and plans for public employees, nonprofits, small businesses, and even churches. The retirement industry has exported its tactics, using them to achieve similar outcomes in retirement plans in Canada, Europe, Australia, and elsewhere, and has big plans for Social Security and its overseas equivalents as well. Unless it is reined in, the global retirement industry will continue to capture retirement wealth earned by many to enrich a relative few.

CHAPTER 1

Siphon: HOW COMPANIES PLUNDER THE PENSION PIGGY BANKS

I N NOVEMBER 1999, a group of the nation's leading pension experts met at the Labor Department in Washington to discuss a $250 billion problem. After eight years of double-digit returns, the pension plans at American corporations had more than a quarter of a trillion dollars in excess assets. Not a shortage of assets—excess assets. At some companies, the surpluses had reached almost laughable levels: $25 billion at GE, $24 billion at Verizon, $20 billion at AT&T, $7 billion at IBM.

One might expect that such lush asset balances would be something to celebrate.

Pension assets had been building for years, the result of downsizings, a robust stock market, laws enacted in 1974 that required employers to adequately fund pensions, and a 1990 law that made it harder for them to raid the surplus by terminating their pensions.

Thanks to this, many employers hadn't contributed a cent to their plans since the 1980s, yet they still had enough money to cover the pensions of all current and future retirees even if they lived to be one hundred. With so much money, the plans would cost the companies nothing for years to come.

But employers weren't celebrating. The money was burning a hole in their pockets. In theory, surplus pension assets are supposed to remain in the pension plans, to provide cushion for the inevitable times when investment returns are weak and interest rates fall. But employers felt that requiring companies to use pension money only to pay pensions made no sense.

"Rigid and irrational legal restrictions trap these surplus assets in the pension plans and prevent them from being used productively," maintained Mark Ugoretz, the head of ERIC, a group that lobbies for employers on benefits matters.

Complaining that the pension assets were "locked up," employers had asked the ERISA Advisory Council to study the issue. Employers had good reason to believe that the council would recommend changes they wanted. The council consists of fifteen members, appointed by the secretary of labor, to advise the department on benefits matters.

The revolving cast includes representatives from think tanks, academia, unions, and pension administrators. But the council has often been dominated by corporate representatives, who influence the choice of topics and suggest which expert witnesses should testify. Nine of the fifteen appointed members of the council at the time were representatives of employers and financial firms, and many of the experts they invited to testify not surprisingly shared employers' views.

At the 1999 hearings, executives from DuPont, Northrop Grumman, and Marathon Oil strongly advocated allowing employers to withdraw pension money to pay for their retiree health benefits. This would not only be good for retirees, they said, but good for retirement security overall.

John Vine, a lawyer from Covington & Burling, a Washington law firm that had advised clients on myriad methods to monetize their pension surplus, discussed ways employers could extract the assets in mergers or use them to pay severance costs or even to "provide enhanced pension benefits to a subclass of the plan's current participants" (e.g., the employer's executives).

Michael J. Harrison, human resources vice president at Lucent

Technologies, the giant AT&T spin-off, liked the idea of using surplus assets to pay executive benefits. (The language was less blunt; he and others advised using surplus assets to pay for pension benefits "in excess of qualified plan limits (such as 415 and 401[a][17] limits).")

Like other witnesses, he maintained that allowing employers to drain the surplus assets from pension plans would actually enhance retirement security. "We believe making excess pension assets more freely available for other constructive purposes would encourage more companies to voluntarily sponsor defined benefit pension plans and encourage companies to enhance participants' security by funding these plans at a higher level," he testified.

DuPont's chief actuary, Ken Porter, minced no words regarding on whose behalf the company managed the pension plans: "As a publicly traded company, DuPont has a fiduciary responsibility to its owners. We have been entrusted with the owners' assets with the expectation that we will allocate our resources efficiently and appropriately to provide for all of our corporate obligations," he said.

A witness from the AFL-CIO had the temerity to suggest that employers use the surplus to increase benefits or provide cost-of-living increases for retirees. Porter dismissed this notion, saying that using the surplus to pay benefits would dilute reported earnings. "Accordingly, business competitiveness issues, not pension asset values, dictate when and whether benefits levels are changed."

Ron Gebhardtsbauer, senior pension fellow of the American Academy of Actuaries, echoed this trickle-down concept, testifying that if employers could use pension assets for their own benefit, it would actually help the employees and retirees. "Strengthening employer solvency can create more security for the pension plan . . . surplus assets could be helpful to strengthen a company at an important time . . . the best insurance is a strong employer."

The experts who testified also included consultants from Watson Wyatt Worldwide and Mercer, two of the largest global benefits-consulting firms, which for years had helped large employers use all these strategies to tap their pension plans like piggy banks. They felt that these were all great ideas, as did the chairman of the working group, Michael J. Gulotta. As chief of AT&T's actuarial consulting unit, he had helped the company and many others convert billions of dollars in its pension assets into company assets. They all had much to gain by helping employers further unlock the riches in their pension assets, and they already had plenty of experience doing so.

Not surprisingly, their final report concluded that "for the good of America," the government ought to loosen the withdrawal rules. The irony is that all these employers, and many others, had already been quietly siphoning billions from their pension plans for years. They were merely seeking "reforms" that would open the spigots even further.

The arguments sounded plausible: Pension plans already had too much money and would only become even more overstuffed. After all, the stock market, like real estate, would only go up: The economy was buzzing, the government had a massive budget surplus, and interest rates were low.

One of the few dissenting voices was David Certner's. AARP's legislative affairs watchdog, Certner was adamant that pension assets be used for no purpose other than providing pension benefits. "The funds are put into the pension trust for the exclusive benefit of the participants," he said at one of the council's meetings.

Allowing employers to use the money for anything else would put the plans at risk, Certner warned, because employers would be tempted to skim off excess funds in good times and then face shortfalls when the markets declined. He warned that the recent bull market would end and that changes in the economy, interest rates, or market returns could quickly erase the surplus, putting individuals at risk. If the plans failed, participants could see a big chunk of their benefits wiped out.

If his warnings sound familiar, it's because every single one of Certner's predictions came true. But nobody was listening. And nothing has changed. These are the strategies employers were using—and have continued to use—to drain their pensions.

PARTING GIFTS

One common use of pension assets has been to finance restructurings. In 1994, Bell Atlantic, formed after the breakup of the Baby Bells in the early 1980s, was transforming not only its technology but also its workforce. In 1994, it had 100,000 employees, many of whom had been on the job for decades. This was exactly the cohort that many industries, including the fast-changing telecom sector, were eager to whittle down. Workers were in their peak earnings years, and the value of their pensions, which was based on tenure, was about to spike. Severance is typically paid for with cash, so shedding this large cohort would be costly.

Fortuitously, Bell Atlantic had a lushly overfunded pension plan and, like many companies, it offered to sweeten the pensions of those it was letting go. Over the next six years the company used $3 billion in pension assets to finance early-retirement incentives for 25,000 managers. Using pension surplus not only saved the company cash but saved payroll taxes, because, unlike severance pay, money paid from a pension in lieu of severance isn't subject to the 7.65 percent Social Security (FICA) taxes.

Pension law doesn't allow companies to use pension assets to pay severance, so companies characterized the payments as "termination benefits," "shutdown benefits," or "additional pension credits" that might provide people additional years of service or the equivalent of, say, an additional year of an employee's pay.

Bell Atlantic merged with GTE (formerly known as General Telephone & Electronics Corp.) in 2000 and changed its name to Verizon Communications, but the pension withdrawals continued. Over the next five years, Verizon continued to pay for retirement incentives using pension assets, even though the surplus, which had peaked at $24 billion in 2000, had shrunk to only $1.7 billion by the beginning of 2005, thanks to market losses and company withdrawals.

Verizon then had to make a critical decision: It could stop withdrawing assets to finance layoffs, and let the pension plan rebuild its cushion of assets to provide employees and retirees with greater retirement security. Or it could cut pensions, which would lop off some of the liability, making the plan better funded.

The company chose the latter strategy, and froze the pensions of its fifty thousand management employees. The move eliminated $3 billion in liabilities from the books and replenished the surplus. Of course, Verizon didn't describe the transaction that way. "This restructuring reflects the realities of our changing world," Verizon chairman and CEO Ivan Seidenberg said in a statement announcing the change. "Companies today, including many we compete with, are not adopting defined benefit pension plans." Verizon subsequently withdrew $5 billion from the surplus, and the 2008 market crisis wiped out the rest. By early 2011, the plan had a deficit of $3.4 billion.

Seidenberg wasn't affected by the pension freeze. His supplemental executive pensions and deferred-compensation plans had grown to $96 million by the beginning of 2011.

In the 1990s, dozens of companies, including utilities, defense contractors, and manufacturers, began relying on their pension funds to finance restructuring. Unfortunately, the companies with the biggest incentive to do this were companies in a downward financial spiral. Delta and United, struggling in the travel slump after the September 11 terrorist attacks, each used roughly half a billion dollars to fund buyouts and pay termination benefits to employees they laid off. Each subsequently declared bankruptcy, and the pension plans they handed over to the Pension Benefit Guaranty Corp. (PBGC), the federal pension insurer, were so underfunded that employees lost billions in pensions they were entitled to.

The Big Three automakers took this route, too. General Motors, the poster child for chronic underfunding, used $2.9 billion in pension assets to pay for lump-sum severance benefits in 2008. In 2007, Ford Motor Co. used $2.4 billion, a move that left it with no cushion when the market cratered in 2008. By 2011, the pension had a $6.7 billion shortfall. Delphi, the eternally troubled auto parts spin-off of GM, entered bankruptcy in 2005, yet the following year used $1.9 billion in pension assets to pay for its "special attrition program," which is what it called its buyout program. The pension never recovered, and Delphi dumped the plans for seventy thousand workers and retirees on the PBGC in 2009. Delphi employees were devastated. Mark Zellers, a Delphi retiree in Columbus, Ohio, lost a third of his pension and took a $9-per-hour job at Home Depot to help make up for the difference and pay for his health care, which was also eliminated in the bankruptcy.

ROBBING PETER TO PAY PAUL

Companies giving their workforces makeovers tapped the pension plans to pay for another essential benefit: retiree health benefits. These health plans continue a retiree's health coverage until age sixty-five, when Medicare kicks in. Employers don't usually fund the plans, instead paying the cost of the coverage each year, the same pay-as-you-go arrangement used for medical plans for current employees. Thus, pulling cash from pension plans to pay for these costs enables companies to avoid using cash to pay the benefits. Over the past two decades, companies have also siphoned billions of dollars from their pension plans to pay for retiree health benefits.

DuPont pioneered the practice. It dipped into its pension assets on more than seven different occasions during the 1990s, drawing out $1.7 billion to pay for retiree health benefits. It also used "a significant amount" of surplus pension assets to finance a number of voluntary retirement programs. The market decline in the early 2000s erased what was left of the pension surplus. DuPont froze its pension starting in 2007, but that wasn't enough to restore it to health, and by early 2011 the plan was $5.5 billion in the hole.

Employers had lobbied aggressively for the right to use pension assets for retiree medical benefits, which are called "420 transfers," after the section of the tax code they fall under. They argued that if a plan had a surplus, why not use it to benefit the retirees? Congress agreed in 1990, but included some limits. To protect the pension plan, employers could withdraw the assets only if the plan had a surplus. But that didn't stop employers from pulling money from their deteriorating pension plans anyway. Despite the market decline between 2000 and 2002, Allegheny Technologies, Qwest, and U.S. Steel continued to transfer millions of dollars from their pension plans to pay for retiree health benefits, moves that contributed to their subsequent deficits.

The practice continues. Prudential Financial transferred $1 billion from its pension plan in 2007 to pay for several years' worth of retiree health benefits, and Florida Power & Light transferred more than $180 million from its pension plan between 2005 and 2010. Their pension plans remain well funded, but so, initially, did the pensions of the companies above.

SELLING SURPLUS ASSETS

Mergers, acquisitions, and spin-offs have also enabled companies to convert their surplus pension assets into cash. The strategy might be as simple as merging an underfunded pension plan with an overfunded one. But there are were less obvious ways to monetize the assets.

One strategy involves selling a unit to another company, then handing over more pension money than is needed to pay the benefits of the transferred workers and retirees, in exchange for a higher sale price. General Electric is a master of the practice. In 1993 it sold an aerospace unit to fellow defense contractor Martin Marietta. In the deal, it transferred thirty thousand employees and $1.2 billion in pension assets to Martin Marietta to cover the liabilities for their pensions. That was $531 million more than was needed to fulfill the pension obligations. By getting a better price for the unit because it came with the surplus, GE effectively got to put half a billion dollars from its pension plan into its pocket.

GE did dozens of such deals over the years, monetizing billions of dollars of pension assets. Thanks to this and other practices, the $24 billion in surplus in its plan in 1999 evaporated in the following years, and at the beginning of 2011 the plan was short $6 billion.

The Defense Department wasn't asleep at the wheel during these deals. It sued GE to recover the surplus, because when the government provides money in its contracts to fund pension and retiree medical benefits, the company is supposed to return the money if it is not subsequently used for benefits. The money isn't supposed to vanish into company coffers.

Contractors get around this by restructuring. If a contractor closes a segment, it has to hand the pension surplus to the government; but if the contractor sells the unit, it can turn the pension over to the acquirer and get some cash for the surplus out of the deal. The new owner can then close the segment, which is what Martin Marietta did to the GE unit it acquired. Government lawyers consider these to be sham transactions intended to help the contractor raid the pension, and the legal tugs-of-war between defense contractors and the government over the scalping of retiree assets have kept a generation of Justice Department lawyers busy for years.

GE countersued the U.S. government in the U.S. Court of Federal Claims in Washington,* saying not only was it entitled to keep the entire surplus, but the government actually owed GE hundreds of millions of dollars. The company's reasoning? Because GE transferred so much pension money to Martin Marietta, the pensions of the aerospace

---

* This court handles disputes between contractors and the government.

workers it didn't transfer were now less well funded. GE wanted the government to pony up the shortfall. This was just one of roughly twenty lawsuits between GE and the federal government regarding retiree assets that have slogged through the courts in the past two decades.

There's no way to know how many billions of dollars in pension assets vanished into the coffers of dealmakers in the frenzy of acquisitions, mergers, spin-offs, and the like, because the details are concealed in non-public-disclosure documents.

Generally, lawsuits are the only way these transactions are flushed into the open. Employees have sued when they learned that the surplus in their pension plans was being used to top up the pension of a newly acquired company, or for some other corporate purpose. But the courts have essentially green-lighted these indirect pension raids.*

Companies keep these arrangements out of the limelight because employers are fiduciaries, meaning they're supposed to manage the plans solely for the benefit of participants and beneficiaries. Actuaries and lawyers discussed this dilemma at a session on "Consulting in Mergers & Acquisitions" at a professional conference in 1996. Their solution? Don't put it in writing. "The parties need to cut a purchase price and that's it," said a partner with the New York corporate law firm Sullivan & Cromwell. "That way nobody can pinpoint what portion of the purchase price, if any, was attributable to the pension surplus."

A principal at Mercer, the human resources and benefits consulting firm, explained that some of the companies he worked with "believe

---

* The question of who owns the surplus assets has provoked numerous lawsuits, but the cases have by and large been resolved in employers' favor. One of the most significant was *Hughes Aircraft Co.* v. *Jacobson* (1999), in which the Supreme Court ruled that employers can use surplus assets even if employees contributed to the plan.

that none of this should be documented, so they don't leave a nice paper trail. You need to decide what situation you find yourself in." The panelists noted that buyers typically pay fifty to eighty cents on the dollar for surplus assets.

PENSION PARACHUTES

Conveniently, when key managers lose their jobs in connection with mergers, spin-offs, and other restructurings, the pension plan can help finance their departure payments. These arrangements also remain off the radar screen of regulators, employees, and the IRS. In 1999, Royal & Sun Alliance, a global London-based insurer, closed a Midwest division and laid off all 228 of its employees. Just before the shutdown, the insurer, commonly known as RSA, amended the division's employee pension plan to award larger benefits to eight departing officers and directors. One human resources executive, for example, got an additional $5,270 a month for life, paid out in a lump sum of $792,963.

Fruehauf Trailer Corp. used a trickier maneuver to deliver departure bonuses to its human resources executives. The truck manufacturer was going over a cliff in 1996, and about three weeks before it filed for bankruptcy protection, the company transferred $2.4 million in surplus assets from the union side of Fruehauf's pension plan into the frozen plan for salaried employees. It then awarded large pension increases to a select few. The most substantial increases went to members of the Pension Administration Committee, including a 200 percent increase to the vice president of human resources and a 470 percent increase to the controller.*

---

* Creditors challenged the payments in bankruptcy court, which halted the payouts to the executives. The case dragged on for years, and in 2005 the bankruptcy court ruled that the pension payments "constituted a fraudulent transfer," and said the pension money should have gone to pay the creditors.

AT&T used pension assets in a variety of ways. In 1997, AT&T offered 15,300 older managers the equivalent of a half-year's pay, in the form of a cash payout from the pension plan as severance if they voluntarily agreed to retire. The move consumed $2 billion in pension assets.

Michael J. Gulotta, who led the ERISA Advisory Council task force as it explored ways to use pension assets, was also the president of Actuarial Sciences Associates, AT&T's benefits consulting subsidiary. In 1998, he helped the company change its traditional pension to a "cash balance" pension (more on these later), which saved the company $2.2 billion by cutting the benefits of more than 46,000 long-tenured employees in their forties and fifties. Many would see their pensions frozen for the rest of their careers.

Employers can use pension assets to pay the actuaries, lawyers, financial managers, and trustees who provide services related to the management of the pension plans, and uncounted millions have gone to pay the actuaries who craft ways to cut benefits and to lawyers who defend suits brought by pension plan participants. For its consulting and administrative services in connection with the cash balance conversion, AT&T paid ASA $8 million from the trust assets of the AT&T Management Pension Plan.

ASA set up a separate cash-balance plan for itself, using assets from the AT&T Management Pension Plan, which provided ASA managers with 200 percent to 400 percent of the value of what they would have if they had remained under AT&T's management plan.

Six months later, AT&T sold the Somerset, New Jersey, unit, ASA, to the managers for $50 million, and transferred $25 million in pension assets to ASA, more than twice the amount needed to cover the pensions owed. In 2000, two years after buying ASA from AT&T, Gulotta sold it to the giant insurance and benefits consultant Aon Corp. for $125 million. He remained a principal of the firm until his retirement.

Surplus pension assets have ended up in executives' pockets in more creative ways. In late 2005, CenturyTel (now CenturyLink), a telecommunications firm based in Monroe, Louisiana, attached a list to its workers' pension plan with the names of select individuals who would get an extra helping of pension benefits from the plan.

Normally, federal law forbids employers from discriminating in favor of highly paid employees who participate in the regular pension plan; everyone in the plan is supposed to have roughly the same deal. There's also an IRS limit on the amount a person can earn under the plans. These restrictions are why companies provide separate, supplemental pension plans open only to executives.

But by using complex maneuvers that take advantage of loopholes in the discrimination rules, many companies do, in fact, discriminate in favor of their executives and exceed the statutory ceiling on how much they can receive from the plans.

CenturyTel used one of these techniques in its pension plan, which covered 6,900 workers and retirees, to boost the pensions of eighteen executives in the plan. One of them was chief executive Glen Post, who before the amendment had earned a pension of only $12,000 annually in the regular pension plan. But the increase bumped it up to $110,000 a year in retirement.

The technique doesn't increase the executive's retirement benefits. When the swap is made, the supplemental executive pension is reduced by an equal amount. The goal, rather, is to enable companies to tap pension assets to pay for executive pensions — and even their pay.

Intel, the giant semiconductor chip maker based in Santa Clara, California, used this method to move more than $200 million of its deferred-compensation obligations for the top 3 percent to 5 percent of its workforce into the regular pension plan in 2005. Thanks to this, when these executives and other highly paid individuals leave, Intel won't have to pay them out of cash; the pension plan will pay them (more on this in Chapter 8).

Using these methods, companies have moved hundreds of millions of dollars of executive pension liabilities into the regular pension plans, and then have used pension assets originally intended to pay the benefits of rank-and-file employees to pay the additional pension benefits for executives. The practice exists across all industries: from forest products (Georgia-Pacific) to insurers (Prudential Financial) to banks (Community Bank System Inc.).

The practice has something in common with the practice of selling pension assets: Employers prefer to keep it under wraps, lest it spark a backlash when employees find out the CEO with millions of dollars in supplemental executive pensions is also getting an extra helping from the rank-and-file pension plan.

To "minimize this problem" of employee relations, companies should draw up a memo describing the transfer of supplemental executive benefits to the pension plan and give it "only to employees who are eligible," wrote a consulting actuary with Milliman Inc., a global benefits consulting firm. Covington & Burling, a Washington, D.C., law firm, advised employers to attach a list to the pension plan, identifying eligible executives by name, title, or Social Security number, along with the dollar amount each will receive. CenturyTel, People's Energy Corp., and Niagara Mohawk Power Corp., a New York utility that's part of London-based National Grid PLC, all used methods like this.

Initially, employers used these executive pension transfers as a way to use surplus pension assets, and some companies with overfunded pensions still do. To "take advantage of the Surplus Funds in the Pension Plan," Florida real estate developer St. Joe Co. amended its employee pension plan in February 2011 to increase benefits for "certain designated executives." These included departing president and CEO William Britton Greene, who was pushed out by a large shareholder. The amendment more than doubled the pension he'll receive from the employee pension plan, boosting the lump sum amount from $365,722 to $797,349. Greene also received an exit package worth $7.8 million.

But moving executive pension obligations into the regular pension plans can not only use up the surplus assets, it can put a dent in the rest of the pension assets as well. Today, many pension plans with special executive carve-outs are underfunded, including Carpenter Technology Corp., Parker Hannifin, Illinois Tool Works (which manufactures industrial machinery), PMI Group (a mortgage insurer), ITC Holdings, and Johnson Controls.

TERMINATORS

When it comes to siphoning pension assets, nothing beats terminating the piggy bank and grabbing the entire surplus at once.

This maneuver was common. In the 1980s, employers terminated more than two thousand overfunded pension plans covering over two million participants and snatched surplus assets in excess of $20 billion. Some were inside jobs. Occidental Petroleum terminated its pension in 1983 and paid no income tax on the $400 million in surplus it captured because the company had net losses that year.

Other pension plans fell victim to pension raiders like financier Ronald Perelman, who took over Revlon in 1985, killed the pension plan, and nabbed more than $100 million in surplus pension assets, and Charles Hurwitz, who took over Pacific Lumber, closed down its pension and used $55 million in surplus pension assets to help pay off the debt he took on with the leveraged buyout. To stop these abuses, Congress slapped a 50 percent excise tax on "reversions" in 1990, and pension terminations at large companies slowed almost to a halt. But there was a huge loophole (there always is): A company that terminated its pension could avoid the onerous 50 percent excise tax—and pay only 20 percent—if it put one-quarter of the plan's surplus into a "replacement plan." A replacement plan could be another pension. Or it could be a 401(k). The only restriction was that companies allocate the surplus into employee accounts within seven years.

Montgomery Ward was a big beneficiary of this loophole. The stodgy retailer, struggling to compete with low-cost giants like Kmart and Wal-Mart, filed for bankruptcy protection in 1997. Its $1.1 billion pension plan was especially fat, because two years before its bankruptcy filing, Montgomery Ward cut the pension benefits by changing to a less generous plan. This reduced the obligations, and thus increased the surplus.

The company then terminated the pension plan and put 25 percent of the $270 million surplus into a replacement 401(k) plan. It paid the 20 percent excise tax, and the remaining $173 million of the surplus went to Ward income-tax-free, because the company had net operating losses. Ward used the money to pay creditors—the largest of which was the GE Capital unit of General Electric. It emerged from bankruptcy in 1999 as a wholly owned subsidiary of GE Capital, its largest shareholder.

The employees didn't have much time to build up their 401(k) savings: The company went out of business in early 2001, closed its 250 stores, and laid off 37,000 employees. What about the 20 percent of surplus assets set aside to contribute to employee accounts? The $60 million or so that hadn't yet been allocated to employee accounts went to creditors, not employees. Creditors have often ended up with the pension surplus. Around the time Montgomery Ward was fattening its plan for slaughter, Edison Brothers Stores, a St. Louis retailer whose chains included Harry's Big & Tall Stores, entered Chapter 11. It killed the overfunded pension plan in 1997 and set up a 401(k). After paying the 20 percent excise tax, Edison Brothers forked more than $41 million in pension money over to creditors and emerged from bankruptcy. Its employees had even less time to build a nest egg in their new 401(k): The company liquidated in 1998.

These strategies ought to make it clear that many companies were terminating pension plans not because the pensions were underfunded or a costly burden, but because the pension plans were *fat* and the companies themselves were in financial trouble. The icing on the cake was that a company with losses would pay no income tax on the surplus assets.

It also puts a less savory spin on the origin story of the 401(k): Companies like Enron, Occidental Petroleum, Mercantile Stores, and Montgomery Ward didn't adopt 401(k)s because they were modern savings plans employees were supposedly lusting after; their 401(k)s were merely the bastard stepchildren of dead pensions.

BLACK BOX

Lack of a pension surplus hasn't stopped employers from raiding their pensions. Even if a plan has no fat, companies have been able to indirectly monetize the assets using the bankruptcy courts. Struggling in the wake of September 11, US Airways filed for Chapter 11 in 2003 and asked the bankruptcy court to let it terminate the pension plan covering seven thousand active and retired pilots. The airline estimated it would have to put $1.7 billion into the plan over the coming seven years, a burden that it said would force it to liquidate. David Siegel, US Airways' chief executive, told employees in a telephone recording that the termination of the pilots' plan was "the single most important hurdle for emerging from Chapter 11." He said the move was regrettable but maintained that "the future of the airline is at stake."

Few challenged the "terminate or liquidate" statement. Cheering the move were US Airways' creditors, lenders, and shareholders with a stake in the reorganized company, because removing the pension plan would wipe out a liability and make the company more likely to emerge from Chapter 11 in a position to pay its debts and provide a return to its shareholders. Other cheerleaders were the Air Transportation Stabilization Board, which was poised to guarantee loans to the carrier, and the airline's lead bankruptcy lender, Retirement Systems of Alabama, which stood to gain a large equity stake in US Airways when it emerged from

Chapter 11. They accepted, without question or independent confirmation or research, the airline's analysis and backed its request to kill the plan.

The pilots suspected that the airline was exaggerating the ill health of their pension to convince the court to let it pull the plug. Why the pilots' plan, they wondered, and not the flight attendants' plan or the mechanics' plan? Had the airline deliberately starved their pension plan while funding the others? There was no way to tell, because the company didn't turn over pension filings that included the critical liability and asset figures—not until the night before the bankruptcy hearing that would decide the pension's fate. Without the information, the pilots couldn't make their case that the liabilities were inflated.

In court, US Airways' team of lawyers and consultants presented reams of actuarial calculations and colorful charts and tables demonstrating the pension plan's deficit and the perils of preserving it. The frustrated pilots, with their lone actuary, couldn't put on as good a show. The bankruptcy judge relied on US Airways' figures and allowed the termination to proceed. In his decision, Judge Stephen Mitchell said that the pilots were less credible, because they had "based their calculation on rules of thumb and rough estimates while [US Airways'] actuary based his on the actual computer model used for administration of the plan."

Bankruptcy raids like this are made possible by a loophole in the bankruptcy code, which coincidentally was enacted at about the same time as federal pension law, in the late 1970s. The law says that when companies go into Chapter 11, banks and creditors take priority over employees and retirees, who have to get in line with the other unsecured creditors, like the suppliers of peanuts and cocktail napkins.

Delta Air Lines filed for bankruptcy in 2005 and terminated the pension plan covering 5,500 pilots. Denis Waldron, a retired pilot from Waleska, Georgia, had been receiving a monthly pension of $1,939 until the pension plan was taken over by the Pension Benefit Guaranty Corp.

But the PBGC guarantees only a certain amount. The maximum in 2011: $54,000 a year ($4,500 a month) for retirees who begin taking their pensions at sixty-five. The maximum is lower at younger ages, and for those with spouses as beneficiaries. The PBGC doesn't guarantee early-retirement subsides, which are enhancements that make pensions more valuable. The payout is further limited for the pilots because they are required to retire at age sixty. After myriad calculations, including various look-back penalties, Waldron's pension fell to just $95 a month.

Pilots were slammed in another way as well: Their supplemental pensions weren't guaranteed at all. Don Tibbs, of Gainesville, Georgia, had put in more than thirty years as a pilot and was receiving $7,000 a month from his supplemental pilots' plan and $1,197 a month from the regular pension plan. The supplemental plan was canceled when the airline filed for bankruptcy, and a year later, when Delta turned the pilots' pension plan over to the PBGC, Tibbs lost that pension, too, thanks to quirks in the insurer's rules.

Though creditors, shareholders, and executives all profited, Tibbs now has only his Social Security and a small military reserve income. "They were able to use the bankruptcy court to walk away from their obligation," Tibbs recalled bitterly. "What happened to me and a lot of my friends was and is criminal."

United Airlines was next in line on the bankruptcy tarmac, and it spread the pain even more widely. In 2006 it terminated all its pension plans—for flight attendants, mechanics, and pilots.

Today the giant surpluses are gone: sold, traded, siphoned, diverted to creditors, used to finance executive pay, parachutes, and pensions. But you'd think the employers had nothing to do with it. Companies blame investment losses for their plight, as well as their aging workforces, union contracts, regulation, and global competition. But their funding problems were largely self-inflicted. Had they not siphoned off the assets, they would have had a cushion that could have withstood even the market crash that troughed in March 2009. Nonetheless, employers continue to lobby for more liberal rules that would enable them to shift hundreds of millions of dollars of additional executive obligations into the pension plans and to withdraw more of the assets to pay other benefits. Meanwhile, their solution when funds run low remains the same: Cut pensions.

CHAPTER 2

Heist: REPLENISHING PENSION ASSETS BY CUTTING BENEFITS

I **N 1997,** Cigna executives held a number of meetings to discuss their pension problem. At the time, the plan was overfunded, but executives weren't satisfied and suggested cutting the pensions of 27,000 employees in an effort to boost the earnings they could report on their bottom line. The only hitch? How to cut people's pensions—especially those for long-tenured employees over forty—by 30 percent or more, without anyone noticing?

Cigna was just the latest of hundreds of large companies, including Boeing, Xerox, Georgia-Pacific, and Polaroid, that had already gone through this charade in the 1990s. These companies had something in common: They all had large aging workforces—with tens of thousands of employees who had been on the job for twenty to thirty years. These workers were entering their peak earning years, and with traditional pensions that are calculated by multiplying years of service by one's annual salary, their pensions were about to spike. With the leverage of traditional pension formulas, as much as half an employee's pension could be earned in his final five years. In short, millions of workers were about to step onto the pension escalator.

Financially, that wasn't a problem. Companies, including Cigna, had set aside plenty of money to pay their pensions, so having a large cohort of aging workers didn't put the companies in peril. The companies had anticipated the growth rates of people's pensions, and the estimated life spans of their workers, and had funded their pensions accordingly. So it didn't matter that the pensions would quickly grow. The companies were prepared.

The problem, from the employers' perspective, was that it would be a shame to pay out all that money in pensions when there were so many other useful ways it could be put to use for the benefit of the companies themselves.

Laying people off was one way to keep pension money in the plan. When people leave, their pensions stop growing, and if this happens just when employees' pensions are poised to spike, all the better. In the 1990s, companies purged hundreds of thousands of middle-aged workers from the payrolls at telephone companies, aerospace and defense contractors, manufacturers, pharmaceutical companies, and other industries, reducing future pension outflows by billions of dollars.

Employers couldn't lay off every middle-aged worker, of course, but there were other ways to slow the pension growth of those who remained. They could cut pensions, but there were certain constraints. Pension law prohibits employers from taking away pensions being paid out to retirees, and employers can't rescind benefits its employees have locked in up to that point. But they can stop the growth, by freezing the plans, or slow it, by switching to a less generous formula.

That was the route Cigna took. The company estimated that the move would cut benefits of older workers by 40 percent or more, which meant that as much as $80 million that had been earmarked for their pensions would remain in the plan.

The challenge was how to cut pensions without provoking an employee uprising. Pushing people off the pension escalator just when they're about to lock in the fruits of their long tenure would be like telling a traveler that his *nearly* one million frequent flier miles were being rescinded—they weren't going to like it.

Cigna's solution to this communications challenge? Don't tell employees. In September 1997, consulting firm Mercer signed a $200,000 consulting contract to prepare the written communication to Cigna employees, describing the changes without disclosing the negative effects. One of these was a benefits newsletter Cigna sent employees in November 1997, entitled "Introducing Your New Retirement Program." On the front, "Message from CEO Bill Taylor" declared: "I am pleased to announce that on January 1, 1998, CIGNA will significantly enhance its retirement program. . . . These enhancements will make our retirement program highly competitive."

The newsletter told employees that "the new plan is designed to work well for both longer- and shorter-service employees," provides "steadier benefit growth throughout [the employee's] career," and "build[s] benefits faster" than the old plan. "One advantage the company will not get from the retirement program changes is cost savings." In formal pension documents it later distributed, Cigna reiterated that employees "will see growth in [their] total retirement benefits every year."

The communications campaign was successful: Employees didn't notice that their pensions were being frozen, and didn't complain. "We've been able to avoid bad press," noted Gerald Meyn, the vice president of employee benefits, in a memo three months after the pension change. "We have avoided any significant negative reaction from employees." In the margins next to these statements, the head of Cigna's human resources department, Donald M. Levinson, scribbled: "Neat!" and "Agree!" and "Better than expected outcome."

When employees made individual inquiries, Cigna had an express policy of not providing information. "We continue to focus on NOT providing employees before and after samples of the pension plan changes," an internal memo stressed. When employees called, the HR staff, working with scripts, deflected them with statements like "Exact comparisons are difficult."

Cigna wasn't the only company deceiving employees about their pension cuts, and actuaries who helped implement these changes were concerned, for good reason: Federal pension law requires employers to notify employees when their benefits are being cut. At an annual actuarial industry conference in New York later that year, the attendees discussed how to handle this dilemma. The recommendation: Pick your words carefully. The law "doesn't require you to say, 'We're significantly lowering your benefit,'" noted Paul Strella, a lawyer with Mercer, which had advised Cigna when it implemented a cash-balance plan earlier that year. "All it says is, 'Describe the amendment.' So you describe the amendment."

Kyle Brown, an actuary at Watson Wyatt, reiterated that point: "Since the [required notice] doesn't have to include the words that 'your rate of future-benefit accrual is being reduced,' you don't have to say those magic words. You just have to describe what is happening under the plan. . . . I wouldn't put in those magic words."*

Just to make sure this sunny message had sunk in, in December 1998, Cigna sent employees a fact sheet stating that the objectives for introducing the new pension plan were to:

- Deliver adequate retirement income to Cigna employees
- Improve the competitiveness of our benefits program and thus improve our ability to attract and retain top talent
- Meet the changing needs of a more mobile employee workforce, and
- Provide retirement benefits in a form that people can understand.

---

* When later asked to comment about this piece of advice, a spokesman for Watson Wyatt maintained that Brown was actually advocating clear communication to plan participants. "The term 'magic words' was a lawyer's reference to the triggering words in the [disclosure] statute," he said.

The letter went on to say that "Cigna has not reduced the overall amount it contributes for retirement benefits by introducing the new Plan, and the new Plan is not designed to save money."

This was true, literally. Cigna had indeed not reduced the *overall* amounts it contributed for retirement benefits. It had lowered the benefits for older workers and increased benefits for younger workers (slightly) and for top executives (significantly). Looked at this way, the plan wasn't designed to save money, just redistribute it.

The communications campaign was successful. Janice Amara, a lawyer in Cigna's compliance department, didn't learn that she had not actually been receiving any additional benefits until September 2000, when she ran into Cigna's chief actuary, Mark Lynch, at a farewell party for two other Cigna employees. "Jan, you would be sick if you knew" how Cigna was calculating her pension, she recalled him telling her. "Frankly, I *was* sick when I heard this," Amara said. Under Cigna's new pension formula, Amara's pension would effectively be frozen for ten years.

Cigna was a relative latecomer to the hide-the-ball approach to pension cuts. The cash-balance plan it implemented was initially developed by Kwasha Lipton, a boutique benefits-consulting firm in Fort Lee, New Jersey, as a way to cut pensions without making it obvious to employees.

Helping employers hang on to pension assets had been a Kwasha Lipton specialty for years. In the early 1980s, Kwasha Lipton helped companies like Great Atlantic & Pacific Tea Co. kill their pension plans to capture the surpluses. Pension raiding became more difficult as Congress began implementing excise taxes on the surplus assets taken from the plans, so Kwasha devised the cash-balance plan as a new way for employers to capture the surplus.

Changing to a cash-balance pension plan was a way to boost surplus because it reduced the growth rate of employees' pensions, and thus their total pensions. Unlike a traditional pension plan that multiplies salary by years of service, producing rapid growth at the end of a career, a cash-balance plan grows as though it were a savings account. Every year, the pension grows at a flat rate, such as 4 percent of pay a year. At a benefits conference in 1984, a Kwasha Lipton partner stated that converting to this formula would "immediately reduce pension costs about 25 percent to 40 percent."

Bank of America was the first company to test-drive the new pension plan, in 1985. The bank was cash-strapped because of soured Latin American loans and didn't want to have to contribute to its pension plan. The pension change saved the company $75 million.

The bank's employees didn't complain when their pension growth slowed, because they didn't notice. "One feature which might come in handy is that it is difficult for employees to compare prior pension benefit formulas to the account balance approach," wrote Robert S. Byrne, a Kwasha Lipton partner, in a letter to a client in 1989.

The cuts were difficult for employees to detect because they didn't understand how pensions are calculated, let alone these newfangled versions, which appeared deceptively simple.

In reality, cash-balance plans are complex. When companies convert their traditional pensions to cash-balance plans, they essentially freeze the old pension, ending its growth. They then convert the frozen pension to a lump sum, which they call the "opening account balance." The lump-sum amount (i.e., the "balance") doesn't grow each year by multiplying years and pay, both of which would be growing, and thus generating the leveraged growth seen in a traditional pension. Instead, the pension "balance" grows by a flat percentage of an employee's pay each year, say, 4 percent. Voilà: no more leveraged growth.

Ironically, employers were able to capitalize on the growing popularity of 401(k)s by presenting cash-balance plans as merely 401(k)-style pensions. Cigna told employees that the new cash-balance plan was like a 401(k), only better, because the company made all the contributions and departing employees could cash out their accounts or roll the money into IRAs. Employees didn't realize that there was no actual "account" receiving actual employer "contributions" or "interest"—just a frozen pension, and a new pension that had a formula producing very low growth, with no leverage. The pension plan was still one big pool of assets, and the only thing that was changing was the formula used to determine how much each employee would get.

In other words, after a company changed to a cash-balance plan, most employees were no better off than if they had changed jobs or been laid off (which would have stopped their old pension from growing) and now had only a 401(k) at their new job, growing at only 4 percent a year.

But it was even worse than that at Cigna and other companies: Older workers weren't even getting the annual increase. That's because at many companies the "opening account balance" was worth less than the value of the lump sum. For example, if at the time of the pension change someone had earned the equivalent of a $300,000 payout, the opening account balance might be only $250,000. Consequently, it could take years for the pay credits to build the "balance" back up to where it had been when the pension change was made. As a result, following the change to a cash-balance plan, the pensions of older workers were frozen—in some cases for the rest of their careers. Employees didn't notice because the amounts on their "account statements" always appeared to be growing.

In the pension world, this period of zero pension growth is called "wear-away," because a person has to wear away his old benefit before his benefit begins growing again. Creating a wear-away is an employer's way of saying, "We should have had this less generous pension all along, and if we had, your pension would be smaller. Bottom line: You've been overpaid and won't get any pension until you've worked off the debt."

It was little different from an employer cutting someone's pay, then telling him he wouldn't get a paycheck for five years, because he should have been paid less all along. Employees would notice if their pay was frozen, but they didn't notice that their pensions weren't growing because the opening account balance had been lowballed. Amara's opening balance was $91,124, instead of the $184,000 she had earned. Under the new formula, she wouldn't begin to build a new benefit until 2008. Essentially, wear-away is like a retroactive pension cut.

Under pension law, it's illegal to retroactively cut someone's pension (though employers can slow the pension growth or end it altogether by freezing the pension plan). Cash-balance plans provide a way around this prohibition against retroactive pension cuts because if employees leave before their accounts have caught up to their old pensions, they always receive at least the value of the benefit they had when the pension was changed. In this case, Amara would receive the lump sum of $184,000 if she left; but if she didn't, she could work another ten years with no increase in her pension.

Gerald Smit, a longtime AT&T employee, was forty-seven when AT&T changed its pension plan in 1998. At the time, his pension would have been worth $1,985 a month when he reached age fifty-five. Though he continued to work at AT&T for eight more years, when he left, his pension was still worth just $1,985 a month. For other employees, the waiting period could be longer. Minutes of a 1997 meeting of AT&T's pension consultants noted that "employees in their 40s could lose, [and] have to wait 10 years for benefits. By contrast, the benefit would build "immediately for younger employees." (The benefits for younger employees and new hires would grow immediately, because they had accumulated little or nothing under the old pension.)

From the beginning, the cash-balance plan's ability to disguise the pension cuts was one of its selling points with employers. In 1986, Eric Lofgren, an actuary and principal with Mercer-Meidinger (later called Mercer), discussed the newfangled cash-balance plans on a panel discussing new kinds of pension plans at an actuaries conference. The cash-balance plan, he explained, was a pension plan "masquerading as a defined contribution" savings plan, like a 401(k). It was, he commented, "a very worthy concept."

Lofgren went on to provide two definitions of the cash-balance plan. "Both definitions are true, but they slant in different directions," he said. "The first definition is the upbeat definition: 'Dear employee: A cash-balance plan is an exciting, modern, flexible new plan designed with the advantages of both defined benefit and defined contribution. Easy to understand, each employee quickly vests in a portable lump sum account which is guaranteed to increase at the CPI [consumer price index] for inflation protection. There are many benefit options at retirement.'"

He continued: "The second definition goes like this: 'Dear employee: We've got for you a cash-balance pension plan. It's our way to disguise the cutbacks in your benefits. First we're going to change it to career average [meaning that the benefit would be based on an average of one's salary, not the highest amount, as in a traditional pension]. We'll express the benefits as a lump sum so we can highlight the use of the CPI, a sub-market interest rate. What money is left in the plan will be directed towards employees who leave after just a few years. Just to make sure, we'll reduce early-retirement subsidies.'" These subsidies allow a person to retire at age fifty-five or sixty with roughly the same pension as if they'd stayed to age sixty-five. Taking away the subsidy could reduce a pension by 20 percent or more.

The desired effect of the pension change, from the employer's point of view, was not just that it froze the pensions of older employees, but redirected some of the savings to younger workers. Publicly, employers emphasized that the new pension was better for "young, mobile workers" (a phrase that appeared in virtually every piece of marketing material issued by a company to help explain why it had changed the plan). In fact, two-thirds of young workers leave their jobs without vesting in their pensions, meaning that they got nothing. The forfeited amounts remained in the plan.

Initially, other consulting firms were skeptical of this radical design. But as Kwasha Lipton converted pension plans at Hershey, Dana, Cabot, and other companies, competing consulting firms saw a lucrative opportunity. Soon Mercer, Towers Perrin, and Watson Wyatt developed their own hybrid plans, and they too emphasized the ability of the plans to mask pension cuts.

WISE GUYS

Not everyone was fooled when their employers changed to a cash-balance plan. Jim Bruggeman was forty-nine when his employer, Central and South West, a Dallas-based electric utility, took this step in 1997. "The changes being made are good for both you and the company," the brochure noted. Bruggeman, an engineer in Tulsa, was eager to find out how, and was uniquely qualified to do so. He also had a background in finance, his hobby was actuarial science, he had taken graduate-level courses in statistics and probability, and he knew CSW's old pension plan inside and out. After considerable tinkering with spreadsheets, he was able to finally figure out that the supposedly "better" pension would reduce the pensions of many employees by 30 percent.

He wasn't about to keep this finding to himself. At a question-and-answer session on the new plan, Bruggeman spoke up and told co-workers how their pensions were being reduced. He had a sheaf of spreadsheets to prove it. The next day, his supervisor went to his office with a message from CSW management in Dallas. They were concerned that his remarks would cause an "uprising" and warned him that if he continued to talk to other employees about the pension change, they'd think he wasn't a team player and his job could be in jeopardy. In his next performance evaluation, his supervisor's only criticism was that he "spends too much time thinking about the pension plan." CSW saved $20 million in the first year it made the change. Bruggeman was fired in 2000.

Another engineer one thousand miles away was equally perplexed. Steven Langlie had spent three decades designing military engines, but he couldn't figure out how the cash-balance plan his employer changed to in 1989 worked. The skeptical engineer relentlessly pestered his employer,

Onan Corp., a unit of Cummins Engine in Minneapolis, for answers. When they refused to spill the beans, the increasingly apoplectic Langlie wrote to local lawmakers, complained to the Minnesota Department of Human Rights and the IRS, and traveled to Washington, D.C., to deliver a petition signed by 460 fellow workers to the Department of Labor.

As Langlie's pension complaints escalated, he was transferred, denied training, and demoted, despite favorable job-performance reviews. The company also refused to upgrade his computer from a primitive IBM 286—the industry equivalent of an Etch A Sketch, which couldn't run engineering software or communicate with the company's servers. Finally, the human resources department told Langlie's supervisor that it would "help retire him" and eliminated his job. After Langlie's thirty-seven years with the company, his pension, which would have been $1,100 a month under the old pension plan, was just $424 a month.

Deloitte & Touche, the giant accounting firm, made a big miscalculation when it tried to switch to a cash-balance plan in 1998: The finance guys apparently forgot that a large number of the firm's employees were older, experienced actuaries and accountants, who took a professional interest, as well as a personal one, in the plan's novel design. They were horrified when they connected the dots and saw that their pensions would go over a cliff. They went ballistic, and the firm backtracked, allowing all who were already on the staff when the cash-balance plan was adopted to stick with the old benefit if they wished.*

IBM also underestimated the über-nerds on its staff, though it's not hard to understand why the company was so complacent: It had cut pensions several times in the 1990s, and no one had noticed. Traditionally, it provided 1.5 percent of pay for each year of service, which resulted

---

* A number of companies "grandfathered" older workers under the prior plan. But these transition periods typically lasted only five years, merely postponing, and ultimately increasing, the wear-away.

in a pension that replaced roughly one-third to almost one-half of a person's salary in retirement. The calculation was simple: years of service times average pay in the final few years times .015. For example: If someone worked thirty years, and his average pay in the final years was $50,000, the pension would be worth $22,500 a year in retirement ($50,000 x 30 x .015).

Reducing any of these factors would produce a smaller pension. In the early 1990s, IBM reduced all three. In 1991, it capped the number of years of service that got taken into account when calculating pensions, limiting it to thirty years. This meant that if people worked longer than that, their pensions wouldn't grow. Next, it lowered the multiplier from 1.5 percent to 1.35 percent, again reducing the pensions. Finally, it reduced the salary component; instead of basing the pension on the average salary an employee earned in the final five years of service, it began to use an average based on the entire time of service, including the early years when pay was low.

These early cuts were like gateway drugs: The first one produced a mild high; the next two were more potent; then IBM moved on to the equivalent of heroin: the "pension equity plan." The very name was deceptive, like "low-fat" and "organic." "Equity" suggested fairness. More than that, the pension equity plan looked as though it *favored* older workers.

At first glance, pension equity plans, which went by the zippy acronym PEP, looked similar to cash-balance plans. An employee received an "account" that would grow with an employer "contribution" based on the employee's average pay over the prior five years or so. This pay figure would then be multiplied by a factor that increased the longer a person worked at the company. This sounded fair since, if the figure is rising, the pension must be increasing each year, too—right?

Well, here's the beauty of the hat trick: If you multiply three items—all positive numbers—which keep growing each year (the years on the job, the salary, the multiplier), the result is an account with a rising balance. But if you then multiply the result by a declining number, the result can be a pension that isn't growing—and might even be declining—in value.

That's what happens in pension equity plans: The interest rate used to calculate the pensions—a rate that wasn't disclosed—would get smaller as people got older. It was 5 percent for employees under age forty-five, 4 percent for those aged forty-five to fifty-five, and 0.5 percent less for each year above age fifty-five. So, even though the company "contributions" rose as a person got older, multiplying it by a declining (embedded) interest rate caused the pension's rate of growth to shrink as a person aged. The "easy-to-understand" pension equity plan was a Rube Goldberg contraption of moving parts. "The plan took me months to understand," Donald Sauvigne, head of retirement benefits at IBM—who had twenty-five years' experience with pensions—told an audience at a 1995 actuaries conference in Vancouver.

After warming up with the series of modest pension trims, IBM was looking for something that would enable it to ditch its costly "early-retirement subsidy," which allowed employees in their fifties to retire with nearly the pension they would have at sixty-five. This feature was once common at larger companies, and IBM had added it to its pension plan in the 1980s as an incentive to get workers to leave in their fifties rather than hang around until sixty-five to max out their pensions. It "encouraged departures," so it "served us well," Sauvigne told his colleagues at the conference. But IBM found that the subsidy also had the unwelcome effect of encouraging people to stick around until at least age fifty-five so they could lock in the subsidy.

IBM couldn't just pull the plug on the subsidy, because pension law doesn't allow a company to take away a benefit a person has already earned or take away a pension right or feature the company has granted. "So we had to design something different," Sauvigne said. Enter Louis V. Gerstner Jr., IBM's new president. He'd headed RJR Nabisco in 1993 when it faced a similar dilemma: how to reduce pensions and remove the retirement subsidy without obviously violating the law or provoking an employee backlash. Gerstner and IBM turned to Watson Wyatt, the same consulting firm that had helped Nabisco solve its pension problem.

Watson Wyatt had been marketing its "pension equity plan" design to large employers, with considerable success. Its brochure summed up the benefits: "Younger employees are happier because they see an account-based benefit; older employees are happy because benefits are still rich enough to achieve retirement security at long tenures; the CFO is happy because the PEP eliminates the expensive—and from a business sense counter-productive—early retirement subsidy."

The brochure didn't point out another benefit—deception—but it was no secret among the consulting community. "It is not until they are ready to retire that they understand how little they are actually getting," said a Watson Wyatt actuary at a 1998 panel entitled "Introduction to Cash Balance/Pension Equity Plans." That got a good laugh from the audience, as did the response by a fellow panelist, who was with Mercer: "Right, but they're happy while they're employed. . . . You switch to a cash-balance plan where the people are probably getting smaller bene-fits, at least the older, longer-service people; but they are really happy, and they think you are great for doing it." More laughter.

Watson Wyatt epitomized the new breed of benefits consultants that was revolutionizing the compensation-and-benefits landscape. In prior decades, benefits specialists handled the garden-variety tasks of pension administration and human resources consulting. That began to change in the 1980s as consultants began more aggressively prospecting for business and developing niche specialties in cutting retiree benefits, boosting executive compensation, and managing mass layoffs and early-retirement windows.

Watson Wyatt was particularly innovative. It developed a suite of demographically inspired services specifically aimed at helping employ-ers evaluate—and reduce—the cost of their older workers. One service was the firm's "Aging Diagnostic," which marketing material described as "a tool designed to measure how the cost of compensation and benefits is affected by an aging workforce, so organizations can detect this trend early . . . and begin managing it, before it manages them."

> With one baby boomer turning 50 every eight seconds for the next 10 years, the economic issues of an aging workforce could become a major issue for your company. For every 50-year-old employee in your company, you are likely to pay:
>
> - Twice as much in health care as for a 30-year-old.
> - More in base salary and vacation leave, because of longer job tenure.
> - Up to twice the employer match on defined contribution deferrals than you would for a 20-year-old, due to higher participation and savings rates.
> - More than twice the pension plan contribution rate that you would pay for a 25-year-old.
> - Companies that manage this trend early—before it manages them—will create a significant competitive advantage. . . . That's where Watson Wyatt's Aging Diagnostic™ comes in. Our state-of-the-art modeling system uses your data and the latest demographic research to project the total impact of an aging workforce on your compensation and benefits costs. . . . Companies that want to combat the cost spiral of changing demographics should take a careful look at their current workforce demographics, hiring practices and benefits design, paying special attention to retirement packages.

With little fanfare, IBM rolled out the pension equity plan in 1995 and heard not a peep from the employees. Three years later, it was ready for yet another pension cut. This time it decided to convert the pension equity plan to a cash-balance plan. IBM's consultants at Mercer Human Resource Consulting and Watson Wyatt calculated that when it switched to the cash-balance plan, approximately 28,300 older IBM employees would stop earning pension benefits for one to five years, while younger employees would begin to build benefits immediately. The net result, though, would be that the pension plan would pay out $200 million less, and most of the savings would come from older, long-service employees, like Dave Finlay.

Finlay was exactly the kind of employee the company was taking aim at: He was fifty-five and had been at the company twenty-six years. As a senior engineer, he had a comfortable, though not lavish, salary. He expected his pension to be the same, and it would have been if IBM hadn't engineered its series of secret cuts. He began to figure this out in early 1999, after he got a brochure from IBM in the mail announcing that the company was modifying its pension plan to make it "more modern, easier-to-understand, and better suited for a mobile workforce." Finlay was close to retirement, so he scrutinized the document, trying to figure out how the new pension compared with his old one. The description of the new pension was thin on details, noting only vaguely that employees "will see varying effects" and that those retiring early will "see lower value." Not good enough.

Finlay went to the internal company Web site, where IBM had long offered a "Pension Estimator" that enabled employees to estimate how much their pension was—and would be—worth, depending on how long they'd worked, their estimated annual pay raises, and other factors. But IBM had taken the pension tool offline. When Finlay called administrators in IBM's human resources department to complain, they told him the company had taken the estimator down because "it really does not seem appropriate to be modeling a plan that no longer exists."

This response was common. The corporate finance departments that hatched these schemes typically kept most of the lower-level human resources managers and peons in the dark and fed them the same hooey they served up to the employees. For example, when IBM switched to a pension equity plan a few years earlier, it had sent a memo to managers stressing that the new pension equity plan was "the result of a recent study which concluded that the plan should be modified to meet the evolving needs of IBM and its increasingly diverse work force, and align more with industry practices and trends." It didn't tell the HR staff any more than it told the employees that it was cutting pensions (including theirs) and that it was doing so to keep more money in the plan to enrich the company.

After getting no help from the benefits administrators, Finlay began to suspect that IBM was hiding something. Though Finlay didn't have the online pension estimator at his disposal, he had saved every benefits booklet, announcement, statement, and handout he'd ever received since he joined the company in 1972 and was able to reconstruct the estimator. It became a personal challenge. For weeks, he bicycled home from work to his subdivision on the outskirts of Boulder, Colorado, and stared at his computer until nearly midnight. He spent weekends developing spreadsheets and reverse-engineering the algorithms with the information he hauled up from his basement. Finlay eventually figured out that the earlier 1995 change, one that he hadn't examined so thoroughly, had reduced his prospective pension from about $69,500 a year to about $57,700, a 17 percent drop. And the latest switch would cut his annual pension a further 20 percent, to about $45,800.

Finlay showed his spreadsheets to his manager and suggested sending them to the human resources department. Don't bother, his manager said: The human resources people wouldn't believe his figures and would tell the managers that he didn't know what he was talking about. At that point, the self-described Republican and Vietnam vet was steamed enough, he said, that he would have joined a union if the company had had one.

BACKLASH AT BIG BLUE

To make up for the loss of the pension estimator, some IBMers launched a Web site on Yahoo! to compare notes and air gripes about the anticipated change. Finlay posted his spreadsheets and calculations, which gave his colleagues a way to measure how much their pensions would shrink. The site began getting fifteen thousand hits a day as many of IBM's 260,000 employees around the world began picking apart virtually every actuarial assumption related to IBM's calculation of benefits. "I'd like to think this group is too intelligent and motivated to let a bunch of corporate actuaries sell us down the river and think we're too stupid to figure out their half-truths," noted NiceGuys-Win-in-the-End.

The HR department was not popular. "The mathematically disadvantaged half-wits in HR can't hold up a conversation on the topic of calculating anything," remarked IBM-Ghost. "They are more like used-car salesmen trying to sell a car with a sawdust filled transmission (my apologies to any used-car salesmen as you probably have more integrity than HR)," wrote idontknowaboutyou.

CEO Louis Gerstner was unpopular, too. One employee suggested hiring an airplane to drag a banner over the IBM facilities in Silicon Valley during lunchtime, with the message HEY LOU, "THOU SHALT NOT STEAL."

Meanwhile, IBM insisted that it was instituting the change to make the plan more "modern" and not to save money. This was a common, though disingenuous, claim. Sure, IBM wasn't literally saving money, because it wasn't spending any money. (The pension plan was overfunded.) Rather, the pension cuts were enabling the company to keep $200 million, which otherwise would have gone to pay benefits to long-term employees.

Another popular whopper used by Lucent, AT&T, and so many others, was that the change wouldn't reduce a person's retirement benefits. What they didn't say was that in these calculations, they were also counting 401(k) savings as "pension benefits" and assuming that employees would be contributing a large percentage of pay that would receive double-digit returns. So, yes, the pension change wouldn't, perhaps, collectively reduce the employees' retirement benefits, as long as one included the fantasy portion. The pension change took place anyway, in July 1999, but employees didn't drop their demands that the company change it back. The irony was that they wanted IBM to change the cash-balance plan back to the pension equity plan, which the employees didn't realize—then or before—had already cut their pensions.

Employees formed the IBM Employee Benefits Action Coalition, which began to complain to the Equal Employment Opportunity Commission (EEOC), the IRS, Congress, and anyone else who would listen. August is usually a slow month that finds lawmakers at state fairs and pie-judging contests, but that year lawmakers in areas with large IBM populations were besieged in town hall meetings by angry IBM constituents. The largest was in Vermont, where eight hundred people jammed into an art center in Winooski for a meeting held by then Congressman Bernie Sanders. Sanders, a feisty independent, thought the IBM employees, who were asking IBM to let them remain in the old plan, had a point. "If converting to a new pension program doesn't save a company any money, as some companies say, it should not be too expensive for companies to offer all of their employees the choice to remain in their original pension plan."

A Senate committee decided to hold a hearing on whether employers were adequately disclosing pension cuts to employees. During the session, PricewaterhouseCoopers, a leading benefits consultant and accounting firm, circulated a briefing memo to lawmakers and the media stating that recent newspaper articles "leave readers with the unsubstantiated conclusion that corporate America uses cash-balance plans to mask significant reductions in pension benefits and costs." The memo also noted, "It is unfair to imply that employers chose to switch to cash-balance plans in order to mask benefit reductions."

But the impact of the consultants' briefing material was extinguished when a witness at the hearing played an audiotape of William Torrie, a Pricewaterhouse actuary, telling a Society of Actuaries meeting the previous year that "converting to a cash-balance plan does have an advantage, as it masks a lot of the changes. . . . There is very little comparison that can be done between the two plans," he said.

The witness played other audiotapes of discussions among actuaries made in the 1990s at other professional conferences. "If you decide your plan's too rich, and you want to cut back, and you only want to do it for new hires, changing to a totally different type of plan will let you do that without being obvious about it," said Norman Clausen, a principal at Kwasha Lipton, which had become a unit of Pricewaterhouse-Coopers. An article about the tapes' contents had earlier appeared in *The Wall Street Journal*, and then NBC got hold of the tapes and played excerpts on the *Nightly News*.

Gerstner and other top managers were caught flat-footed by the backlash, and before long they were staging a partial retreat. The company agreed to allow 35,000 older employees to stay in the old pension, but it still saved plenty of money. The cash-balance plan boosted IBM's pretax income in 1999 by $184 million, or 6 percent.

A MOVING STORY

Despite the negative attention its pension changes were getting, IBM continued to devise sly ways to cut benefits. One was to pay them out as lump sums. Companies championed the lump-sum feature as something that made cash balance and other hybrid pensions better for "a more mobile workforce." Because employees change jobs more frequently than they did in the past, employers maintained, they need a portable pension, like a 401(k), that they can cash out when they leave and roll into an IRA (or blow on a bass boat or a Taco Bell franchise).

One flaw in this construct is that employers have always been free to provide lump sums from traditional pensions; lump sums aren't intrinsic to cash-balance plans. And in any case, most employers automatically distribute pensions in lump sums when the pensions are worth $5,000 or less, to spare themselves the trouble of keeping track of them over many years.

Watson Wyatt, ever the innovator, offered employers the Single Payment Optimizer Tool (SPOT), a software program that enabled employers "to compare the cost of lump-sum cash outs to the costs of keeping employees on the retirement rolls." "Often, lump sums are the most cost-effective form of pension payout because of lower administrative costs over time," the accompanying marketing material says. It went on to note that sometimes employers are better off not offering lump sums if they can earn a higher rate of return on the assets than they will have to pay out to employees, adding that "SPOT can tell an employer when it is more cost effective to pay a lump sum and when an annuity is best. . . . With organizations scrutinizing every expense for bottom-line impact, every bit of savings helps." So much for the concern about providing lump sums to help more-mobile workers build retirement benefits.

Another fallacy is that workers are more mobile. Younger workers are, indeed, more mobile—Bureau of Labor Statistics data show that they tend to change jobs seven times before they're thirty-two. But pensions, including cash-balance plans, require five years on the job before one vests, so few younger, more-mobile workers remain in place long enough to collect a pension at all.

Older workers, by contrast, aren't mobile at all (at least not voluntarily). As IBM and other employers were painfully aware, older workers tend to stay on the job until they lock in a bigger pension. That was the portion of the workforce IBM and other companies wanted to dislodge. Lump sums offered a twofold solution. For one thing, they were an enormous carrot to get people out the door. Companies knew that employees found lump sums irresistible. "Choosey Employees Choose Lump Sums!" was the title of one of Watson Wyatt's surveys.

The carrot was especially effective when presented along with a stick: As part of their retirement "windows," numerous companies told employees that if they agreed to leave now, they could take a pension as a lump sum. If not, they could take their chances and get laid off next year and have only the option of a monthly check in retirement. Another benefit of lump sums—from employers' perspective—is that they shift longevity risk to retirees. Employers have been acutely aware that life spans are increasing, which explains why companies with a large percentage of women and white-collar professionals have been eager to provide lump sums.* If the pension is based on a life expectancy of seventy-eight, then an engineer who lives to age ninety will have drawn a pension for roughly twelve years longer than the amount the lump sum would have been based on.

By contrast, coal miners and factory workers tend to have shorter life spans than the national average, so it's no surprise that they are less likely to have a lump-sum option. General Motors, for instance, doesn't allow most of its factory workers to take a lump-sum payout. But it does allow its white-collar workers to take a lump sum if they leave before retirement age.†

Government data show a strong correlation between longevity and payout options: Bureau of Labor statistics show that about one-third of blue-collar workers have a lump-sum option in their pension plans, while 60 percent of white-collar workers do.

This concept is understood by noncorporate pension managers as well: The Marine Engineers' Beneficial Association, which covers ship engineers and deck officers, requires workers to take a medical exam before being eligible for a lump sum. Retirees in good health can take a lump sum, but those in poor health may not be allowed to.

Thus, despite all the talk about the burden of longer life spans, employers that pay out pensions in lump sums actually face none at all: The longevity risk has been passed on to the retirees.

---

* Employers began using unisex mortality tables in the 1980s, which has been disadvantageous for women taking lump sums rather than annuities.

† In recent years, some employers have argued that their workers are actually dying younger; this would enable employers to contribute less to their pension plans. Lawmakers bought it: The Pension Protection Act of 2006 allows large companies to use their own mortality assumptions when they figure out how much money to contribute to pension plans. Lower life spans mean lower contributions.

TAKING THEIR LUMPS

Lumps sums provided employers with yet another benefit. Companies used them to secretly cut pensions even as people walked out the door. The mechanism was simple: If someone's pension, converted to a lump sum, was worth $400,000, the employer could offer a lump sum worth, say, $350,000. How can this be legal, given anti-cutback rules?

Simple: Companies didn't tell employees that the lump sum was worth less, and employees couldn't tell. But as long as the employee chooses the lump sum—unknowingly cutting his own pension—the anti-cutback law hasn't been violated. (A key reason the lump sums are smaller is that they might not include the value of any early-retirement subsidy, which can be worth 20 percent or more of the total value.)

Few employees would knowingly give up tens of thousands of dollars' worth of pension, but unless employers provided apples-to-apples comparisons of the actual values of the monthly pension and the lump sum, there was no way to compare. In 1999, Mary Fletcher, a marketing services trainer and fourteen-year veteran of IBM, had to decide between taking a lump sum and a monthly pension when IBM sold a unit with three thousand U.S. employees to AT&T. She hired an adviser who calculated that while the monthly pension would be worth $101,000 if cashed out, the lump sum IBM offered Fletcher was worth only $71,500. Still, she took the lump sum. Almost all employees do, figuring they can invest the money and eventually end up with more. She was forty-seven and figured she was better off having nothing more to do with the IBM pension plan.

Employee advocates, including the Pension Rights Center and AARP, demanded better disclosure rules, but employers fought back. Lobbyists for the American Society of Pension Actuaries, the ERISA Industry Committee, and the U.S. Chamber of Commerce told Senate staffers that employees would only become confused if they were presented with too much complex information, and that providing more disclosure would be a "daunting task." Lawmakers didn't completely buy this, so in 2004 the IRS began requiring employers to tell people more clearly if the value of the lump sum wasn't equal to the monthly pension.

In 2006, the Pension Protection Act banned wear-away prospectively, meaning that if an employer set up a cash-balance plan after the 2006 law went into effect, it couldn't include a wear-away period.

But the issue of pension deception is still playing out in the courts. Cigna employees, who hadn't been told their pensions were essentially frozen when the company changed to a cash-balance plan, sued the company in 2001. In 2008, a federal court concluded that Cigna deliberately deceived its employees when it changed its pension plan in 1998, gave them "downright misleading" information about their pensions to negate the risk of an employee backlash. "CIGNA's successful efforts to conceal the full effects of the transition to [the new pension] deprived [plaintiffs] of the opportunity to take timely action . . . whether that action was protesting at the time [the change] was implemented, leaving CIGNA for another employer with a more favorable pension plan, or filing a lawsuit like this one."

The district court ordered Cigna to restore the pension benefits it had led employees to believe they would be receiving. Cigna appealed to the Second Circuit, and lost, but that wasn't the end of it. Cigna didn't try to appeal the court's finding that it deceived its employees—the memos and documents that surfaced in the case were too damning.

But in a kind of hail Mary pass, Cigna appealed to the Supreme Court, arguing that in order to get the benefits, each individual employee must prove he'd acted on the misinformation–that is, didn't change jobs or save more money, and thus suffered financial harm.

During oral arguments before the Supreme Court late in 2010, it became clear that the majority of justices were troubled by the fact that if they adopted the "detrimental reliance" standard Cigna was advocating, then employers would suffer no consequences even for the most egregious deception. "Doesn't this give an incredible windfall to your client, Cigna, or to other companies that commit this kind of intentional misconduct?" Justice Elena Kagan asked Cigna's attorney. In May 2011, the justices sent the case back to the lower court with instructions that it review its decisions, based on the portion of pension law that requires employers to tell employees, clearly and unambiguously, when it is cutting their pensions.

If the judge comes to the same decision to award the benefits to the employees—a total of $82 million—this would be the biggest award for employees whose employer hid pension cuts.

But Cigna has already taken steps to soften the blow: It froze the pension plan in 2009 and cut health, disability, and life insurance benefits for retirees, giving it a gain of $92 million.

CHAPTER 3

Profit Center: HOW PENSION AND RETIREE HEALTH PLANS BOOST EARNINGS

I**N ACTUARIAL CIRCLES**, there's a joke that goes something like this: A CFO is interviewing candidates for a job as a benefits consultant. He calls the first one, an accountant, into his office and asks, "What's two plus two?" The accountant says "Four." The CFO sends him away, calls an actuary into the room, and asks, "What's two plus two?" The actuary closes the door, pulls down the blinds, then leans in and whispers, "What do you want it to be?" He gets the job.

As much as this anecdote unfairly maligns the vast majority of actuarial professionals, it nonetheless sums up the view that some in the profession have toward their more aggressive brethren. Until the 1990s, benefits consulting firms generally handled standard pension tasks, like helping companies figure out how much to put into their pension plans, based on the ages and life expectancies of their employees, plus other factors. More closely aligned with the human resources department, they were one of the costs of operating a business, like accountants and the janitorial staff. But over the next two decades, large benefits consulting firms began aggressively marketing themselves to the finance departments. Their pitch? They could help employers turn pension plans into profit centers.

Their primary tools included the new accounting rules* that employers implemented in 1987, which require employers to disclose the size of their pension obligations, as they do other kinds of debts, and show how these pension debts affect income each quarter. Though the new accounting standard, FAS 87, was intended to increase transparency—allowing shareholders to see the full liability on a company's books—it was the beginning of the end for pensions. Before the new rules went into effect, employers got only one benefit from cutting pensions: The money that would someday have been paid to retirees would instead remain in the pension plan. Under the new accounting rules, employers got a second benefit when they cut pensions: Reducing the liability generated gains. These are paper gains, not cash, but when it comes to calculating earnings, the gains are treated the same as income from selling software or trucks. IBM's pension cuts in 1999 reduced its pension obligation by $450 million, resulting in a pot of gains worth roughly $450 million that the company could add to income either right away or over time. IBM added $200 million of these gains to its 1999 income.

The ability to convert pension benefits that would have been paid out to retirees over the coming decades into immediate profits for shareholders, today, changed the game: Pension plans weren't just piggy banks to tap for cash. They were also cookie jars of potential earnings enhancements.

It works something like this: Let's say a person earns $1,000, but he and his employer agree that he won't be paid until next year. Under FAS 87, this IOU is a debt, which the employer records on his books: Deferred compensation, $1,000.

But what if the employer decides to cut the employee's salary to $600 after the company has already recorded this debt on his books? Two things happen. The following year, the employer pays only $600—a cash savings of $400—and enjoys a secondary benefit: It has reduced its

* The rules, developed by the Financial Accounting Standards Board (FASB), went into effect for large companies in 1987 and a bit later for small employers.

debt by $400. Under accounting rules, a forgiven debt is recorded as a gain, and boosts income.

To see how this plays out in the retirement heist, add a few zeros to the $400 and think of the deferred pay as a pension: You're earning it today, but it will be paid later. Add ten thousand colleagues and the resulting obligation is billions of dollars. Reducing that obligation by $400 million generates gains.

PENSION TEMPTATION

There's nothing magical about these accounting rules. What made pension debt different from other kinds of debt was that it was easier to erase. A company that borrows $100 million to build a factory can't later wave a wand and make the debt go away; it can restructure the debt, or shed it in bankruptcy, but otherwise it's sticking around.

Pensions are different. Companies have a lot of leeway to change the benefits, and thus the size of the pension debt—but not all of it: A company can't touch the retirees' monthly checks. And it can't take away amounts people have already earned. But it can slow the growth of their pensions or halt it altogether by freezing the plans or laying off workers. This explains why, even when a pension plan has plenty of money, a company will profit if it cuts benefits.

It didn't take benefits consultants long to realize that every dollar a company had promised a retiree—for pensions, prescription drugs, dental coverage, life insurance, or death benefits—was the equivalent of a dollar that could potentially be added to a company's income. Suddenly, the $1 trillion that companies owed three generations of employees and retirees for pensions and retiree health benefits became potential earnings enhancements. Cuts generate gains, which lift earnings, which help the stock price, which boosts the compensation of the executives whose pay is based on performance. What CFO could resist that?

Not too many, and not for long. By the late 1990s, roughly four hundred large companies, most of which had well-funded or overfunded pension plans, had cut pension benefits, primarily by changing to a less generous cash-balance plan, which for many older workers was no different from freezing their pensions.

Pension managers faced a fresh conflict of interest: Should they manage the plans for the benefit of shareholders (and themselves) or for the benefit of retirees? Pension law requires that the plan be managed for the "exclusive benefit" of its participants. But on this point, pension law is like a toothless dog: It might sound scary, but it has no bite. Short of outright theft of pension assets, employers have been fairly free to make a lot of self-interested decisions when it comes to managing pensions.

Accounting professors at Cornell and the University of Colorado examined hundreds of companies that had converted their pensions to a cash-balance formula and found that the average incentive compensation for the chief executive officers jumped to about four times salary in the year of the pension cut, from about three times salary the year before. When companies didn't change their pensions, CEO pay also didn't change much. "You could have real economic wealth transfers away from employees," concluded Julia D'Souza, a Cornell associate professor of accounting and lead author of the study.

Pensions with Benefits

Gains from benefits cuts were only one way the pension plans were lifting earnings. The investment returns in the plan were another. Under the old system, employers got only one benefit from the investment returns in the pension plan: If the investments did well, the company would have to contribute less to the plan to keep it well funded.

Under the new rules, employers got a second benefit: If investment returns on pension assets exceed the pension plans' current costs, a company can report the excess as a credit on its income statement. Voilà: higher earnings. The bigger the pool of assets, the greater the potential gains.

This gave employers an incentive to cut benefits, even when the plan had a surplus. By the end of the decade, ten of the twelve companies with the most pension income had cash-balance or similar benefits-reducing pension plans. In 1998, Bell Atlantic Corp.'s pension plan produced a $627 million pretax credit for the company, and GTE Corp. reaped a $473 million pretax credit. US West, Boeing, IBM, and Ameritech had pension income ranging from $100 million to $454 million.

The desire for pension income also encouraged employers to increase stock holdings in the pension plans, in an effort to generate more income. The percentage of pension assets invested in stocks rose from 47 percent of assets in 1990 to more than 60 percent since the mid-1990s. A peculiar result of the accounting rules was that, instead of earnings driving the stock price, the stock market was driving earnings. In 1998, more than $1 billion of GE's pretax profit of $13.8 billion came from the pension plans. Caterpillar Inc. scored a $183 million credit. At Northrop Grumman Corp., 40 percent of first-quarter pretax profit was attributable to the surplus. USX–U.S. Steel Group would have reported a first-quarter loss except for its overfunded pensions.

In the euphoria of the bull market, few analysts noticed that a big chunk of company profits was coming from the pension plans. Patricia McConnell, a senior managing director at Bear Stearns, was one of the few who noticed the trend. Concerned that investors didn't understand that pension income was the result of smoke and mirrors, not improved sales or some other tangible achievement, she conducted an eight-month study and found that pension income accounted for 3 percent of the operating income of the S&P 500 companies in 1999. At some, it made a big difference. Without pension income, the income at People's Energy, Westvaco, U.S. Steel, and Boeing would have been 20 percent to 30 percent lower. Northrop Grumman's income would have been 43 percent lower.

Pensions not only generated profits; they also became tools to manage earnings, thanks to the enormous control employers had over the size and timing of pension profits. Need to lift the stock price before a merger? About to miss earnings targets by a few cents per share? No worries: The pension plan could get you there. The new accounting rules gave a whole new meaning to the words "pension fund management."

The mechanics aren't that complicated. Pension managers make a number of assumptions when they estimate the size of their pension liability, such as how long employees will work, what their annual pay increases are likely to be, whether they're married, and how long they'll live. One of the most powerful assumptions used to determine the size of the pension obligation is the "discount rate." A lower discount rate produces a higher liability, because if a company assumes that the assets in the pension plan will grow at a rate of 5 percent a year, it will need more money in the fund today than if it's assumed to grow by 7 percent.

Pension managers can't just pull any number out of a hat; they generally use a rate based on long-term, high-grade corporate bonds to calculate their benefits obligations. But companies have some wriggle room, and even seemingly small differences can have a big impact. In 2009, for instance, Lockheed decreased its discount rate from 6.4 to 6.1 percent, which boosted its pension obligation by $1.7 billion.

Great Expectations

Another key assumption is the "expected rate of return" on pension assets. This isn't the assumption used to measure the size of the liability; it's the assumption used to measure the pension plan's impact on quarterly income. Odd as it may sound to people who hear about it for the first time, accounting rules permit pension managers to use hypothetical or "expected" returns on their pension assets—instead of the actual returns. This is intended to smooth out the impact of the investment returns, so that a year of large increases or decreases doesn't affect earnings dramatically. This "smoothing mechanism," which employers insisted on having when the rules were developed, gives companies a great deal of control over the amount of pension income or expense.

Researchers at Harvard University and MIT analyzed filings from more than 2,000 companies and found that companies near critical earnings thresholds had boosted their estimated returns the prior year. One of the companies was IBM. As its operating performance was deteriorating in 2000 and 2001, in the wake of the tech bubble bust, the company raised its expected return from 9.25 percent to 10 percent. The increase in the assumed return accounted for nearly 5 percent of IBM's pretax income in 2000 and 2001.

The researchers also found that firms used higher expected returns on pension assets prior to acquiring other firms. "Managers may want to raise reported earnings . . . both to boost the price of stock that might be used as currency in such transactions and to generate greater bargaining power in the bidding process," they concluded. In addition, they found that firms raise their assumed returns when they issue equity and when their managers exercise stock options.

Using expected returns to boost income isn't the only way companies can use pensions to manage earnings, but these other ways have received little or no scrutiny. For example, underestimating the return on the pension assets can also render a benefit. For much of the nineties, the average expected rate of return companies used was 9 percent, even though returns were usually in the double digits, and exceeded 30 percent in some years. When the assumed (i.e., "expected") return is lower than what the pension assets actually return, the excess gains—the amount that exceeds the expected returns—are set aside. Over time, companies add some of these excess gains into future years' earnings calculations, a process called amortizing. By 2000, there were billions of dollars in "actuarial gains" sitting in reserves. When pensions had huge losses in the early 2000s, companies used these gains to cushion and delay the impact on earnings. (The reverse is also true: If losses are greater than the expected returns, the excess losses are parked on the sidelines and get added to the income calculations in subsequent years.)

Contributing Factors

Stuffing money into a pension plan is another way companies manage the timing and size of an income boost. When Lockheed Martin contributed $2 billion to its pension in 2010, the 8 percent expected return on assets guaranteed the aerospace-and-defense giant a $160 million boost to the bottom line in 2011, regardless of whether the company made any money selling jets. And because pension contributions are deductible, Lockheed was able to shave $64 million from its taxes.

The accounting and tax breaks explain why companies with well-funded pension plans happily shovel money into them. Why let a billion dollars in cash sit around unproductively when parking it in the pension can be so rewarding? Being able to park money in pension plans has so many rewards that employer groups have perennially lobbied to be allowed to put as much as they'd like into the plans. (Current law doesn't let companies deduct contributions to pension plans once the level of assets reaches 150 percent of the plans' liabilities.)

Companies also have a variety of reasons to adjust their assumptions to make their pension appear less well funded, or even terminally ill. This might be helpful prior to union negotiations or layoffs.

Mergers and acquisitions can offer companies an opportunity to monkey with the numbers. Prior to putting itself up for sale, a company may want to cut benefits or take other actions to make itself look more profitable.

Or perhaps it might want to sell some of the surplus. This was a common enough scenario that it was the topic of a panel at an annual actuaries conference in Colorado Springs in the summer of 1996. The panelists put on a skit involving a company that has asked its actuary to help increase the liability for the pensions of the transferred employees and retirees, so the company can justify transferring more assets than necessary and get cash in return, built into the sales price. The actuary does this, but is later called before a standards board and asked to justify the assumptions he used.

The "prosecutor," played by the chief actuary at the American Academy of Actuaries, asks the actuary to defend his decision to use a 1951 mortality table to calculate the liability.

> PROSECUTOR: Didn't you choose these assumptions . . . so you could transfer as much money as possible to the buyer?
> BAD ACTUARY: No, these are miners, so their life expectancy is not nearly as great as that of the general population.
> PROSECUTOR: How much did you get for them in the purchase price? Is it 80 percent or 90 percent?
> BAD ACTUARY: Well, it turned out that way in this transaction.

But he defends his actions saying he was just doing what his client wanted.

The skit concludes with the "prosecutor" telling the "bad actuary" that he's done a good job. "Someday the PBGC is going to . . . make an example of somebody. So when you get involved in these areas, make sure you're ready to answer all those questions. Have your answers ready."

None of this was illegal, but it shows how routine these sales transactions were.

ACCRUAL WORLD

The pension income charade began to change after the market tanked in 2001. When the market was rising in the nineties, few analysts noticed that falling pension obligations and 30 percent investment returns were fluffing up profits, and companies didn't go out of their way to call attention to it, preferring instead to let investors give company executives all the credit.

But when pension plans began losing money from 2000 through 2002, in part because managers had loaded them up with stock to boost pension income, companies quickly blamed the pension plans for their financial woes. Securities analysts who had been oblivious when pensions were pumping up income began cranking out reports dissecting the many ways pension plans were hurting earnings. These newly minted pension critics didn't notice that companies could manage earnings by adjusting discount rates, dumping money into the plans, or cutting benefits. But they did notice that companies were using expected returns of between 8 percent and 10 percent. In 2002, for example, GM assumed a 10 percent return, even though assets actually lost 5.2 percent. Companies had been using the same 8 to 10 percent assumptions for years, including those when assets were earning 30 percent, but analysts acted as if they'd discovered the next Enron, and they cranked out even more reports. Even Warren Buffett, chairman of Berkshire Hathaway, weighed in, scolding companies for "legal but improper accounting methods used by chief executives to inflate reported earnings. The most flagrant deceptions have occurred in stock-option accounting and in assumptions about pension-fund returns. The aggregate misrepresentation in these two areas dwarfs the lies of Enron and WorldCom."

The market plunge had smoked out accounting innovations at Enron, Lucent, Nortel, Tyco, Waste Management, and WorldCom, most of which involved management efforts to bump up the share price by manipulating earnings. Many of these practices involved "accrual accounting," i.e., the way companies report such things as debts and reserves. Retiree benefits are a form of accrual accounting, too, subject to the same manipulation but not to the same scrutiny.*

---

* In 2003, the Securities and Exchange Commission began investigating whether companies were using retiree plans to manage earnings. It sent subpoenas to Boeing, Delphi, Ford Motor, General Motors, Navistar International, and Northwest Airlines, asking the companies whether they had used pension and health-benefit funds to adjust their earnings in recent years. The companies said "Of course not," and the investigation fizzled out. The SEC was focusing on discount rates and other assumptions used to calculate liabilities, not the use of pension cuts and other maneuvers.

CHAPTER 4

Health Scare: INFLATING RETIREE HEALTH LIABILITIES TO BOOST PROFITS

COMPANIES HAVE BEEN PLAYING even more elaborate games with their retiree health plans. These health plans are essentially medical pensions that employers have promised to decades of workers. If someone worked long enough to earn retiree health benefits, then, when he retired at fifty-five or later, his employer's medical plan would continue to cover him until he qualified for Medicare at age sixty-five. Some plans, particularly for unions, provided a Medicare supplement, covering things like prescription drugs.

And then, in 1992, companies began sending letters to hundreds of thousands of retirees, all of which contained eerily similar messages: "Health care costs continue to skyrocket," wrote McDonnell Douglas. Health care costs were "skyrocketing," wrote R.R. Donnelley. In these letters, Sears, Caterpillar, Unisys, and scores of other employers, citing "spiraling" health care costs, all informed retirees that, regretfully, they had no choice but to cut benefits.

The companies blamed a new accounting rule—FAS 106—for the changes. The rule was similar to the one employers had adopted with pensions a few years earlier in that it required companies to estimate their obligations for the health coverage they would provide to retirees—current and future—and report the obligation to shareholders. When the companies did this, they claimed to be shocked to find that the costs were so high. This, they said, called for hard choices, and regretfully, they would have to cut benefits. It was a matter of survival.

Though corporate America acted as though it had just discovered it was sitting on a neutron bomb, CFOs knew well ahead of time what the charges would be. Major companies, including IBM and GE, had worked with the Financial Accounting Standards Board (FASB) to create the rules, as they had with the pension rules, and had persuaded the accounting board to build in as much flexibility as possible. As with pensions, companies had substantial leeway to raise or lower their obligations by changing the assumptions they used, including interest rates, expected returns on assets, employee turnover, marriage rates, retirement age, and mortality rates. But companies had another powerful lever for manipulating the numbers: the health care inflation assumption (also known as a "health care trend rate"). Despite its name, this isn't an actual measure of inflation in the cost of hospital stays, premiums, or prescription drugs. Rather, it's simply a company's estimate of the increase in what it might pay, based on undisclosed factors. In other words, they can pretty much make it up.

With so much control over the size of the liability, one might expect employers to use a low health care inflation rate, since this would make their obligations look smaller. But many companies did just the opposite, choosing to assume that double-digit health care inflation would persist for decades. They did this even though most experts at the time believed that the worst period of health care inflation was over and the rate of increase was declining, thanks to the spread of managed-care programs, which were intended to reduce unnecessary health care costs. (By 1995, in fact, health care costs were flat, before trending upward again.) Among the pessimists who continued to predict steady inflation were Kimberly-Clark (16 percent), Teledyne (11.5 percent), and Allied-Signal (12 percent).

These high inflation assumptions, combined with other assumptions, including that benefits plans would never change and that the retirees would live a really long time, led to whopping obligations. As the companies had hoped, the media was awash in stories about this new, unexpected threat to the viability of the nation's largest companies. A sample from late 1991: "Automakers Face Massive Charges" (Associated Press); "Rude Awakening on Health Costs. . . . The numbers are shocking many" (*Los Angeles Times*); "New Medical-Benefits Accounting Rule Seen Wounding Profits, Hurting Shares" (*The Wall Street Journal*). The industry-funded Employee Benefit Research Institute estimated that the total impact on companies could be as great as $2 trillion.

There was little downside to putting huge retiree liabilities on their books. Securities analysts and shareholders tend to ignore earnings hits that are the result of accounting changes that all companies must adopt. Speaking candidly to consultants at an actuarial conference in 1996, Ethan Kra, then the chief retirement actuary at William M. Mercer, summed up Wall Street's sentiment: "The Street views FAS 106 obligations as ephemeral."

Reporting a giant retiree liability was also an opportunity for some big-bath accounting, a process in which publicly traded companies pile a lot of bad items into a single year, so subsequent years' income will look better by comparison. It could also be called "you can't fall off the floor" accounting. Expecting costs from layoffs? Need to write off that bad loan? Doing badly anyway? Get all the bad news out of the way at once, so when net income rises in subsequent quarters, even if only a little, management will look like a hero for turning things around.

PUMP AND DUMP

McDonnell Douglas was one of the first companies to claim the sky was falling. In 1991, the giant aerospace-and-defense contractor lost a lucrative Department of Defense contract to develop a stealth aircraft because of perpetual delays and cost overruns. It was in need of an earnings lift, and FAS 106 came at a fortuitous time. McDonnell Douglas adopted the new accounting rule in January 1992, estimating that health care costs would rise 15 percent a year and that the benefits would remain unchanged. This produced a shocking obligation, for which the company took an immediate $1.5 billion after-tax charge.

But just nine months later, McDonnell Douglas pointed to those whopping costs and announced it would phase out all health coverage for its twenty thousand nonunion retirees. "Health care costs continue to skyrocket," explained John McDonnell, then the company's chief executive, in an October 7, 1992, letter to retirees, adding that there was also a new accounting standard that "threatened to deal a heavy blow to our bottom line."

> I'm writing to tell you we've found a solution. It may seem complicated at first glance, but, when all is said and done, you will have the same coverage under the new plan. . . . So here's what we're going to do. First, health care coverage provided by McDonnell Douglas to non-union retirees will end Dec. 31, of this year, and retirees are then responsible for obtaining and paying for their own coverage. BUT, second, as of that date, coverage identical to what you have had (but *arranged* by McDonnell Douglas, rather than *provided by* McDonnell Douglas) will be made available to you.

What was really happening: McDonnell Douglas would be paying for the additional coverage—using pension assets—for four years. After that, well, the retirees would pick up 100 percent of the costs (with their premiums being subtracted from their pensions). McDonnell maintained in his letter that this plan, which supposedly would enable retirees to continue their benefits "without denting your pocketbook," would save the company millions. In fact, McDonnell Douglas's pump-and-dump maneuver gave it a pretax gain of $698 million. Without the gains from cutting retiree medical benefits, the company would have had a loss for the year. Companies could take the gains all at once, even if the cuts wouldn't take effect until later; the bigger the bath, the bigger the pile of gains.

CFOs and consultants didn't call attention to this, and most analysts were oblivious to the way non-cash gains from benefits plans were enhancing income. But one prescient observer, Jack Ciesielski, an independent accounting analyst in Baltimore, warned in a 1994 client newsletter that the new rules gave employers an incentive to inflate their liabilities. "Companies that were the most adversely affected may have made the most dire assumptions in setting up their postretirement benefits liabilities—and thus have the largest 'reserves' to call upon should they need a little earnings help in the next economic downturn," he wrote. "It's programmed-in earnings improvement. . . . By bulking up their assumptions, they created a piggy bank of earnings improvers."

McDonnell Douglas illustrates another key difference between pensions and retiree health plans. While federal law dictates that companies can't cut pensions that have already been earned, this is not the case for health plans. Unless the benefits were protected by a union contract (and sometimes not even then), companies could pull the plug on benefits that employees, including retirees, had already earned.

McDonnell Douglas's profits came at the cost of thousands of retirees like Robert Taylor, who joined the company shortly after the Second World War and retired in 1979. He died four years later, at age seventy-nine, just when the company started passing the costs on to the retirees. As the company phased out its share of the coverage, the retirees' share grew, until they were paying 100 percent of the costs. Rhada Taylor, Robert's widow, continued to get the coverage, which supplemented Medicare and covered such things as prescription drugs. Initially, the premium she paid for this was $168. As is common practice, the company deducted the ever-increasing premium from her widow's pension of $420 a month. The premiums increased bit by bit each year, and by

2000 her pension had disappeared altogether, leaving her with only a Social Security check of $1,009 a month to live on.

R.R. Donnelley, a printing company based in Chicago, dispatched a similar letter to its retirees in October 1992, also blaming "skyrocketing" health-care costs and FAS 106: "We have another problem—a new accounting rule we must use, beginning in 1993. This of course has a serious negative impact on our earnings." Regretfully, the company began to charge retirees for their once free health care, "to remain competitive." That last part was true: It remained competitive with the other companies that were cutting retiree health coverage.

While some companies like McDonnell Douglas chose to report all of its gains in a single year, R.R. Donnelly took the more common approach and spread them over several years. Donnelley's gains were fed into income throughout the nineties.

LET THE GAINS BEGIN

Few noticed that companies were gaming the system, and people who pointed it out didn't score any points with private industry. Jeffrey Petertil had been an adviser to the accounting-board task force that drafted the new rule, and he wasn't happy with the outcome. "FAS 106 not only overstates the value of future retirees' health benefits, but its complexity presents another hazard," he wrote in a 1992 editorial in *The Wall Street Journal*. "The value a company assigns to future health benefits can be wrong, whether by mistake or by design, and nobody will much know. The FASB rule leaves loopholes that let a company reduce or increase cost almost as it wishes. One reason there has been little outcry, considering its estimated financial impact, is that some consultants and managers know that by making minor changes to the plans they can greatly reduce the FASB cost."

He also pointed out something that ought to have been obvious:

Employers could make their retiree health liabilities go away. "There is a question of whether there is a liability at all," he wrote. "Many companies extend health benefits to retirees but change them often. Recent court cases indicate that the employers' right to change or terminate the benefit will be upheld." Within twenty-four hours of the editorial's publication, his largest client, a Big Six accounting firm, fired him.

Defense contractors and public utilities had an additional incentive to inflate their obligations, because they could use the high figures to ask for more money in their government contracts or to ask utilities commissions for rate increases to offset the cost of the benefits. Pacific Gas & Electric reported a large liability in 1993, then asked the California Public Utilities Commission for permission to raise rates to cover its retiree health costs. It obtained a $181 million rate increase that year. But PG&E then reduced what it would pay for benefits and cut its workforce by 17 percent. By 1999 it had reduced its annual retiree-benefits expense by 90 percent.

California ratepayer advocates ultimately caught on and pointed out PG&E's retiree-liability two-step to the utilities commission. The commission required the company to credit $191 million to ratepayers for the years 1993 through 1995. By the late 1990s, more ratepayer advocates were hiring auditors to review utilities' requests for rate hikes to pay for retiree health costs. When evaluating a request by New Jersey water utilities for a rate hike, the advocates' office hired an expert who found that virtually every assumption—health care inflation, mortality rates, salary increases, expected rates of return on the assets, and so on— was unrealistic. The rate board nixed the increases. Similarly, the Massachusetts Attorney General's Office and the Rhode Island Division of Public Utilities and Carriers, an agency that represents consumers, hired a consultant to conduct an audit of New England Electric System's retiree health costs. The auditors determined that ratepayers had overpaid for the benefits, and the utility was forced to refund $20 million.

HUSTLING THE JUDGES

The giant liabilities that companies reported for retiree health care also had a powerful effect on the courts. Unisys, like many other companies in the late 1980s and 1990s, promised lifetime, company-paid health coverage to older employees as an inducement to get them to retire. Albert Shaklee was one of thousands of Unisys career employees who took the deal. But the coverage didn't last long. In October 1992, Unisys sent a letter to 25,000 former employees saying that because of "increasing medical costs and growing worldwide competition" the company would shift 100 percent of the cost of coverage to the retirees over three years. "This new plan will be cost-effective, will provide financial protection against the high cost of illness or injury, and will continue to be available at group rates," the letter said.

Shaklee, who had moved to Lake Kiowa, Texas, when he retired, hung on to his coverage as long as possible, because his wife, Doris, hadn't yet hit the Medicare eligibility age of sixty-five and, with a cancer diagnosis, was uninsurable. When his premiums reached $784 a month in 1996, exceeding his $727 monthly pension, he dropped out of the plan. Though he had earned $70,000 a year, in order to get health coverage Shaklee had to take a minimum-wage midnight-shift job at a parts-grinding factory in nearby Gainesville. He was seventy at the time.

Unisys retirees sued, pointing to the written promises, but the court rejected their claim. "Just as in war, there are no winners," wrote a U.S. district court judge in Philadelphia in a 1996 decision. "This is a corporation that provided a generous benefit and may have continued providing it if medical costs had not escalated and FAS 106 had not become a reality."

HITTING THE CEILING

For all their talk of skyrocketing costs and burdensome accounting regulations, these companies weren't facing as much peril as the public assumed. Generally, the benefits cover only people who retire between fifty-five and sixty-five, assuming the person had worked long enough to be eligible—usually a minimum of fifteen years. Employers had largely closed that barn door long ago, shutting out people hired after a certain date, so the population of employees eligible for benefits had largely stopped growing. Another factor that limits employers' liabilities: When the retiree turns sixty-five, employer coverage, if it continues, becomes secondary to Medicare, which provides basic hospital and doctor-visit coverage. That means the employers' costs drop sharply. As unlikely as it sounds, the older retirees get, the less expensive they become to their former employers.

Nor did employers face much exposure to rising costs. That's because when they adopted FAS 106, most companies, including Sears, R.R. Donnelly, Delta Air Lines, and Caterpillar established ceilings on how much they would spend for retiree health care, regardless of how high they rose in the future. What this means is that, once these companies hit their pre-set spending ceilings, say, at $20 million a year, or at an annual limit for an individual, they're protected from rising health care costs, no matter how sick their retirees get or how long they live.

In 1993 IBM set ceilings on its future spending. For retirees under sixty-five, the cap was $7,000 or $7,500 depending on when they retired. For those on Medicare, the cap was $3,000 or $3,500. The ceilings effectively shifted the risk of rising health care costs to the retirees, because once the costs increased enough to hit the company's pre-set ceiling, any costs over the cap are passed on to the retirees. When IBM hit its spending ceiling around 2002, its spending stopped growing. All the increased costs were passed on to the retirees, whose health care premiums rose 67 percent, while IBM's spending declined 18 percent. With spending caps in place, companies see a steady decrease in costs as their aging retirees become eligible for Medicare, drop the coverage, or die.

RETIREE DROPOUTS

By the late 1990s, about two-thirds of retirees were dropping their employer-provided coverage within several years after retiring, according to Labor Department figures. Among them was Elaine Russell, a Sears retiree in Seattle, who dropped the coverage when it had reached one-third of her pension. Medicare didn't cover medications for her thyroid condition and colitis, so she paid for her prescriptions with her grocery budget and relied on the $2.50 lunches at the senior center and on the local food bank, where she got free canned food for herself and her cat.

Though the retirees' share of costs was rising, Sears's was shrinking, not just because of the cost shifting, but because it changed its estimate about health care inflation. By 1999, the retailer had slashed the health care trend rate to 6 percent from 14 percent. Revising that assumption downward, of course, lowered the obligation on the books. So did the benefits cuts. By the end of the decade, Sears's IOUs for retiree health care had fallen 69 percent, to $900 million.

When retirees like Russell drop coverage they can no longer afford, companies benefit in two ways. One is that they no longer have to pay their share of the benefits. That's a cash savings. The other is that because the company will no longer have to pay anything for the retiree dropouts, for the rest of their lives, the company can total up the overall lifetime savings and reduce its obligation by that amount. That produces gains that boost income.

By 2005, when Sears merged with Kmart, the number of retirees in the Sears plan had fallen from 100,000 to 50,500. Sears doesn't disclose how many had died and how many had dropped out. Liz Rossman, Sears's vice president for benefits, dismissed the notion that retirees were dropping out because they couldn't afford the benefits. Apart from those who had died, others might have gotten jobs with health coverage. "We were trying to strike a balance between duty to shareholders, so they could get an adequate return on investments, with our duty to retirees." And the Sears plan was "far more generous with benefits than others in our industry." She pointed out that the company had boosted other retiree benefits, such as doubling the discount retirees receive on clothing purchases at the store, from 10 percent to 20 percent.

In 2006, Sears stopped paying retiree medical costs altogether.

DEATH SPIRAL

These ceilings not only protect companies from rising health care costs but also provide them with a perverse incentive: A company that has hit its spending cap has little incentive to negotiate the lowest possible prices with medical providers. In fact, it has an incentive not to: Rising expenses not only won't hurt the company but will tend to drive more retirees from the program.

Meanwhile, retirees with preexisting conditions and serious health problems remain in the health plan, driving up costs further. Robert Eggleston, an IBM retiree in Lake Dallas, Texas, had brain cancer, so even when his monthly costs for retiree coverage exceeded his pension, he remained in the plan, which also covered his wife, LaRue. To get by, he cashed out his 401(k) account and took out a second mortgage on his home. Luckily, he was eligible for free supplies of a tumor-fighting drug through a program for low-income families, but this was an unexpected end for a career IBM employee.

Some employers hastened the death spiral by segregating retirees into their own risk group rather than keeping active employees and retirees in the same "risk pool" and spreading costs among a wider group of people, as had been common practice in the past. When retirees are segregated into their own pool, the per capita costs rise, because an older, sicker population needs more medical care.

After Xerox split its active and retired employees into two pools in 2003, its retirees under sixty-five began paying 50 to 60 percent more than employees their age. Eugene Nathenson, a retired controller of Xerox Financial Services, saw his premiums shoot up from $1,645 in 2003 to $3,196 the following year, while the deductibles he and his wife paid pushed their out-of-pocket costs beyond $6,000 a year.*

REPLENISHING THE COOKIE JAR

By the late 1990s and early 2000s, many companies had used up the actuarial gains they'd stockpiled after the early rounds of cost shifting and benefits cuts, just as they had spent the surplus in their pension piggy banks. So they turned to a tried-and-true solution: Cut more benefits.

Companies continued to cut retiree health benefits throughout the 2000s. International Paper cut benefits in 2000, 2001, and 2002, telling retirees that health care costs were spiraling. What had actually happened was that it had used up the pool of accounting gains generated after the company recorded a huge liability in 1991, and then set a cap on benefits. Unlike McDonnell Douglas, which took all the gains at once, International Paper trickled the gains into income in subsequent years, to the tune of $17 million a year. After this stockpile was used up, cutting the benefits generated a fresh pool of accounting gains that added a total of $65 million to its income by 2004. In 2004, the company then closed the plan to salaried employees whose age plus years of employment with the company totaled less than sixty as of January 1, 2004. Another cut in 2009 whittled another $40 million in obligations.

IBM's cookie jar of earnings enhancements was also running low by the end of the 1990s. IBM's solution was to establish "health care accounts" for future retirees, which was essentially a way to further limit the amount it would pay for their health benefits. This step, which

---

* This explains why COBRA costs can be so high: Employers can segregate former employees—regardless of their age—into the retirees' risk pool.

the company took in 1999, reduced the company's liability by $127 million and generated a fresh pool of accounting gains that the company added to income over a period of years.

Benefits consultants helped their clients replenish the cookie jars. William Falk, who oversaw the retiree medical consulting practice at Towers Perrin, addressed the problem of diminishing income at an actuarial conference in the late 1990s: "So the clients are saying, 'Well, what can we do about this? We don't want our costs to jump up next year. Management and shareholders won't accept it.' Well," he told his fellow consultants at the meeting, "they're doing a lot of things. They're looking at reduction in benefits again."

Towers Perrin sent marketing materials to current and potential corporate clients, saying employers needed to think about "new strategies and approaches to managing health benefits." Among them: tightening eligibility by requiring higher ages and years of service; getting some dependents out of the plan, such as dependent children; and increasing premiums, deductibles, and out-of-pocket expenses, "especially when you can't get people [like union retirees] out" of the plan. Companies could also adopt "more aggressive assumptions" for health care inflation, administrative expenses, and participation rates. Health care inflation trends "have been low, but we've kept them high. Now we have room to move back down" and generate some new accounting gains.

Of course, companies that announce benefits cuts don't say they're cutting benefits because they've run out of accounting gains generated by earlier cuts. They generally just blame rising health care costs. That was what Aetna did in 2003 when it announced it would phase out health care benefits for workers who retired starting in 2004. The reality: Aetna's costs were going up because it had used up the pool of gains generated when it capped the benefits in 1994. It had used as much as $23 million a year from this pool to reduce its annual expense. By 2002 those gains had run out, and to keep its expense from rising, Aetna needed to cut benefits again.

But was Aetna actually spending more money? Not really. Thanks to the ceiling on spending, the amount the company actually paid—that is, dollars out the door—remained roughly flat from 1998 through 2002, ranging between $35 million and $39 million. Asked to explain why it was cutting benefits when it wasn't spending more, Aetna responded by saying that it needed "to reduce expenses in order to be competitive." That answer, at least, made more sense: The maneuver increased Aetna's pretax income by $34 million in the first quarter of 2003. That was 6.4 percent of its earnings. The gains continued to lift Aetna's pretax earnings about $45 million a year for several more years.

Companies could time the cuts to generate gains at opportune moments. With a little preparation, companies can determine how many cents per share they need to meet earnings targets, and then identify which bits of their retiree plans to trim to generate the gains the company needs to clear the earnings hurdle. Caterpillar increased retirees' premiums and made other benefit cuts in 2002 that reduced obligations by $475 million. This resulted in a $75 million accounting gain that year, which amounted to 9.4 percent of pretax earnings. The flexibility built into the accounting rules—and employers' ability to trim benefits—has enabled companies to cannibalize their retiree health plans whenever they need to generate gains to boost income.

At Whirlpool, the retiree health plan has offset the cost of defective appliances over the years. In the second quarter of 2003, trims to its retiree medical benefits generated a one-time gain of $13.5 million. This added 19 cents a share—enough to offset a one-time after-tax charge of 16 cents a share to cover the cost of recalling defective microwaves, with three cents left over. This enabled the company to report earnings of $1.35 a share—beating the $1.31-a-share consensus estimates.

In March 2009, Whirlpool made another benefits trim: It suspended the annual credit it provided to the retiree health savings accounts. The

$89 curtailment gain this cut generated neatly offset a one-time charge for a voluntary recall of 1.8 million refrigerators sold in the United States and Canada between 2001 and 2004. And in March and June 2010, the $62 million in gains from other cuts to the retiree health care plan largely offset the $75 million charge for recalling 1.8 million dishwashers sold in the United States and Canada between 2006 and 2010.

CHAPTER 5

Portfolio Management:

SWAPPING POPULATIONS OF RETIREES FOR CASH AND PROFITS

ONE OF THE LAST LETTERS Bill Jelly received before he died in 2003 was from his benefits administrator, informing him that the death benefit from his employer, Western Electric, was going to be canceled—in one month. He'd earned the benefit decades ago, when death benefits, like retiree health coverage, were commonly offered to people who'd spent most or all of their careers at a particular company.

The benefit wasn't much: $39,000, the equivalent of the salary he had the year he retired in 1979. But he had been counting on it to pay his burial costs and the medical expenses the couple faced, thanks to cuts to their retiree health coverage. "I guess I'm going to have to die before then," Jelly, who was seventy-nine, told Margaret, his wife of fifty years.

But even though Jelly had spent his entire career at Western Electric, the letter had come from Lucent Technologies, based in Murray Hill, New Jersey. At that point, Jelly had barely heard of Lucent, a spin-off created seventeen years after he had retired. But like millions of retirees across the country, his pension and retirement benefits were under new management thanks to mergers and restructurings that took place after he retired, thereby shuffling his benefits to a new company. From a management point of view, pools of retirees are essentially portfolios of debts and assets. The debts are the pensions and retiree health benefits the workers earned, and the assets are the funds set aside to pay them. When a business unit is sold, merged, acquired, or spun off, a portfolio of retirees is often packaged along with the rest of the business.

To the new owners, the retirees in the portfolio aren't former engineers, managers, or factory workers. They're a resource to be managed with an eye toward profits. Retirees find it unsettling that their pensions have migrated to new owners, especially when the new portfolio owners send them "Dear Retiree" letters, telling them that their health coverage is ending, their pension has been incorrectly calculated, or other benefits are being cut. When the retirees' increasingly frantic appeals fall on deaf ears, they conclude that the new company has no loyalty to them. But they don't realize the half of it. They've literally become human resources, to be consumed for cash and profits.

PENSION ASSETS

Chuck Ackerman discovered this with a shock in early 2000. The first sign of trouble was when his pension check didn't arrive on time. At first he thought it was a Y2K glitch. Then he received a letter from Raytheon, a company where he had never worked, telling him that not only was he not going to get his pension check but that he actually owed the company $31,904 that he'd been mistakenly paid over the prior five years. The letter explained that the company would be withholding his pension payments for the next year and a half until the "debt" was paid off. It was like a punch in the gut for the retired pilot, who was already battling cancer.

Ackerman had flown corporate jets for Hughes Aircraft for twenty-six years, delivering executives, including C. Michael Armstrong, then the chairman of Hughes Electronics, to meetings around the globe, ski vacations, and private homes in places like Baja and Taos. He loved being a pilot, but regulations required that he retire at age sixty, in 1992. He plowed his retirement savings into an eighteen-acre farm outside of Santa Maria, California, where he and his wife, Audrey, cleared land and grew grapes to sell to local wineries.

Five years after he retired, in 1997, defense giant Raytheon acquired Hughes. The acquisition brought with it a portfolio of thousands of retirees, along with pension and health care liabilities of $5.6 billion, and $6.4 billion in assets to pay the retirees' benefits. In other words, as part of the acquisition, Raytheon got a pool of assets that was more than large enough to pay every cent of the retirees' pension and healthcare benefits until they died. Hughes, in effect, sold roughly $1 billion in pension surpluses to Raytheon. This boosted the price Raytheon paid for Hughes, but the acquisition had an immediate payoff: The infusion of billions of dollars of pension assets into Raytheon's pension plan generated roughly $500 million of income in the first year.

Despite having acquired $1.2 billion more than needed to pay the retirees' pensions, Raytheon did what other companies typically do when they acquire a portfolio of assets: It set about trying to maximize its investment. Under pension law, a company can't cut pensions once retirees start receiving them. But if it determines that the retirees are mistakenly receiving benefits that are too large, it can claw the overpayments back.

One of the first things companies do is assign their benefits consultants to flyspeck the records and ferret out mistakes in the company's favor. Given the complexities of pensions, it's no surprise that they find some. It might be that an incorrect interest rate was used, or that twenty years earlier, a prior owner of the portfolio miscalculated a cost-of-living increase. Raytheon hired Hewitt Associates for this task. On its Web site at the time, Hewitt boasted that one of its audits had "uncovered $4.1 million in savings per year by eliminating participants erroneously left on the carrier's system."

Hewitt concluded that Ackerman's pension had been incorrectly calculated. Pilots are required to retire by age sixty, so many receive a pension supplement until they reach age sixty-five. The pension administrator had forgotten to end the supplement when Ackerman turned sixty-five. Now Raytheon wanted its money back.

Pension law requires that pension overpayments be returned to the pension plan, but it doesn't say who should return the money: the employer that made the mistake, the current portfolio owner, or the retiree. Companies usually pursue repayment from the retirees or their surviving spouses, by reducing the person's pension or even stopping it altogether until the overpayment is recovered. Private employers like Hughes are allowed to offset 100 percent of a retiree's pension to recoup an overpayment. Multiemployer pension plans, which cover retirees at different companies, are limited to 25 percent, while the Pension Benefit Guaranty Corp., which takes over failed plans, can reduce a pension by no more than 10 percent, and doesn't charge interest.

Ackerman made increasingly frantic calls to the toll-free number of the pension administrator, arguing with the clerk, who didn't know how pensions work, let alone the kind of pilot's pension Ackerman had. Ackerman couldn't prove he hadn't been overpaid—he was a pilot, not an actuary. He scrambled to find the details in pension stubs going back years, documents he'd received, or forms he'd signed. He couldn't figure out how the pension was calculated. "When your pension gets shifted from one company to another," his wife, Audrey, concluded, "they've got you over a barrel."

Seniors' advocates say it's unfair for retirees struggling with small pensions on fixed incomes to pay for a company's mistakes. "Our clients are often confused and shocked to learn that their pension plan overpaid them," says Justin Freeborn, a legal-aid lawyer with the Western States Pension Assistance Project in Sacramento, California, funded in part by the U.S. Administration on Aging. He has seen a steady stream of frightened retirees in recent years coming for help when they receive demanding letters from the pension administrators. "In most cases, they had no idea they were receiving the wrong amount. They've already spent the overpaid money, and they have no way to pay it back."

Chuck Ackerman didn't have the money or the time to fight in court: Just four days before he got the letter from the pension administrator, he learned that the esophageal cancer he'd been treated for had spread to his liver and lungs. Figuring his days were numbered, he appealed to the company to forgive the debt. While awaiting an answer, he began chemotherapy treatments at a hospital near Santa Barbara, where he ran into a retired vice president of Hughes and told him about his pension problem. A few weeks later, when he checked his mailbox, he found a note from the retired executive, with a personal check for $5,000. He also found a letter from the retirement board of Raytheon, denying his appeal to review their decision to dock his pension.

Raytheon refused to forgive the debt and demanded that the Ackermans repay it within a year. The couple appealed this decision, because it would have consumed all of their pension plus most of their Social Security, leaving them with nothing to live on. Raytheon relented, and later that year agreed to let them repay $500 a month. Between chemotherapy treatments and battles with the pension administrator, Ackerman poured himself into farmwork. Even as his six-foot-four-inch frame dwindled to 140 pounds, he also made various improvements on the farm—fixing the roof, mending outbuildings. What bothered him the most, Audrey recalled, was that after he'd spent so many years as a pilot making sure the Hughes executives were safe, "he felt like the company considered him a liar and a cheat."

Ackerman died in 2002, and it took his wife two and a half years more to repay the debt to Raytheon, out of her diminished widow's pension. Then, for three months, even after she'd finished paying the debt, Raytheon mistakenly continued to withhold the $500 monthly repayments. Only after she complained a number of times did Raytheon correct the mistake.

BLINDSIDED

A portfolio of retirees can change hands so many times that even the new owner of the retiree portfolio can't keep track of who's owed what. In the late 1990s, British Petroleum, or BP, as it is now called, acquired a portfolio of retirees from a variety of companies when it merged with Amoco. In 2000, it hired a new pension administrator, Fidelity Investments Institutional Operations Co., which handles benefits plans covering about nineteen million employees and retirees. The BP plan, thanks to its promiscuous rounds of acquisitions and mergers, had close to fifty thousand U.S. retirees, plus seventy thousand workers and former employees who'll get pensions someday. Fidelity audited the plan in 2004 and concluded that 316 retirees had mistakenly been paid a total of $100 million that some other predecessor company owed. BP began the process of recouping the money.

One of the retirees was Charlie Craven, a retired mine supervisor in Tucson. Craven had been receiving a pension of $346 a month for eighteen years, until January 2005, when, instead of a pension check, he received a letter from Fidelity informing him that a recent audit revealed he was receiving benefits in error.

"You must repay the overpayment of $18,363 in one lump sum by January 21, 2005. If you are unable to make a one time lump sum repayment and wish to set up a repayment plan, your payments are as follows: $1,530 per month for (12) months." The letter added: "If you do not comply within the stated timeframe, the plan sponsor may take additional steps to correct this overpayment.... Such steps might be to reclassify the [overpayment] as miscellaneous income," issue a corrected 1099-R, and report him to the Internal Revenue Service, "or take more formal collection action against you."

"I thought when you retired, that was it," Craven said. "How can they come to me all these years later and tell me this?" Craven, a widower with macular degeneration who is nearly blind, had a friend read him the letter, which said that a company called Foundation Coal Corp. should have been paying Craven's pension, and directed him to write to Foundation Coal, in Linthicum Heights, Maryland, for information about his benefit. In the meantime, he needed to begin repaying the debt to BP. "Please accept our apologies for any inconvenience this may have caused," the letter concluded.

Craven had never heard of Foundation Coal. He'd earned the pension working for Cyprus Mines, a copper-and-minerals company, and had bounced among several mines in Arizona and Nevada over the years. He didn't know which company bought what; he only knew that his check had been coming from BP.

He was still thinking about this dilemma two weeks later when a second letter from Fidelity Investments arrived, reiterating the demand for repayment. This letter, like the preceding one, was delayed because it had been sent to his prior address in Kingman, Arizona. This second letter noted that Craven had originally earned his pension under the Amoco pension plan, which had merged with the BP plan, "but the liability for that benefit and the associated pension assets were subsequently transferred to Cyprus Minerals in 1985 . . . and therefore not payable under the BP pension plan. This letter didn't mention Foundation Coal, but directed him to write to Fidelity Investments in Cincinnati or call a toll-free number. Craven asked his friend Ruth Emley, a widow from Nevada he'd met online, to make the call. Ruth, who, like Craven, was seventy-nine at the time, called but got an automated system and was put on eternal hold. "We never got to talk to anyone there," Ruth said.

This second letter told Craven that if he disagreed with the demand for payment, he should send a claim, "stating specific grounds upon which your request for review is based," along with supporting documents, to BP's claims-and-appeals coordinator in La Cañada Flintridge, California. By the time he got the second letter, Craven had been without his pension for three months.

So who should have been paying Craven's pension? Even if Craven had been able to see, his computer was broken, and his research skills were limited. His math wasn't so great, either: He hadn't noticed that eighteen years of monthly payments of $346 added up to a lot more than the $18,363 Fidelity's letter was demanding. Like many retirees, he had not followed the mergers-and-acquisitions activity of his former employer, and kept few records (or, in his case, no records, other than canceled checks). His companion, Ruth, started digging through old boxes of canceled checks and looked in the Yellow Pages under "Senior," hoping to find someone to help.

Though Craven was a little hazy on his employment history, this is what records later showed. He first went to work at a company called Cyprus Mines in 1962 and left in 1979, the year Amoco Corp. bought the company. He returned to Cyprus two years later and retired in 1985. The year he retired, Amoco spun off Cyprus as an independent company called Cyprus Minerals, transferring to it the pension liabilities of current employees. Cyprus Minerals began paying Craven a pension for his last five years of work, $52 a month. In 1993, Cyprus Minerals Co. merged with Amax, forming Cyprus Amax Minerals Co. Phelps Dodge Corp. acquired Cyprus Amax Minerals Co. in 1999 and continued paying the small pension. Meanwhile, Craven also had begun receiving a second monthly pension for his earlier work stint, for $348. Amoco paid this, and when Amoco became part of British Petroleum in the late 1990s, the combined company paid this second pension. Got it?

By the time BP acquired the portfolio of old miners, it had already passed through so many hands that the pedigrees of many of the pensions were in question. Benefits audits rarely turn up any mistakes in the retirees' favor. As it turned out, though, there *was* a mistake with Craven's pension: Following a second review of the paperwork, prompted by a reporter's call to BP, Fidelity concluded that BP was responsible for Craven's pension after all. It sent him a letter saying it would resume paying his pension and he would receive his back payments, with interest. Unfortunately, most retirees don't have reporters interested in figuring out how much pension money they're owed.

LUCENT'S SPIN JOB

Recovering overpayments is just nickel-and-dime stuff when it comes to managing a portfolio of retirees for cash and profits. No one has done a better job at squeezing retirees than Lucent, the AT&T spin-off. Over its short life, Lucent reaped billions of dollars in cash savings and profits from its retiree portfolio, even as the company persistently maintained— to analysts, shareholders, employees, retirees, and lawmakers—that its 130,000 retirees were crushing the company. The argument sounded plausible. Lucent had five retirees for every worker, putting it in the same club as automakers and steel companies. But whatever financial problems Lucent was having, the retirees weren't the cause. They were merely the scapegoats.

Lucent was created in 1996 when AT&T spun off its equipment-manufacturing business, including Western Electric and Bell Laboratories, along with their more than fifty thousand retirees. These included telephone operators and linemen, middle managers, engineers who developed missile systems, transistors, lasers, and fax machines, and the factory workers who built them. Some had been retired for months; many had been retired for decades. Some had worked for the business units included in the spin-off, and others had worked in other parts of AT&T.

Loading up the retirees into a new unit and spinning it off enabled AT&T to unload a $29 billion liability for pensions, health care, dental coverage, and death benefits. But the retirees weren't a burden to the newly formed company: The retiree portfolio also contained a $29.8 billion pension fund, and two trusts to pay retiree health benefits. All told, Lucent started out with $33.5 billion in assets, to cover a $28.7 billion obligation. In short, the company started out with almost $5 billion more than it needed to pay 100 percent of the retirees' benefits.

Lucent, nevertheless, began trimming benefits. It cut the salaried employees' pensions in 1998, and in 1999 it eliminated discounted long-distance phone rates for anyone who retired after 1983. The move, combined with other changes, lessened the retiree-benefits obligation on Lucent's books by $359 million.

Pension cuts and the telecom bubble caused the assets in Lucent's pension plan to balloon. At its peak, in 2000, it had $45.3 billion in assets—a surplus of almost $20 billion. The vast pool of pension assets boosted Lucent's income by hundreds of millions each year, from $265 million in 1996 to $975 million in 2000. By 2003 it had added an additional $1.6 billion to income.

In its early years, Lucent focused on growth: acquiring companies, hiring people, borrowing heavily, and generally operating as if the roaring telecom market would last forever. It didn't. When the bubble burst in 2000, demand for telecom products and services fell sharply, and Lucent began frantically downsizing. It spun off business units, made early-retirement offers, and cut staff, which the pension plan helped pay for. The company used $800 million in surplus pension assets to pay termination benefits as it cut 54,000 employees from its payroll in 2001 and 2002. It learned this move from parent AT&T, which in 1998 had provided 14,700 managers the equivalent of one half-year's pay, in the form of a cash payout from the pension plan, as severance. At Lucent, the move consumed $4.7 billion in pension assets. By 2003 Lucent's workforce had shrunk from 118,000, in 1999, to 22,000.

Lucent also used the retiree health plan as a downsizing tool. In 2001, Lucent offered retiree health coverage to a pool of managers who were not yet eligible for the benefit, because they had not worked fifteen years at the company and had reached age fifty-five. Ultimately, more than 23,000 accepted the offer in 2001 and 2002 and left the company. Taken together, Lucent used the pension and the retiree health plans to finance a massive downsizing without paying a cent from its own pocket.

As its workforce shrank, its retiree population grew. By 2004, Lucent had 127,000 U.S. retirees—a fact that Lucent pointed out over and over. But increasing its number of retirees didn't boost Lucent's pension burden. Just the opposite: When an employee turns into a retiree, his pension stops growing; as the pension is paid out, the liability declines, dollar for dollar. If the pension is properly funded, as Lucent's was, it has adequate assets to pay all the pensions owed to current—and future—retirees. This isn't something unique to Lucent—it applies to all companies with pensions. So it didn't matter how many Lucent employees retired; the company still wasn't losing any money.

Nor did the growing number of retirees boost Lucent's health care burden. The *total* amount of money Lucent spent on medical benefits didn't change. The amounts the company paid in medical benefits were essentially transferred from the employee side of the ledger to the retiree side. In 2003, Lucent spent about $1.1 billion in health care costs, roughly the same amount as in 1999. The only difference was that the amounts it spent for employees shrank (because there were fewer of them), while the amounts it spent for retirees grew (because there were more of them). In 1999, it paid $517 million for employees and $539 million for retirees; by 2003 the company was spending about $850 million for retirees and $264 million for employees. Once retirees reach age sixty-five and are eligible for Medicare, the employer's costs for them fall—to an average of about $1,200 a month.

The downsizing helped Lucent financially in a number of ways. For one thing, it didn't have to pay for the health benefits of laid-off workers who weren't eligible for retiree health benefits, a group that included any salaried employee hired after June 1986. That was a cash savings. And for salaried workers hired earlier, the company established a ceiling on what it would pay for their benefits. Adopting the cap in 1999 reduced Lucent's retiree health liability by $359 million.

But the biggest benefit was that Lucent no longer had to pay for their health care benefits from corporate cash: It could tap the pension plan. By 2003 Lucent had taken out more than $1.2 billion in assets from the pension plan to cover health benefits.

There was a limit on how much pension money Lucent could transfer from the pension plan to pay for retiree health coverage. Companies can do this only when they have a surplus. By 2003, most of the nearly $20 billion surplus it had in 2000 had evaporated. It was consumed by Lucent to pay for severance and medical benefits, and erased by stock market losses and low interest rates. This meant that there wasn't any more money in the piggy bank for Lucent to take out. Something would have to be done.

TAPPED OUT

Up to this point, Lucent had not spent a penny on the retirees it claimed were so burdensome. Faced with the prospect that it might actually have to spend cash on retiree benefits for the first time, Lucent had a better idea: It chose to cut them—again. Knowing that this would be an unpopular move, Lucent had to put a positive spin on the news. So it called Henry Schacht, a former CEO, out of retirement and sent him on a ten-state road show to deliver the bad news.

One of his stops, in October 2003, was at the Sheraton Hotel in Buckhead, Georgia, where Schacht made a presentation to a group of more than a hundred retirees. Security was tight, and as the retirees tottered in, some propped on walkers and canes, uniformed officers searched their handbags and briefcases, confiscating cameras and recording devices. Only after their photo identification had been checked and their hands stamped were they allowed into the chilly auditorium. No reporters were admitted.

Schacht took the podium, and in his lengthy PowerPoint presentation he explained the burden Lucent faced from spiraling health care costs and rising numbers of retirees. It was a message that has grown commonplace in the media. Lucent just could not afford to sustain the generous level of benefits it had been paying. The company had five retirees for every U.S. worker, Schacht said. "Unfortunately, the numbers just don't work."

The retirees were resigned: Unless the company cut benefits, it might just go bankrupt, and they'd end up with nothing. Lucent couldn't cut the retirees' pensions—pension law didn't allow that—but it would be legal to cut the other benefits: health care, dental coverage, death benefits, coverage for spouses, Medicare Part B premiums, even telephone discounts. Lucent went after them all.

Even the oldest retirees were hit hard. Lucent eliminated dental coverage and Medicare Part B payments, which retirees used to pay for their Medicare premiums. For Howard O'Neil, who was ninety at the time, losing the premium coverage for himself and his wife, Mabel, cut his $970 monthly pension almost in half. (Premiums are deducted from the pension.) He'd earned the benefits working at Western Electric from 1939 until he retired forty years later. He thought this was pretty rough treatment, akin to getting a pay cut in retirement. That, in fact, was accurate: Retiree benefits are a form of deferred compensation, so cutting them is the equivalent of a retroactive pay cut.

Lucent couldn't unilaterally reduce benefits for the union retirees, because their benefits were protected by negotiated contracts. The retired managers and salaried employees were another matter, however. This dynamic is endemic: Companies go after salaried retirees' benefits first, since they have fewer legal protections. Among those who suddenly had their benefits cut were managers who had been induced to retire two years before, with the promise of subsidized health coverage. Lucent told them this was a shame but pointed out that the fine print gave the company the right to change their coverage. Most companies have these "reservation of rights" clauses in their benefits documents, so even if the retirees had been promised the benefits—orally, by the human resources managers, or in writing—the plan documents would override them. Lawsuits were futile. The odds of winning this type of benefits case are about on a par with the Chicago Cubs winning the World Series. The cases are heard in federal court. Retirees rarely bring them and rarely prevail. And even when cases make it to court, they take years to resolve.

Joseph Parano, a retired engineer and manager for the Bell System with Stage IV colon cancer, knew he didn't have time to make a federal case out of it. So he tried something creative. Shortly after Schacht's road show, Parano went to superior court in San Mateo, California, paid his $30 filing fee, and sued Lucent in small claims court. Normally the battleground for neighborhood spats and debt collectors, small claims courts are not a venue for federal benefits cases. But Parano had successfully sued both a moving company that lost his sister's belongings and a bank for not paying interest on a dead relative's passbook savings account, so he thought it was worth a shot. In his complaint, Parano sought $5,000 (the maximum amount recoverable under a small claims action) "for loss of spousal death benefits" and also had a claim for $2,300 in medical bills he said should have been paid from Lucent's retiree health plan.

Lucent's big-league lawyers were flummoxed, and in February 2004 they settled the claim for an undisclosed amount. "But it was a lot more than $10,000," Parano said afterward, with a certain amount of satisfaction. He also got his digs in one last time, in his self-published obituary, which ran in the *San Francisco Chronicle* in February 2006:

> He retired from AT&T after 32 years of service with a secure benefit package. After retirement he was reassigned against his wishes to Lucent Tech. Inc. who reduced his health benefits and eliminated his spousal death policy that was promised. He is survived by his loving wife of 24 years, Susie Cronin Parano.

The notice provided the time of the funeral mass and said that in lieu of flowers, donations could be made in Joe's name to: PETA, 501 Front St., Norfolk VA 23510. Joe was sixty-nine.

OLD WIVES' TALES

Most retirees and their spouses, however, didn't have a chance. Connie Sharpe, a widow in Las Cruces, New Mexico, had been a classic corporate spouse, moving many times as her husband, George, set up missile programs in Cape Canaveral, Florida, Vandenberg Air Force Base in California, and White Sands, New Mexico.

When George retired in 1975 after working for Bell Laboratories for thirty-four years, he had a pension, retiree health coverage, and a death benefit. The couple hadn't taken out life insurance, because they were relying on the death benefit of $34,080, which was what George had been earning when he retired.

But when George died in 2003, his wife's health coverage ended six months later, and his pension ended, too. Lucent maintained that Connie Sharpe had waived her right to a survivor's pension; she didn't remember doing so and asked to see the paperwork. Lucent told her she would have to subpoena the records. With just $950 a month in Social Security, hiring a lawyer was out of the question. "If I don't live too long," she said, "I won't have to go on welfare. I sure do feel sorry for the big executives who make millions when they retire."

Margaret Jelly, Bill Jelly's wife, also found herself in a fix she never expected to be in. She had been a classic stay-at-home spouse in the golden age of benefits. If anyone was likely to have a secure retirement, it was this postwar cohort, whose paths followed a common trajectory.

Bill had begun working as an electrician's apprentice for Western Electric when he was seventeen. After serving in the Air Force in Italy during the Second World War, he returned to New Jersey, and to Western Electric, as a full-fledged electrician. There were millions like him: ex-servicemen and others, swelling the postwar workforce. Companies were growing rapidly and competing for workers. In lieu of higher salaries, employers offered deferred compensation in the form of pensions and health care in retirement. This mutually beneficial arrangement enabled companies to have more cash to plow into growth and ensured that workers would have a stream of income in their old age. The young electrician met Margaret in 1949, and in 1954, when the first of their three children was born, Bill was still making only $64 a week, but he was also building up retirement benefits.

When Bill got Lucent's letter in early 2003, he knew that if he didn't die before February 3—a mere three weeks later—that death benefit would vanish. He figured the odds were good that he'd beat Lucent to the punch. "I have a deadline," he told his wife when he went back into the hospital on January 14 for what they both knew would be the last time. He didn't make his deadline. Bill celebrated his eightieth birthday in the hospital on February 14, 2003, which was also his fiftieth Valentine's Day with Margaret. The nurses had a small party for him. He died on February 24, 2003. Lucent saved $39,000.

SLIDE SHOW

In its January 2003 letter to retirees, Lucent said it felt terrible about the move. "Eliminating the death benefit was one of the very difficult decisions we had to make over the past few years," it told retirees. But the more than $464 million savings were crucial for the company's survival, it claimed.

Lucent's letter to the retirees didn't mention that the savings it would get by killing a benefit earned by 100,000 retirees over three decades would help it pay a new retiree obligation—one that was only a little more than five years old: the special supplemental pensions and retirement benefits for its executives. In a few short years, the obligation had grown to $422 million.

Lucent enjoyed another perverse benefit from cutting retiree benefits: Even though it had never spent a cent for its retirees' benefits, cutting them generated instant profit. The cuts announced in 2003 reduced Lucent's liability for its "postretirement benefit plans" by $1.1 billion—a 13.5 percent reduction that year. This generated more than $1 billion in accounting gains, which the company added to income in subsequent quarters.

Lucent used $280 million in such gains in its 2003 income calculations; these gains enabled the company to report its first profits in three years. Lucent executives achieved their performance goals and were awarded handsomely. In 2004, chief executive Patricia Russo was awarded a $1.95 million bonus on top of her $1.2 million salary, $4.6 million in restricted stock, plus $4.8 million in options. Though Russo had been at the helm of the company for only two years, she had already received compensation worth $44 million.

While Schacht was lobbying the retirees, Lucent was lobbying Congress, which was about to enact the Medicare Prescription Drug Plan, which would provide government-paid drug benefits to retirees. Lucent and other companies said that unless the government gave them a subsidy to continue providing prescription drug coverage, they would likely cancel their plans altogether, which would put more of a strain on the government budget. This was largely a bluff, given that the companies had already been cutting health coverage for salaried retirees and would have loved to do the same for its union retirees, if they hadn't had those pesky collectively bargained contracts.

Lucent, in fact, had never paid a cent for its retirees' prescription drugs: It had used money from the trusts it acquired in the spin-offs or had tapped the pension plan to pay for them. Nonetheless, with the passage of the Medicare drug plan, Lucent received a tax-free subsidy that enabled it to whack $500 million off its liabilities. Another way to look at it: Lucent killed the death benefit to be able to hang on to $400 million in the pension plan, even as it won a subsidy of $500 million.

One retiree who didn't buy Schacht's plea of poverty was Walt Ehmer. He had been the chief executive of Lucent Technologies Denmark, and he scoffed at the notion that the company needed to throw the retirees overboard to survive. For one thing, he pointed out, the company was sitting on $4.3 billion in cash. Couldn't it use some of that to pay for retiree benefits? Not possible, Schacht said. Lucent needed to commit its cash to "securing its future."

It also needed it to pay the executives who helped engineer the retiree cuts. The year of the Schacht road show, Lucent's cash payments to its top five executives totaled $12.5 million. That was roughly the amount of benefits paid for health care for 3,396 retirees and their dependents that year.

The following year—for the very first time—Lucent actually had to shell out something for the benefits of its 129,000 retirees: It paid $159 million. To put this figure in perspective, it also paid $300 million in executive bonuses. Schacht later defended the bonuses, saying it was necessary to pay competitive compensation to executives, "because that's what it's going to take to continue to attract and retain the talent required to build this company back to where we want to go."

The spin job didn't stop. In a financial filing discussing its pending merger with French telecom giant Alcatel SA in 2005, Lucent referred to its "costly" retiree plans and said that the combined company might have to take steps to reduce those costs.

It didn't mention that the pension plan, which by then covered 230,000 retirees and employees, was again so flush that it pumped $973 million of noncash income into Lucent's earnings in fiscal 2005—about 82 percent of the company's pretax profit for the year. The only U.S. pension creating a drag on earnings was the supplemental pension for its 2,500 executives—its liability had grown to $422 million.

In 2005, Russo was awarded $3.6 million on top of her base salary of $1.2 million, and was granted an additional $8.7 million in restricted stock and options, a total of $13.5 million in 2005, a year the company would have been unprofitable were it not for the gains from its pension.

Lucent continued to benefit from the retiree plans. It used another $2 billion in pension assets to pay for retiree health care, and when it merged with Alcatel in 2006 to become Alcatel-Lucent, it still had a dowry of $5 billion in surplus pension assets.

The new French owners of the portfolio of American retirees

continued to benefit from their investment: Alcatel-Lucent continued to pick away at the benefits. Thanks to gains from benefits cuts, plus pension income, the pension plan generated $1.7 billion in income in 2007, without which the company would have reported a loss of $1 billion. Alcatel-Lucent executives achieved their performance targets and were awarded their bonuses.

In 2008, Lucent eliminated its prescription drug plan for salaried retirees altogether, which generated $358 million in income. Russo stepped down at the end of the year, taking with her $8 million in severance.

In October 2009, the company froze the pensions of its 11,500 management employees. Their loss was Alcatel-Lucent's gain: a $531 million boost to profits.

CHAPTER 6

Wealth Transfer: THE HIDDEN BURDEN OF SPIRALING EXECUTIVE PENSIONS AND PAY

WHEN HENRY SCHACHT was delivering the bad news to Lucent retirees, there was one retiree in the room who wasn't going to feel the pain. That was Schacht himself. As a former CEO, Schacht had accrued a small fortune, joining the club of executives with enough retirement wealth not only to retire to an island but to buy it.

While Lucent and other companies were cutting benefits for hundreds of thousands of retirees to the bone, they were lavishing increasingly enormous sums on top management. This isn't simply an issue of disparity; it's a transfer of wealth. Billions of dollars earmarked to pay pensions and health care benefits to retirees were consumed, one way or another, by management teams who profited from the short-term income lift these maneuvers generated.

The dismantling of retiree plans did something more than boost profits. It helped fuel the growth of a parallel universe of executive pensions and benefits. Largely hidden, these growing executive retirement liabilities are slowly replacing pensions and retiree health obligations on corporate balance sheets.

The retirement party got started in the early 1990s when Congress, in a futile attempt to rein in executive pay, capped the tax deduction a company can take for an individual's salary at $1 million. Undeterred, managers and compensation consultants simply recharacterized a lot of compensation as "performance-based," which isn't subject to the deduction cap.

Compensation committees maintained that tying executive pay to performance would incentivize managers to do a good job. Whatever it may have done, executives with mountains of stock options and awards were motivated to boost earnings, whether that was accomplished by improvements in productivity, layoffs, offshoring operations, creative accounting, or cutting benefits.

Unfortunately for employees and retirees, this new era of incentive pay coincided with companies' newfound ability to use the pension and retiree health plans to boost income. Knowingly or not, when top management ordered cuts for retirees, they were indirectly boosting their own retirement wealth.

Spiraling executive pay in turn led to spiraling executive pensions. Commonly called SERPs—supplemental executive retirement plans— these top-level pensions generally provide millions of dollars in pension benefits.

Ed Whitacre, AT&T's former chief executive, was president of the company when it froze pensions, and slashed retiree health benefits. When he retired in 2007, he was granted the usual executive entitlements, including the use of corporate aircraft, AT&T office facilities and support staff, home security, and club memberships, plus payments to cover the taxes he pays on the benefits. Whitacre would also be paid $1 million a year under a three-year consulting contract. On top of all that, he also left with a $158 million payout. This type of retirement package, which no longer shocks people, is detailed in the SEC filings that disclose the compensation of the handful of top officers at a company. But they're the tip of a well-hidden iceberg.

Spiraling executive pay doesn't just lead to growing executive pension obligations. It has been creating another giant liability: deferred-compensation obligations. As pay has grown, top earners have channeled more of it into deferred-compensation plans, which enables them to postpone receiving the money and delay paying taxes on it. The deferrals grow with interest and employer contributions, tax-deferred, which further boosts the IOU.

Deferred-comp plans have been called 401(k)s on steroids, because employees contribute pay, employers typically match it, and the employees allocate the funds among a selection of investments. But there's a critical difference: The compensation employees contribute to 401(k)s is actual cash that goes into a separate account at an outside investment firm. These "defined-contribution plans" don't create a pensionlike liability. Deferred-comp plans do. The participant doesn't actually receive the pay before he defers it; it is merely an IOU from his employer. Another way to put it: Employers have been putting much of their spiraling executive pay—pensions and deferred compensation—on the equivalent of a giant credit card.

SCAPEGOATS

Combined, executive legacy liabilities have grown to multi-billion-dollar obligations. General Electric owes an unknown number of executives a total of $5.9 billion in retirement, which amounts to 15 percent of the total pension liability for more than 500,000 workers and retirees. Currently, executive legacy liabilities account for 8 percent to as much as 100 percent of pension obligations at some of the largest *Fortune* 500 companies.

For accounting purposes, executive liabilities are no different from regular pensions and retiree health benefits. They're debts, and can drag down earnings. There's a critical difference, though. Unlike pensions (which employers fund) and 401(k)s (which employees fund), supplemental executive pension and savings plans are *unfunded*. This is due to taxes: If a company set up a pension fund for executives, it wouldn't be allowed to deduct the money, and the assets wouldn't grow tax-deferred.

With no pool of assets that are earning returns, which offset the annual interest cost on the debt, the IOUs for executives always have an interest cost, which can hit earnings hard. But guess which pensions get the blame?

Employers typically aggregate their regular pensions and executive pensions when reporting pension liabilities and costs, so even if the only costly pensions are for the executives, the public doesn't know. Nor do many analysts, whose reports overstate the amount of underfunding, because the pension obligations include executive pensions, which aren't funded. The data, which comes from SEC filings, also includes pensions at companies like Nordstrom. Its pension tables indicate that it owes $102 million in pensions and is 100 percent underfunded. That's because the cheery shoe clerks and store managers don't have pensions. The pensions are only for "certain officers and select employees."

But don't expect employers to bemoan their spiraling executive obligations. In a letter to stockholders dated March 16, 2006, the chief executive of Unisys, Joseph McGrath, blamed "higher pension expense" for the loss the company had reported the previous year. This was partly true: Financial filings show that pension expenses reduced Unisys's earnings by $104 million.

But he left out a critical detail: Most of the increase in cost was from a half-dozen supplemental pension and savings plans for top Unisys executives. The regular pension plan had actually been a benefit to the company. From 1995 to 2001, the company's pension plans actually increased corporate earnings—by an average of $91 million a year. That was because the income on assets set aside for regular workers' pensions more than covered all of Unisys's pension expense, with the remainder flowing to the bottom line. In 2003, however, Unisys started to incur pension expenses, because of investment losses, falling rates, and because its executive pensions had become so costly that the gains produced by the regular pension plan were no longer enough to make up for it.

The day after McGrath's report to shareholders, Unisys announced that it would freeze the regular employees' pension plan to control "the level and volatility of retirement costs." McGrath said that "we think these changes have struck the appropriate balance between controlling our pension costs and continuing to help our employees prepare for retirement." On balance, it was good for Unisys: Freezing the regular pensions generated a quick gain of $45 million and will add a total of about $700 million to earnings over ten years.

A variety of companies froze their pensions in 2006, taking advantage of low interest rates, which had inflated their obligations. Curtailing pensions at a time when the obligations are artificially high results in a larger drop in the obligation, and bigger gains.

Even when a company postpones the effective date of the freeze, it can reduce its obligation immediately. In early 2006, IBM announced that it would freeze the pensions of about 117,000 U.S. employees starting in 2008, citing pension costs, volatility, and unpredictability. Only by drilling into its pension filings would one notice that $134 million, or a quarter of its U.S. pension expense the prior year, resulted from pensions for several thousand of its highest-paid people. The rest of IBM's U.S. pension expense, $381 million, related to pensions for 254,000 workers and retirees. The only U.S. pensions dragging down earnings are the executive pensions, which have continued to rise. The freeze didn't hurt CEO Sam Palmisano's retirement: He'll receive at least $3.2 million a year in retirement.

Now, thanks to the pension freeze, the employee pension plan no longer has any expense: In the years since the freeze was announced, the gains from curtailing benefits have added nearly $3 billion to IBM's income.

GM also took advantage of low interest rates to lock in a bigger liability. When the automaker announced in 2006 that it would freeze the pensions of 42,000 U.S. salaried workers, it blamed its troubles on "legacy costs," including pensions for its U.S. workers. The move wiped $1.6 billion from GM's pension obligations.

How costly were the pensions of GM's workers at the time? The pension covering nearly 700,000 U.S. workers and retirees had a $9 billion surplus and was adding $10 billion to its income calculations. The executive pension was another matter. The $1.4 billion in executive legacy liabilities for an unknown number of executives generates an expense that hurts GM's bottom line each year. GM has often claimed that its U.S. pension plans add about $800 to the cost of each car made in the United States. But it doesn't say how much of this cost is for executive legacy liabilities.

A MERCANTILE DECISION

It's possible that the widening retirement gap is just an unintended by-product of a trend to reduce benefits and enhance executive pay. But at some companies, the disparity was deliberate. In 1996, the pension committee of the board of directors of Mercantile Stores met at the exclusive Union Club in New York City to vote on some critical changes in their retirement plans. The chain of department stores in the Midwest and the South had a pension plan covering 21,000 employees and retirees. The pension plan wasn't a burden: It had a surplus of about $200 million. The average pension of the retired cashiers and clerks was $138 a month, and employee turnover was so high that many workers never qualified for a pension anyway.

But the company was in financial trouble, and the pension plan was one place to look for relief. Benefits consultants pondered the situation and concluded that pension cuts would be appropriate. Why? Because the Mercantile pension plan was more generous than those of other retailers, the consultants said. At the same time, the consultants concluded that the executives' pensions weren't "competitive" with others in the industry. To resolve this supposed imbalance and bring Mercantile's retirement benefits in line with those of its peers, the board voted to reduce the pensions of low-paid workers and boost executive pensions. Two years later, Dillard's Inc., a Little Rock, Arkansas–based retailing chain, bought Mercantile, terminated the pension plan, and captured the surplus.

Towers Perrin, the consulting firm that helped Mercantile with these kinds of decisions, merged with Watson Wyatt in 2010. Now called Towers Watson, the global consulting firm continues to help the largest companies in the United States, Canada, the United Kingdom, the Netherlands, and Germany shrink retiree benefits and boost executive pay and pensions.

Towers Watson practices what it preaches. Its employees have a cash-balance pension plan, while top executives have a supplemental pension with all the bells and whistles that have been stripped from rank-and-file pensions, including a generous formula based on final pay, which spikes in value in the later years, and the ability to retire at sixty with full benefits. The company reimburses executives for their FICA (payroll) taxes and "grosses up" the payments (i.e., it pays the taxes on the tax payments). When top managers depart, the company uses an unusually low interest rate, 3.5 percent, to calculate their lump-sum payouts, which results in a larger payment. In fiscal 2010, the executive pension liability for the combined company stood at $627 million, 32 percent of the total pension obligation. The company also paid out $496 million in "discretionary compensation," i.e. bonuses, of which most, or all, went to executives.

UNDERSTATEMENT

Like many public pension plans, executive liabilities have been growing quietly behind the scenes, producing a mounting obligation, much of it hidden. Even when a company owes its executives billions of dollars, it can be almost impossible to tell because of the way companies bundle all their pensions together in securities filings.

When companies mention executive pensions at all, they typically use terms that only pension-industry insiders would recognize, such as "nonqualified obligations" and "unfunded defined benefit pension plans." Comparing the obligation and cost of executive pensions to regular ones is possible only at the few companies that actually break out the figures (like GE) or provide enough clues to enable a determined researcher to back the figures out of the totals.

Executive pensions are like public pensions in another critical way: The liabilities are often lowballed. So even if one is able to identify the current liability for executive pensions, the figure may provide an unrealistic view of what the company will ultimately pay out, for a variety of reasons, including the way they are calculated.

Like most public pensions, executive pensions are calculated by multiplying years of service and pay—the formula many private employers have abandoned for regular employees because the benefits grow steeply in the final years. With pensions based on final pay, an individual has a big incentive to make sure the final pay is as high as possible. A firefighter or police officer, for example, might work hundreds of hours in overtime in their final years on the job, a move that might add $50,000 a year to a pension.

Executives do essentially the same thing, with bigger payoffs, and have a variety of ways to boost their pay—and thus their pensions—by millions of dollars prior to departure or retirement. One way is to simply change the definition of "pay" to include more types of compensation. ConocoPhillips included "certain incentive payments" when it totted up CEO Jim Mulva's pension in 2008, which increased it by $9.5 million and brought it to a total of $68 million. The same year, a $6 million pay increase for Merck's chief executive, Richard T. Clark, pushed his pension from $11.9 million to $21.7 million.

Awarding a substantial bonus to executives who are on the verge of retirement or departure can also generate a huge pension windfall. One of ExxonMobil's two supplemental pension plans for executives calculates executive pension benefits using the three highest bonuses in the five years prior to retirement. A well-timed bonus can make a big difference. A $4 million bonus to CEO Rex Tillerson in 2008 pushed the total value of his pension up by $8 million in a single year, to $31 million. "By limiting bonuses to those granted in the five years prior to retirement," the company states blandly in its proxy filing with federal regulators, "there is a strong motivation for executives to continue to perform at a high level." It also encourages top management to make some short-sighted decisions, because a large award can lead to bigger pension benefits for the rest of their lives.

Awarding additional years of service, a practice that compensation watchdogs have perennially snapped at, is alive and well. PG&E, the giant West Coast utility, awarded its CEO, Peter Darbee, an additional five years, which boosted his pension 38 percent to $5.2 million in 2008. The company said it was doing this because it felt that his pension was less generous than what other executives were receiving. This kind of peer pressure drives executive pay and pensions steadily higher. That same year, the compensation committee of Constellation Energy awarded its chairman and CEO, Mayo Shattuck, an additional 2.5 years of service, boosting his pension by $10.3 million, a 97 percent increase.

Executive pensions have another characteristic that has been widely criticized in public pensions: Employers have an incentive to boost the benefits and hide the growing (unfunded) liability. In contrast, when it comes to rank-and-file pensions, employers have an incentive to inflate the liabilities and cut benefits.

Using unrealistic (and sometimes undisclosed) assumptions to estimate the executive liability can shrink it substantially. Some companies assume that executive salaries don't rise; others, like Towers Watson, calculate the executive obligation using an unusually high discount rate, 7.5 percent in 2010, which results in a lower reported liability.

Companies can delay reporting some of the liability by waiting until the executive is headed out the door to apply some feature that inflates the total payout. A small change in the interest rate used to calculate a lump sum payout, for example, can increase a pension by millions of dollars.

In 2008, Goodyear Tire & Rubber adjusted the interest rate and compensation assumptions it used to calculate top executives' pensions, which increased chief executive Robert Keegan's pension by $6.3 million, to a total of $17.5 million. (The company earlier credited him with eighteen additional years of service, which has boosted his pension by $10.5 million.) At the end of that same year, Goodyear froze salaried employees' pensions, saying its obligations under the plans were so onerous that they "could impair our ability to achieve or sustain future profitability."

Joel Gemunder, the CEO of Omnicare, a provider of pharmaceutical care for nursing homes, had amassed retirement benefits worth roughly $91 million by the time he retired at age seventy-one in 2010. As lofty as that figure was, it got even bigger when he left. His retirement triggered immediate vesting for his stock options and restricted shares, which were worth more than $21 million, and he received $16.2 million in cash as a severance payment. Small perks included payments for tax and financial planning ($134,250) and "executive bookkeeping services" ($27,500). Altogether, the total retirement payout was more than $130 million. And ordinary Omnicare workers? Their pensions were frozen years ago, and in 2009 the company imposed salary cuts even as it reported record profits.

The pension and deferred-comp tables included in annual proxy statements provide a limited snapshot of the value of a top manager's benefits. But these amounts aren't what the person is likely to receive. Those numbers are tucked away lower down, under various provisions, such as "voluntary retirement" or "disability." If someone relied on the pension table in Wells Fargo's proxy statement, they might conclude that president John Stumpf's pension in 2008 was $9.6 million, a 3 percent decline from the prior year. But elsewhere, the filing notes that the value of the pension he would receive if he left spiked to $17.7 million from $11.2 million—a 58 percent increase.

The biggest trigger of a huge pension boost can be a change in control. Scott Ford, president and chief executive of Alltel Corp., had accumulated a pension of $16.8 million through 2007. But after the company was acquired by Verizon, change-in-control provisions tripled Ford's salary and awarded three additional years of service. He left the company in 2008 with a pension payment of $51.7 million. Altogether, the five departing top executives received pension payouts of $131 million.

Despite their limitations, the executive pension tables in the proxy are better than nothing. In the S&P 500, 160 companies don't have the kinds of retirement benefits that they are required to disclose in the proxies' pension tables. This doesn't mean that those executives receive no retirement benefits, just that the companies characterize the benefits as something other than a pension, so the benefits don't fall under the enhanced SEC disclosure rules that companies were required to adopt in 2007. These require companies to place an overall value on their executives' pension benefits.

Omnicom, for example, established a Senior Executive Restricted Covenant & Retention Plan in 2006 to provide top executives at the global advertising giant with an annual payment, based on salary and years of service, for fifteen years after they depart. John Wren, the company's chief executive, will receive $1.3 million a year for fifteen years. The retirement payments will grow with a cost-of-living adjustment, a feature that most companies have discontinued in the pensions for regular employees. The liability for this? Anyone's guess.

Some companies even give the impression that they've cut executive retirement benefits. Companies that freeze their regular pension plans sometimes freeze their executive pensions, too, especially when the plan is a so-called makeup, or excess, plan that mirrors the regular 401(k) but allows greater deferrals. But companies may take steps to soften or eliminate the impact. State Street Corp. froze its executive pensions effective January 1, 2008, but awarded executives "transition" benefits that postponed the freeze for two years. Thanks to this feature, and a drop in interest rates and other factors, their pensions rose 47 percent in 2008, and CEO Ronald Logue's pensions (like most top executives, he has more than one) rose by $7.8 million to $25.3 million. The company also added a retirement savings component to the plan and will contribute $400,000 a year in cash and stock to each executive's account.

Lincoln National Corp. also froze both its regular and executive pensions in 2008. When it did, it converted the executive pensions to lump sums, enhanced their value by $6.3 million, and added the benefits to a new deferred-compensation plan, to which the company will contribute a minimum of 15 percent of the executives' total compensation each year. That year, it contributed $12.3 million to the new account for CEO Dennis Glass. The company didn't enhance the 401(k) plans of regular employees whose pensions it froze.

One thing people can count on: Unlike the pensions of regular employees, executive liabilities aren't going away. They're protected by contracts. Though lower-level executives can lose their deferred comp in bankruptcy, the pensions and savings of top officers are usually protected by bankruptcy-proof trusts. Chesapeake Energy, the second-largest natural gas producer in the United States, doesn't disclose the total amount it owes executives, but it's no doubt a hefty sum. Aubrey K. McClendon, the chief executive, had compensation that totaled $156 million in the last three years. He's also owed $120 million in pension and deferred-compensation benefits. In its annual report, Chesapeake needs thirty-four pages to describe its executives' retirement benefits. The benefits for 8,200 employees require only half a page to describe—they don't have pensions.

DEFERRED GRATIFICATION

Pensions aren't the only executive liability. So is much of their pay. Unlike salary paid out to factory workers or the CFO, deferred compensation creates huge, and largely hidden, obligations. The plans can cover thousands of lower-level executives and other highly compensated employees, who participate in so-called excess plans. These enable employees to defer some of their salary that they can't put into the 401(k) because of tax laws that limit total employee contributions to $15,000. So if a 401(k) allows employees to contribute 15 percent of pay, someone making $200,000 will be allowed to contribute only a total of $15,000 to the 401(k), and can defer the rest in the excess plan.

These are also called mirror plans, because they "mirror" the 401(k). The only difference is that the amount deferred into the excess plan isn't actual cash, as it is with a 401(k), but an IOU from the company for the pay. Nonetheless, the employee allocates it among virtual mutual funds—usually the ones available in the 401(k)—and may also receive virtual employer contributions.

Upper-level executives often have more elite deferred-compensation plans that enable them to defer upward of 100 percent of their salary and bonuses each year, and sometimes restricted stock or the gains from exercising stock options.

The deferred pay can grow quickly. Companies might contribute a percentage of what the executive defers or make an outright contribution, no strings attached. The savings grow with returns pegged to investment, or with guaranteed returns—as high as 14 percent at GE. The accounts also grow with company contributions, such as the 20 percent match that drug giant Wyeth provides its top executives. John Stafford, the former chairman, one year collected $3.8 million in interest alone on his deferred-compensation account, valued at nearly $38 million. Together, the value of the company contributions and tax-deferred returns can boost the value of the pay by 40 percent.

Companies are required to report only guaranteed above-market interest paid annually into the accounts of the five highest-paid executives, and include the size of each individual's accounts in a separate table. But the total amount of all the deferred compensation of hundreds of executives is typically hidden.

Totting up the total amount a company owes its executives can take some creativity. One way to get a sense of their size is to look at a reporting item called a "deferred tax asset." Companies can deduct compensation they pay, but only when they actually fork over the money (or put money into the pension or 401(k) plan).

When compensation is deferred, companies record a deferred tax asset for the compensation, which is essentially an estimate of how much the company will be able to deduct in the future—when it actually pays executives what it owes them. JPMorgan Chase, for instance, reported a $3.4 billion deferred tax asset for employee benefits in 2007. Assuming a 40 percent combined federal and state tax rate—and backing out obligations for retiree health and other items—this indicates that the financial giant owed its executives $8.2 billion just before the market crisis. Applying the same technique to Citigroup yields roughly a $5 billion IOU, primarily for restricted stock shares of executives and eligible employees. Fannie Mae had a liability of roughly $500 million for executive pensions and deferred compensation at the end of 2007, judging by the size of its deferred tax assets. The liability remained even as the troubled company was placed into conservatorship.

PAY DIRT

By many means, including the relentless cuts to pensions and retiree health benefits, executive pay tied to stock performance and earnings continues to climb. But how much are executives really taking home? For all the hand-wringing by compensation critics, the magnitude of executive pay has remained an elusive figure. But given that so much of it creates an ongoing liability for both the supplemental pensions and deferred compensation, knowing how large the total is can help investors, at least, gauge the pension headwinds ahead.

An indirect way to calculate the percentage of pay executives collectively receive at U.S. companies is to look at payroll tax data compiled by the Social Security Administration, which most people know as FICA. The key: Only earnings up to a certain ceiling are subject to a U.S. payroll tax of 12.4 percent, split between employer and employee, which finances Social Security retirement benefits. The ceiling, which is indexed to the average growth in wages, was $106,800 in 2010. (Employers and employees also each pay 1.45 percent on an individual's total income, with no salary ceiling, to fund Medicare.)

The Social Security data shows that 6 percent of wage earners have pay that exceeds the taxable earnings base, and that their "covered earnings" above the taxable maximum totaled $1.1 trillion in 2007. Adding the portion of their pay below the taxable wage base, $991 billion, produces a total of $2.1 trillion. In other words, by 2008, executives were receiving more than one-third of all pay at U.S. companies—more than $2.1 trillion of the $6.4 trillion total compensation.

The 6 percent of those taking home one-third of all pay includes everyone earning more than the wage base. But the top 2 percent of earners account for the lion's share of the $2.1 trillion. And that's just the pay top earners receive or defer. The figure understates executive pay because it includes just salary and vested deferred compensation, including bonuses.

It doesn't include unvested employer contributions and unvested interest credited to deferred-compensation accounts. Nor does it include unexercised stock options (options aren't subject to payroll tax until exercised) and unvested restricted stock (which isn't subject to payroll tax until vested; the subsequent appreciation is taxed as a capital gain).*

---

* An executive's ability to delay paying payroll taxes on compensation is in itself an economic benefit that ultimately boosts executive paychecks. And at some companies, they don't pay payroll taxes at all: The companies reimburse them for their FICA payments.

Also not included in the total compensation figures are types of executive pay that are never subject to payroll tax at all. This category includes incentive stock options (which are generally taxed as capital gains) and compensation characterized as a benefit (certain benefits, including pensions, aren't subject to any Social Security taxes). The compensation data also leave out compensation paid to hedge fund and private equity managers. The billions they receive isn't considered pay; it's treated as "carried interest," which is taxed as a capital gain.

And what about the other half of the compensation equation— benefits? In addition to $6.4 trillion in wages and salaries, private companies pay $1 trillion in benefits, which include contributions to retirement plans—both pensions and 401(k)s—health care, and life insurance contracts. It isn't possible to tell what portion represents benefits—and liabilities—for executives.

At the giddy height of the mortgage bubble in 2006, economists at Goldman Sachs analyzed what had been the biggest contributors to record corporate profits. The lead items on their list weren't productivity, innovation, or the quality of management. "The most important contributor to higher profit margins over the past five years has been a decline in labor's share of national income," they wrote. They weren't talking about pensions and benefits, but the patterns are parallel.

SHADOW PLAN

Even if the public doesn't know or care how big the executive liabilities are, finance officers certainly do, and they have come up with various ways to deal with it.

The life cycle of pension plans at drug wholesaler McKesson Corp. may provide a hint about how this trend will play out at the many companies with frozen pensions and growing executive liabilities.

McKesson froze its employees' pensions in 1997, and the next year established a SERP for top management. The frozen pension plan soon had a surplus because workers were no longer building pensions and the liability was falling with every dollar paid out to retirees. Thanks to gains from curtailing the pension, plus asset returns, the frozen plan began to generate income. This offset the annual expense of the unfunded executive pensions.

Essentially, frozen employee pensions, like the one at McKesson, provide shadow funding for executive pensions. This isn't necessarily a cash resource (see Chapter 8, "Unfair Shares"). Rather, the pension income offsets the drag the unfunded executive pensions create on income. This is one reason why companies freeze pension plans rather than terminate them: They can be worth more alive than dead. Why kill the fatted calf when you can continue to milk the cow for years?

In 2007, McKesson acquired Per-Se Technologies and merged that company's underfunded frozen pension with McKesson's overfunded frozen pension. This relieved McKesson of the need to contribute to the Per-Se plan. Indirectly, McKesson had monetized the surplus assets in its frozen pension plan. Over time, assuming McKesson doesn't extract the assets, the plan will have a surplus that will continue to build, especially when interest rates begin to rise from their historically low levels. Once again, the frozen plan will be a shadow fund for the executive pensions, including the more than $90 million owed to chief executive John Hammergren.

CHAPTER 7

Death Benefits: HOW DEAD PEASANTS
HELP FINANCE EXECUTIVE PAY

J UST BEFORE CHRISTMAS 2008, Irma Johnson, a widow in Houston with two young children, got a check in the mail for $1,579,399. It was the death benefit proceeds from the life insurance policy on her husband, Daniel, who'd died of a brain tumor at age forty-one the summer before. But the check wasn't payable to the Johnson family. It was made out to Amegy Bank, the company that had fired her husband six years before he died.

The check was accompanied by a note from the U.S. Postal Service, saying that the original envelope had become damaged in processing. But there was no other explanation. Mystified, Johnson called the insurer that had issued the check, Security Life of Denver Insurance Co. The person she spoke to told her that Amegy Bank of Houston was the beneficiary of a life insurance policy on her husband's life. The insurer had already sent the bank a check to replace the one lost in the mail.

This was the first time Johnson had ever heard of the policy, and she was appalled. The bank had taken out a life insurance policy on her husband and now was going to keep the money. But she would have been even more outraged if she had known where the money would go.

In recent years, as the costs of salaries and benefits for executives have put huge IOUs on corporate books, companies have begun stuffing billions of dollars into new and existing life insurance contracts taken out on the lives of their employees. The insurance policies serve as pseudo pension funds for executives: companies deposit money into the contracts, which act like giant IRAs. Like an IRA, the money in the policies is allocated among investments and grows tax-free. When the employees die—no matter how long it's been since they've left the company—the death benefit goes to the company tax-free. The primary goal, though, isn't to harvest the death benefit but to reap tax benefits and to use the investment income to offset the cost of the executive obligations.

Technically, it's illegal for companies to buy life insurance on workers as a tax dodge, but companies can buy it to finance "employee benefits." This loophole was created in the 1990s when companies and life insurance lobbyists convinced lawmakers that they could use the insurance to pay for "retiree benefits." What they didn't tell Congress was that the retiree benefit they were referring to was executive deferred compensation.

This corporate-owned life insurance, or COLI for short, was initially nicknamed "janitors insurance," because when companies first started taking out the coverage in the 1980s and early 1990s, the policies could cover almost anyone at a company, even the janitors. More recently, it has become known as "dead peasants insurance," which is how an insurance consultant for Winn-Dixie Stores, who had apparently watched too many Monty Python movies, referred to it in some memos in the mid-1990s.

Although the companies receive the death benefits, it isn't really the cash that the companies are looking for. The big money, and the big benefit they get, comes from keeping the money in the contracts. This is thanks to a cascade of tax breaks and accounting rules that enable these pseudo pension funds to generate income that boosts profits. It works like this. Let's say a company owes its executives $1 billion in deferred compensation. Since the obligation is unfunded, the interest on the debt hurts the company's earnings. Essentially, the executives, by deferring their pay, are making a loan to the company; the company owes them interest on the loan. The interest cost on the debt reduces the company's income. Unlike regular pensions, executive pensions aren't funded, so there are no investment returns to offset the cost of carrying the debt. And whereas other debt burdens, like retiree health benefits, can be—and often are—cut, companies rarely cut executive benefits.

Enter life insurance policies. The kind companies buy aren't the simple ones that pay a death benefit, but "cash value" policies, like "whole life" and "universal life" contracts, which are investment accounts with a death benefit attached. Because the account is wrapped in an insurance policy, the investments within it accumulate untaxed. In other words, the life insurance contract is a stand-in for a tax-favored pension fund.

The life insurance contracts not only provide some of the same tax benefits as pension funds; they also provide the same accounting benefits. Investments in insurance policies not only grow tax-free, but their returns pump up company income. If the investments had a return of $100 million, the company could add the $100 million to its income that year, which would offset the interest cost on the executive obligations. This tax-free flow of investment income—like the income from investments in pension funds—offsets the interest cost of the executive obligations.

If the investments weren't wrapped in an insurance policy, the company would have to sell the investments, then pay taxes on the gains, if it wanted to be able to report the income. Bottom line: Even though companies aren't supposed to get tax breaks for funding executive deferred comp and pensions, they get essentially the same tax breaks—and accounting benefits—by taking out life insurance on workers.

TO DIE FOR

Though the investments are essentially locked up in the insurance policies, companies receive tax-free cash when employees and former employees die whether in car accidents, in plane crashes, or from illness. Even people who are murdered or accidentally killed at work produce death benefits for their employers.

Companies report the death benefits as income, though they usually refer to them by opaque terms. The St. Louis–based Panera Bread Company calls them "mortality dividends" and refers to a death benefit as a "mortality income receivable" in its filings.

Banks have the largest obligations for executive pay and pensions, so it's not surprising that they are also the biggest buyers of life insurance on workers, which they call "bank-owned life insurance," or BOLI. Industry consultants estimate that over the coming decades, banks will receive more than $400 billion in death benefits as their retirees and former employees die. Financial filings occasionally disclose income triggered by deaths. Pacific State Bancorp, of Stockton, California, reported $2.6 million in income from a death benefit in 2008. A subsidiary of Conseco, Bankers Life and Casualty, bought life insurance on employees in 2006 and got an almost immediate payout of $2.7 million that year after an employee died.

Most families have no clue that their relatives are covered. Irma Johnson certainly didn't. Her husband, Daniel, had been a credit-risk manager for Southwest Bank of Texas, which was a predecessor to Amegy Bank. He was diagnosed with two cancerous brain tumors in 1999 and underwent two surgeries and radiation treatment that initially impaired his speech and left him unable to walk. He eventually returned to work, but in 2000 the bank criticized his communication skills and job performance and demoted him.

Despite the demotion, in May 2001, a manager took Daniel aside and told him that the compensation committee of the board of directors had selected him to be eligible for supplemental life insurance of $150,000. All he had to do was sign an agreement to receive the coverage, and a consent form authorizing the bank to purchase an insurance policy on his life. Four months later, the bank fired him. When Daniel died in

August 2008, his family received no life insurance death benefits, because the company had terminated the family's policy when it fired him.

Irma Johnson says her husband didn't have the "necessary capacity" to make financial decisions when he signed the agreement in 2001, and that the bank should have told him how much it would get when he died. She sued in state court in Houston in February 2009; under Texas law, material omissions can constitute a form of fraud. During the proceedings, Irma learned that the bank, which maintained that it had bought the policies to offset the cost of providing "employee benefits," had received $4.7 million when her husband died. It settled the case in 2010 for an undisclosed sum.

DEATH AND TAXES

Initially, insurance agents touted the death benefits as the most appealing feature of their plans, and some employers were disappointed when employees didn't die quickly enough to generate the anticipated "mortality dividends" for that year. In a confidential memo in 1991, an insurance agent wrote to Mutual Benefit Life Insurance Co. that American Electric Power (20,441 employees covered), American Greetings (4,000), R.R. Donnelley (15,624), and Procter & Gamble (14,987) were "acutely aware" that mortality was running at only 50 percent of projected rates.

The Procter & Gamble plan covered only white-collar employees, which might explain its poor death rate (34 percent of projected mortality), the memo noted. But the disappointing death rate at card maker American Greetings was a puzzle, since the plan covered only blue-collar employees, who are expected to have higher mortality rates. (The white-collar employees were covered by a separate policy with Provident.)

Diebold, the agent wrote, had been expecting $675,300 in death benefits since adopting the plan; so far, it was expecting only one "mortality dividend" of $98,000. "Do you think that a mortality dividend of that size relative to their current shortfall will give them comfort?" the memo said.

A company the agent called NCC had a better death rate, he noted: People were dying at 78 percent expected mortality. "However, this includes three suicides within the first year which is highly unusual"— NCC had not had one suicide in twenty-five years until 1990. "Without these suicides, NCC would be running at 33% expected mortality. This fact highly concerns me."

To keep track of when employees and retirees die, employers regularly check the Social Security Administration's database of deaths. That's how CM Holdings monitored its dead former employees. Page after page of a 1990 document called a "Death Run" lays out the names, ages, and Social Security numbers of more than 1,400 who would be worth more dead than alive. Also included was the amount of money the company was to receive when each employee died, even if the death occurred long after he or she left the job. Older workers would bring the company about $120,000 to $200,000 each, while younger workers would generate $400,000 to almost $500,000 each, the document said. (Younger workers yield bigger payouts because, based on actuarial calculations, they are less likely to die soon, so the premium amount buys more coverage for them.)

One of these workers was Felipe M. Tillman. Born in 1963, Tillman was an unlikely source of revenue for CM Holdings. A music lover whose taste ran from opera to jazz and even country music, he played keyboards and drums, sang, and was choral director at his Tulsa, Oklahoma, church. To make ends meet, he took part-time jobs in record stores, including a brief stint at a Camelot Music outlet owned by CM Holdings. As a minimum-wage, part-time employee, he didn't have health coverage or other benefits. But CM Holdings nonetheless took out a policy on his life. It didn't have to wait long for a payoff. Tillman died in 1992, of complications from AIDS. He was twenty-nine years old.

CM Holdings used the $168,875 death benefit it received when

Tillman died to pay for executive compensation, among other things. Company documents also show that $280 went to Star County Children's Services to help cover child support payments owed by a nephew of Camelot Music's founder, who was working at the company at the time.

Another name on the company's "Death Run" was Margaret Reynolds, of Uniontown, Ohio, born in 1936. Margaret was an administrative assistant and buyer for CM Holdings, making $21,000 a year. In the 1990s, she began deteriorating from the effects of amyotrophic lateral sclerosis, or Lou Gehrig's disease. In her final years, her adult children, who took turns caring for her, begged the company to provide $5,000 to pay for a special wheelchair so they could take their mother to church. "They said it wasn't covered," her son John Reynolds recalled bitterly. His mother died in 1998 at age sixty-two. Her family received a $21,000 benefit from a life insurance policy provided to employees by the company; CM Holdings received a death benefit payout of $180,000.

AN INSURABLE INTEREST

Over time, life insurance began morphing from a tax shelter into a finance tool for executive pay. For decades, if an individual or company wanted to buy life insurance on someone, they had to have an "insurable interest in the person," that is, the beneficiary of the policy would be directly affected by the insured's death. This rule existed for obvious reasons: Without it, a person could buy life insurance on a stranger— say, a skydiver, race car driver, or coal miner—and profit from his demise. And if he didn't die soon enough, the policyholder would have an incentive to push him over a cliff.

Initially, companies bought policies to protect them from the deaths of certain executives, or "key" employees. It made sense for partners in law and accounting firms to buy life insurance on each other. But, encouraged by insurance brokers, companies began buying it on broad swaths of their employees, because by insuring thousands of employees, not just "key men," the companies can place greater sums in life insurance contracts.

Dow Chemical, the Midland, Michigan, company known for its manufacturing of napalm, breast implants, and Agent Orange, was initially skeptical. An internal memo noted that, except for top-paid executives, it was "doubtful that Dow has an insurable interest in any of its employees." But it overcame its qualms and by 1992 had purchased life insurance policies on more than 20,000 employees.

Congress had no idea how widespread this practice had become until someone ratted on them. In 1995, a brown envelope was left on the desk of Ken Kies, chief of staff at the Joint Tax Committee. The envelope contained a list of companies that had bought life insurance on employees—along with calculations showing that a company might take in $1.2 billion over ten years by insuring 50,000 of its employees. It also noted that from 1993 to 1995, Wal-Mart had taken out insurance on 350,000 workers.

Lawmakers did the math and were appalled. They weren't concerned about whether Wal-Mart had an insurable interest in its stock clerks and store greeters, but they did care a lot about the loss of tax revenue. Companies were borrowing money from the policies and deducting the interest. The IRS deemed that the leveraged COLI taken out by seven hundred companies were sham transactions with no business purpose other than to score tax breaks. It filed a flurry of tax court cases, and companies subsequently took big charges for the disallowed deductions for interest on policy loans; among them were American Greetings, the Brooklyn, Ohio, maker of Tender Thoughts brand greeting cards and owner of Holly Hobbie and Care Bears licenses, and W.R. Grace, the Columbia, Maryland, manufacturer of building materials, which took out life insurance on its workers while defending thousands of asbestos-related lawsuits.

Within minutes of the interest-deduction phase-out, companies found a way around it. Instead of borrowing money from insurance companies, they simply borrowed it elsewhere. This was called "indirect leverage." The practice was especially appealing to banks, which can borrow money cheaply. Banks bought fresh policies on employees and in 1997 were floating the idea that they could buy life insurance on depositors and credit card holders as well. Fannie Mae, the giant mortgage buyer, proposed to insure the lives of home-mortgage holders, but the plan didn't go far. Congress nixed those ideas and tried to plug the indirect-leverage loophole in 1998. The Joint Tax Committee's Ken Kies, in classic revolving-door fashion, had quit his government job and was now lobbying for the COLI industry, which led a campaign that blanketed Congress with more than 170,000 letters and faxes and ran radio and newspaper ads targeting lawmakers as anti-business. The effort to close the loophole failed. Former House Ways and Means chairman Bill Archer, who had criticized janitors insurance as a tax shelter in 1995, joined the board of Clark/Bardes, the most influential COLI provider, in 2001.

"RETIREE BENEFITS"

Congress remained suspicious that companies were buying insurance on workers as a tax dodge. Employers said absolutely not: They had a sound business purpose. "The main reason employers are buying life insurance is so that they can provide benefits, in particular retiree medical benefits," maintained Jack Dolan, a spokesman for the American Council of Life Insurers.

Employers were betting, correctly, that the people making the decisions in Washington knew little about life insurance, taxes, accrual accounting, and retiree health plans. For one thing, the assets in the policies aren't cash that companies can pull out and spend; they don't get cash until the covered employees die, so there's no way the companies can use the policies as a piggy bank to "pay" for health care premiums or prescription drugs. In any case, many companies that bought life insurance on their workers didn't provide retiree health coverage, or if they did, few of the workers were eligible for it.

Not everyone was snowed. "We do not believe that the purpose of the [plan] was to fund employee benefits," wrote Judge Robert P. Ruwe in a 1999 U.S. Tax Court ruling against Winn-Dixie. The Jacksonville, Florida, supermarket chain was tussling with the IRS over the legitimacy of deductions it had taken for loans from policies covering 56,000 workers. Judge Ruwe pointed out that staff turnover at Winn-Dixie was so high that few employees were ever eligible for retiree medical benefits, yet the company had continued to collect death benefits on those who left the company before retirement. The judge concluded that the executives "recognized that it was a tax shelter" and that ultimately, over the sixty-year life of the policies, the company hoped to save $2 billion in taxes. The tax court wasn't taking aim at the company's practice of insuring its checkout clerks and bag boys; it was going after the interest deduction. And it ultimately won. In 2001, the U.S. Court of Appeals for the Eleventh Circuit in Atlanta upheld the tax court decision, and in 2008 the U.S. Supreme Court declined to hear Winn-Dixie's appeal. The interest deduction was dead.

Though employers lost the interest deduction, they didn't lose the desire to buy life insurance on workers, because they could still use policies as vehicles to generate tax-free income. In the early 2000s, the practice was proliferating. In 2002, Nestlé USA had policies covering 18,000 workers, Pitney Bowes Inc. had policies covering 23,000, and Procter & Gamble Co. had 15,000 covered workers. The companies all claimed they were using the policies to finance employee benefits. "We have not done this for financial gain," Nestlé said. American Electric Power claimed that the death benefits were "dedicated to retiree benefits." Hillenbrand Industries Inc., a coffin maker in Batesville, Indiana, said it bought the policies to beef up employee benefits.

MANAGERS INSURANCE

By the early 2000s, the days of companies buying policies on masses of low-level clerks and cashiers were largely over as more states, including California, Michigan, Ohio, Illinois, and Minnesota, required companies to secure employee consent to include them in coverage. Some companies had done this in the 1990s, including Walt Disney, which offered workers an incentive of a modest amount of life insurance without charge in exchange for giving the company permission to take out a policy on them.

This didn't dampen sales, because companies figured they could take out larger amounts of death benefits if they bought new policies on higher-paid employees. Janitors insurance mutated into "managers insurance."

Obtaining a manager's consent wasn't difficult. Bank of America appealed to their company spirit, telling managers that letting the bank buy coverage on their lives would help the company. The New York Times Co. offered a carrot: It told eligible executive-level employees they could participate in a deferred-compensation plan if they let the company make itself the beneficiary of insurance on their lives. Employers rarely tell employees how much they're covered for, but the amounts can be substantial.

Focusing on middle managers has an additional advantage: It's easier for employers to make the case that they use the insurance to finance employee benefits, since managers are almost always eligible for benefits, whereas store clerks usually are not. Under tax law, life insurance purchased by a corporation is supposed to have a business purpose. Illegal tax avoidance is not a sanctioned business purpose.

Initially, insurers figured this was a good move: Higher-income employees tend to have longer life expectancies, which meant the policies would eventually be worth more. But the strategy could backfire. They failed to consider that covering a group of people in one place carries additional mortality risk. After the September 11 terrorist attacks, Hartford Life Insurance reported an after-tax charge of $2 million related to the attacks. This didn't mean that Hartford paid out only $2 million; this was how much Hartford lost on having written the policies. Companies like Aon, the giant risk manager and insurer that lost 176 employees in the World Trade Center, reaped tens of millions in death benefits.*

The mass death of heavily insured executives and other employees in the Trade Center attacks was a wake-up call to insurers about the amount of financial exposure they had when there was a high concentration of insureds in a single location. In 2003, at the annual Society of Actuaries meeting in Washington, D.C., a Towers Perrin group-pricing actuary noted that insurers had begun requiring employers to provide not only the ages and Social Security numbers of employees, but also their work addresses, so the employer could assess the potential financial risk of multiple casualties from mass shootings, terrorist attacks, building collapses, and other disasters.

WANTED: DEAD OR ALIVE

Janitors insurance doesn't kill people, but it strikes many people as unseemly, if not creepy, which may explain why the sellers and buyers of the insurance aren't eager to talk about it. Such reluctance to discuss a practice that accounts for one-third of life insurance sales might make CFOs take pause. If they really thought the practice was appropriate, it would be highlighted in the annual report.

---

* Of course, Aon also provided group and executive policies benefiting the victims' families, which it purchased from other insurers. To be clear, Aon and other companies aren't celebrating when they receive death benefits; they're taking out the policies to benefit from the ability to shelter investments in them from taxes, and for the accounting benefits.

A string of lawsuits in Texas beginning in the 1990s, in which employers have been steadily on the losing end, shows that when the practice is put before a jury (a Texas jury, at least), companies have good reason to worry.

One of the earliest suits involved the death of William Smith, in 1991. The twenty-year-old was working at a Stop N Go convenience store in Pasadena, Texas, for extra Christmas money when a robber shot him dead. Angela Smith, his eighteen-year-old widow, who was still in high school, was touched when the company offered her and her one year-old son, Brandon, a payment of $60,000.

Normally, if a worker is killed on the job, his family receives death benefits from the state workers' compensation system. But to save money, the store's owner, Houston-based National Convenience Stores, didn't participate in the program. Still, to protect itself from the cost of wrong-ful death or negligence lawsuits arising from workplace deaths, it took out life insurance on its clerks. The policy, from Lloyd's of London, paid NCS $250,000 after William Smith died.

Angela Smith sued NCS in state court anyway, alleging violation of Texas's insurable-interest rules and seeking payment of the COLI money to Smith's estate. In 1999, the court awarded the estate $456,513, which included insurance, attorney fees, and interest. NCS appealed that judgment, and in 2002 agreed to settle with Smith for $390,000. Valero Energy Corp., in San Antonio, acquired NCS and its COLI pol-icies in 2001, through its acquisition of Ultramar Diamond Shamrock Corp., which had earlier bought NCS.

In a similar case in 1998, in which a family challenged whether NCS had an insurable interest in the deceased employee, the company argued that it did, indeed, have an insurable interest in its workers because, without workers, "NCS would not generate revenue and would cease to exist as a viable entity." The Texas court in that case suggested that NCS consider liability insurance.

A Texas jury was also unimpressed with an employer's claim that it had an insurable interest in a part-time employee. Peggy Stillwagoner was a temporary employee who had been at her job only two months when she died in 1994. A nurse, she had been on her way to a home-care appointment when another driver slammed into her Geo Metro. She underwent emergency surgery, but died soon after. She was fifty-one.

Facing tens of thousands of dollars in medical bills, Stillwagoner's family asked her employer, Advantage Medical Services, if it provided any life insurance or other benefits. The owner of the company said it didn't. But a few months after the accident, when an insurance company investigator contacted Peggy's husband, Kenneth, asking him to sign papers releasing her medical records, he learned by chance that AMS held a $200,000 insurance policy on his wife's life.

The family sued in state court, arguing that the company had no insurable interest in Peggy's life, since she'd been replaced the day after her death. The family was seeking the benefit the company had collected upon her death. The company insisted that it did have an insurable interest, because the field nurse had the "opportunity to attract or create new business and was therefore a valuable employee." The family lost in the lower court, but in late 1998 the appeals court reversed the lower court's ruling and found that Kenneth Stillwagoner had a right to challenge the insurance payment to AMS. Subsequently, the company and Travelers Insurance Co., a unit of Citigroup Inc. that sold AMS the coverage, settled with the family for $395,000.

HOLY BOLI

The bad publicity that lawsuits like these generated spurred lawmakers to draft fresh proposals to rein in the practice. In 2003, Congressman Gene Green, a Texas Democrat, proposed requiring employers to tell all employees, past and present, about any coverage bought on their lives since 1985. Once again, insurance lobbyists fought back. COLI provider Clark/Bardes and insurance-industry groups led the opposition, aided by Ken Kies's lobbying practice, which Clark/Bardes had acquired. The industry took out radio ads in the Washington area attacking proposals to curb what it called "business insurance." The proposals went nowhere.

But lawmakers continued to press for more restrictions on COLI, and in 2006 it appeared they had succeeded. Congress enacted new rules that limit companies to buying life insurance on just the top one-third of earners, who must provide consent.

But the rules turned out to be a boon to insurers and employers. For one thing, they *specifically* permit employers to buy life insurance on the top third of earners—those most likely to participate in deferred-compensation programs. This was the first time the law deemed the practice legal. (Insurance lobbyists aren't paid top dollar for nothing.) And though the new rules require employers to obtain employees' consent, the rules weren't retroactive. Thus, companies still hold old policies covering millions of employees, including lower-level workers and former employees who aren't entitled to benefits of any kind, as well as retirees. The rules don't require employers to notify people covered prior to August 2006.

In fact, these "restrictions" fueled the sale of billions of dollars more in COLI. Banks led the way, not only because of the new rules but because banking regulators in the Bush administration specifically affirmed the use of life insurance to finance deferred compensation.

Banks took out billions of dollars' worth of this life insurance during the mortgage bubble, when executive pay—and the IOUs for their deferred compensation—surged. By the end of 2008, banks had a total of $122.3 billion in life insurance on employees, nearly double the $65.8 billion they held at the end of 2004. (Unlike other companies, banks are required to disclose their total life insurance holdings in regulatory filings.)

At the end of the first quarter in 2009, Bank of America had the most life insurance on employees: $17.3 billion. The bank won't disclose how much it owes executives and insists that "Bank of America uses this insurance to help defray the cost of employee benefits." But filings show that the bank had an unfunded obligation of only $1.3 billion for retiree health benefits; it also owes $2.6 billion for supplemental executive pensions. This suggests that at least $15 billion of the BOLI is intended to back the deferred-compensation obligations. JPMorgan Chase had $11 billion in BOLI and, coincidentally, $10 billion in deferred-compensation obligations. The size of its retiree health obligations? Only $1 billion.

Citigroup had $919 million in unfunded retiree-health obligations, $586 million in supplemental executive pension obligations, and roughly $5 billion in deferred compensation. Offsetting these obligations: $4.2 billion in life insurance. Citigroup said it had bought BOLI because it was "an attractive use of capital" and for "the tax-free nature of the death proceeds."

Wachovia Corp. had $12 billion in BOLI at the end of 2008, when it was acquired by Wells Fargo (which had $5.7 billion). None of the banks would say how many employees it had life insurance policies on, or whether they were still employed by the bank.

UNDERGROUND

Life insurance on employees accounts for an estimated one-third of all sales of cash-value life insurance. The amounts companies hold can exceed the size of their pension plans. Yet companies and insurers are required to report almost nothing on it, making it impossible for employees, regulators, and lawmakers to determine just how much money companies have stashed away in the insurance.

Insurance regulators, who often accommodate the wishes of the industry, help keep the practice a mystery. The National Association of Insurance Commissioners says it has no data about the scope of the sales, and, though banks report their total holdings to regulators, other companies aren't required to.

Even bank regulators, including the Office of the Comptroller of the Currency, the Office of Thrift Supervision, and the Federal Deposit

Insurance Corp., have little data. Banks are required to disclose the total cash surrender value of their policies in quarterly bank filings. This is the amount of money they have stuffed into the contracts, plus interest. But they don't have to disclose anything else, including how much the investments are contributing to earnings. In 2007, the IRS began requiring companies to report the number of employees they purchase insurance on, and the total amount. But companies don't have to provide any figures for insurance they held prior to these new disclosure rules.

The insurance industry won't talk about it, either. The American Council of Life Insurers, which has lobbied strongly to oppose restrictions on COLI, says it doesn't have any data on the product. The National Association of Life Underwriters, despite devoting one-third of its annual conference on life insurance to COLI, says it doesn't know how much companies are buying.

The Life Insurance Marketing and Research Association says it doesn't ask companies how much of the insurance they have, and A.B. Best Co., which sells a report on COLI on its Web site, says it doesn't know how much employers buy or what percentage of life insurance sales it accounts for.

Some insurance consultants used to provide figures to the public, but they stopped. CAST Management Consultants in Los Angeles reported in the early 2000s that sales of new corporate-owned life had risen 60 percent. But it has kept mum since.

Insurance companies that sell COLI don't even mention the products in their SEC filings. Hartford Life, a major COLI provider, used to. In 2001, it had janitors insurance with a face value of $4.3 billion in force among its clients, according to its annual report. COLI in all its forms brought the company $37 million of its $1 billion of net income that year. But Hartford stopped providing such disclosures. The insurers also stopped mentioning in filings that they owned policies on their own employees. Hartford took out an undisclosed amount of insurance on about eight hundred of its own managers in 2002, but current filings don't mention it.

Prudential Insurance Co. of America had four groups of policies on workers' lives, valued at $813 million, in the early 2000s. MetLife Inc., a big seller of corporate-owned life insurance, bought policies on "several thousand" of its own employees in 1993, 1998, and 2001. (There's sometimes a bit more disclosure when insurers buy life insurance on their own employees; if they buy the policies from a subsidiary, they have to disclose the purchases as related-party transactions.)

The SEC requires that companies report increases in the amount of life insurance they have—but only if the increases are "material." *Materiality* isn't defined. "So some large companies with COLI don't need to report it at all," says a former government tax official.

Further, when companies report the holdings, they commonly report all their life insurance in aggregate. This includes "key man" policies taken out on top executives, and split-dollar policies, which are used to funnel lavish retirement benefits to top executives.

For investors, another challenge is knowing how much life insurance might be contributing to a company's bottom line. Companies commonly aggregate the insurance-related income with other items in the "other income" section of their filings.

Clark/Bardes, the COLI consultant, is also vague. A footnote in the income section of its 2000 filing says the "other income" category "includes $1 million in life insurance proceeds." The company received the $1 million when an employee died in a plane crash.

CHAPTER 8

Unfair Shares: USING
EMPLOYEES' PENSIONS TO FINANCE
EXECUTIVE LIABILITIES

BUYING LIFE INSURANCE on workers is one way many companies informally fund executive deferred compensation. Tapping the regular pension plan is another.

Intel, the giant semiconductor chip maker, moved more than $200 million of its deferred-compensation obligations into the regular pension plan in 2005. This move converted an unfunded liability—deferred compensation for the top 3.5 percent to 5 percent or so of its workforce—into a fully funded, regular pension benefit.

When these 12,000 or so highly paid employees and executives at the chip maker get ready to collect their deferred salaries, Intel won't have to pay them out of cash; the pension plan will pay them.*

---

* When companies move deferred-compensation obligations into pension plans, taxpayers not only end up subsidizing additional tax breaks on executive pay, but they also eventually end up on the hook in another way: When deferred executive salaries and bonuses are part of a pension plan, they can be rolled over into an IRA—another tax-advantaged vehicle.

There was another benefit as well: Intel contributed $187 million to the pension fund to cover the executive obligations. Normally, companies can deduct the cost of deferred compensation only when they actually pay it, often many years after the obligation is incurred. But Intel's contribution to the pension plan was deductible immediately. Its tax saving: nearly $70 million in the first year.

Meanwhile, the pension contribution enabled Intel to book as much as an extra $136 million of profit over the ten years that began in 2005 (thanks to the pension accounting rules that let companies immediately record noncash income from pension-plan contributions, based on what they expect the assets to earn when invested). The $136 million was Intel's estimate of the returns on the contribution. The company's effective guaranteed return on the contribution in the first year: 40.6 percent.

Intel's move wasn't illegal, though it had a peculiar result: It turned a pension plan for a company with more than fifty thousand workers primarily into a fund to pay for the deferred compensation of the company's most highly paid employees, roughly 4 percent of the workforce.

If it were this easy for all employers to just shift executive liabilities into their employee pension plans, they would all have done so long ago. But tax rules put up a roadblock. To get tax breaks, pensions have to be open to a broad group of employees and can't discriminate in favor of the highly paid.

Benefits consultants, however, found a loophole in the discrimination rules that has enabled a growing number of large companies to shift hundreds of millions of dollars of executive liabilities into rank-and-file pensions. Using complex and proprietary formulas, the consultants determine how much discrimination a pension plan can achieve without technically violating discrimination rules.

The result might be a dollar amount, say, $200 million, which would be allocated to highly paid employees in addition to their regular benefits from the plan. In Intel's case, the participants got their regular pension, plus an amount of their deferred compensation paid from the pension. These arrangements are often called QSERPs, which stands for "qualified supplemental executive retirement plan."

The shift doesn't increase the total amount a person receives; when the executive liability is moved to the pension plan, an equivalent amount of deferred compensation or supplement executive pension is canceled. The goal of the maneuver isn't to boost executive benefits but to harness the pension plan to pay them. "QSERPs clearly offer a tremendous opportunity for some employers to prefund key executive retirement benefits," noted Watson Wyatt's marketing material.

OVERLOADED

Intel and its pension plan were healthy. But companies in financial distress have an incentive to do this, and when they shovel executive obligations into underfunded pension plans, the result can backfire.

In December 2002, Oneida Ltd., a flatware maker in upstate New York, amended its pension to give then chairman and CEO Peter J. Kallett an additional pension of $301,163 a year in retirement. This was in addition to the $116,000 a year he was already eligible for in the regular pension. The company then transferred the liability for that additional amount from his executive pension.

The company made a similar amendment for another executive in April 2004, boosting his pension from less than $33,000 a year to a minimum of $246,353 a year in retirement. The timing wasn't great. The company was struggling financially, and the pension plan was already significantly underfunded. Two weeks after awarding the pension increase to the second executive, Oneida was supposed to make a mandatory $939,951 contribution to its pension fund. But it didn't. Instead it froze the pension, which meant that employees would no longer build any benefits.

But the freeze didn't affect executives' pensions under the QSERP, because these were already set at a certain amount that wouldn't grow over time anyway. Neither the company nor the plan survived. In 2006, Oneida terminated its pensions in bankruptcy court and transferred the obligations to the PBGC. It also laid off most of its employees. Donald Grogan, who was fifty-two at the time, had worked in manufacturing and shipping at Oneida for twenty-two years before he lost his job. Because the pension plan had been handed over to the PBGC, he had to wait until 2009, when he turned fifty-five, to begin drawing his pension. To make ends meet, he got a truck-driving job with no benefits.

On the other side of the country, a similar drama left Chester Madison with a gutted pension. He had been a middle manager at Consolidated Freightways Corp., a trucking company based in Vancouver, Washington. In late 2001, when the company was clearly in trouble, it transferred most of the retirement IOUs for eight top officers into its pension.*

The executives believed this would protect most or all of their supplemental pensions—which could reach $139,000 a year when they retired—because they'd be paid from the pension plan's trust fund instead of the company's operating cash.

They also felt more secure knowing that once executive liabilities are transferred into a "qualified" pension plan, they, too, are covered by the PBGC. When consulting firms market these strategies to upper management, that's a key selling point. By contrast, deferred compensation and supplemental executive pensions are unsecured promises, which creditors can claim if the employer goes under. Many Enron executives

---

* To help the plan pass the discrimination tests, the company added a minimum benefit of $400 to $500 a year for eligible retirees. "The Company's pension plan passes the test by a wide enough margin to permit the transfer of most of the supplemental retirement benefits to the Pension Plan," noted an internal company memo.

learned about this risk the hard way when they lost millions in deferred-compensation savings when the energy giant collapsed in 2001.

CFC executives soon found out how secure they actually were. The company hadn't been contributing to the pension plan, which was growing steadily weaker. Adding the executive liabilities to the lifeboat swamped it. The plan's funding went from having about 96 percent of the assets needed to pay promised benefits to having just 79 percent.

The next year, Consolidated filed for bankruptcy, and in 2003 it handed its pension plan over to the PBGC. Consolidated executives lost a chunk of their pensions because the maximum PBGC payout at the time was $44,000 a year at age sixty-five, and is far less at earlier ages and when other factors are applied.

When Chester Madison retired in 2002, after thirty-three years, his pension fell to $20,400 a year from $49,200, which forced him, at age sixty-two, to take a job selling flooring in Sacramento.

Consultants have since devised solutions to reduce risk for the top managers. In 2005, when Hartmarx shifted executive liabilities into the regular pension plan, it also established an unfunded trust to benefit fewer than a dozen executives, including chief financial officer Glenn R. Morgan. A Chapter 11 bankruptcy filing would trigger the funding of the trust, assuring that the executive benefits it had transferred into the regular pension would be paid even if the pension plan failed.

That was a smart move by the Chicago-based maker of high-end men's suits. In 2009, when its lenders cut off its credit, the company filed for Chapter 11. The company survived: It was acquired by SKNL North America BV, a subsidiary of an Indian textile maker, and renamed HMX. The pension plan didn't: The new owners had no interest in being saddled with the underfunded pension plan covering thirteen thousand employees and retirees and dumped the plan on the PBGC's doorstep. At that point, the pension plan was only 47 percent funded.

No one knows how many hundreds of millions of SERP and deferred-compensation obligations have been transferred into employee pension plans since the practice emerged in the 1990s. The Milliman consultant who advised employers to tell only the participating executives about the arrangements was also concerned about the IRS's reaction. He advised employers that in "dealing with the IRS," they should ask it for an approval letter, because if the agency later cracks down, its restrictions probably won't be retroactive.

"At some point in the future, the IRS may well take the position" that supplemental executive pensions moved into a regular pension plan "violate the 'spirit' of the nondiscrimination rules," he wrote. Companies have been able to blow the practice past the IRS because, when they file the amendments, they don't explicitly note the purpose of the change and include it with a flurry of other technical amendments. In any case, the IRS staff is stretched too thin to scrutinize the dozens of pages of complex calculations companies perform to prove that they don't discriminate. In contrast with a deduction a freelance worker might take for a home office, the IRS generally accepts an employer's word that its pension plan doesn't discriminate. To halt the practice, Congress would have to end the flexibility that companies now have in meeting the IRS nondiscrimination tests, which is something employers have strongly opposed.

And though companies are supposed to disclose details of the compensation of their top officers, they maintain that, because the executives' benefits are now part of the broad-based plans, they are no longer considered to be executive benefits, so disclosure isn't required.

DISCRIMINATION 101

These techniques were spawned in the early 1990s, when the IRS issued new rules intended to rein in an employer's inclination to set up and run retirement plans for the favored few. To get tax breaks that allow them to deduct contributions and have the money grow tax-deferred, companies had to prove that their pensions, profit sharing, and 401(k)s don't discriminate.

Employer groups hadn't stood idly by awaiting these new regulations. As they had when FASB crafted new pension and retirement benefits accounting rules, employers and their consultants weighed in, demanding flexibility. They got their wish.

As a result, employers don't have to actually treat everyone participating in the pension or savings plan the same. They are allowed to have a certain amount of "disparity," or inequality, as long as they can pass certain tests showing that they weren't going too far.

The first test is the so-called coverage test, which essentially determines that if 100 percent of the higher-paid executives are going to participate in a plan, then at least 70 percent of the lower-paid must also participate.

Thus, in a perverse way, this anti-discrimination rule makes it legal for employers to exclude 30 percent of their low-paid workers from a particular plan right off the bat.

Even before applying the coverage test, employers generally exclude many part-time workers, independent contractors, and "leased" employees, such as janitorial, security, and cafeteria workers. These categories make up about 25 percent of the U.S. workforce.

The diminished pool of employees "eligible" to participate don't necessarily get their feet in the plan right away. They must first pass certain hurdles. These might require that they be twenty-one or older, work one thousand hours, or reach December 31 of the year following the year they were employed.

Excluding employees doesn't just save money: It enables higher-paid employees to receive the maximum benefits. Under IRS rules, the amount higher-paid workers contribute to a 401(k) can't be greater than a certain percentage of what the lower-paid contribute. But if the lower-paid contribute too little, the contribution gap will be too great, and the higher-paid won't be allowed to contribute the maximum ($16,500 in 2011). The simplest way of closing the gap is to exclude as many lower-paid workers as possible. In the fast-food, retail, and hotel industries, it's common for at least half the workforce to be locked out of the savings plans.

Inadvertently, this kind of legal salary discrimination can have a disproportionate impact on women and minorities. For years, Hugo Boss, which makes high-end clothing, excluded the 80 or so workers at its warehouse in Midway, Georgia, from the 401(k) retirement plan that it offered to the 232 employees and managers at its Cleveland headquarters. With their low salaries, the warehouse workers, mostly black women, would have contributed little to their accounts, causing the plan to fail another discrimination test, one that compares the contributions of the low paid and the highly paid. If the gap is too wide, the highly paid can't contribute the maximum to their accounts ($16,500 in 2011). Ironically, the easiest way to prevent this outcome is to exclude low-paid workers altogether.

Countless studies and surveys lamenting the low participation rates of employees barely making a living wage have portrayed low-income workers as apathetic about saving money. Similar studies also trot out statistics about the low savings rates of blacks and Hispanics, and of women compared with men.

Lorenzo Walker, one of the warehouse workers at Hugo Boss, didn't fit this stereotype. Walker, in his fifties, was earning only $6.50 an hour but still wanted to save some money for his retirement. He preferred an account like a 401(k), where his contributions would be withheld automatically from his paycheck, perhaps receive a matching contribution from his employer, and grow untaxed. His wife, a nail technician, had no retirement plan. Social Security was going to be the couple's primary source of income, plus whatever Walker could squirrel away. He'd had a 401(k) at a prior job at a poultry-processing factory and had saved up about $11,000.

So one of the first things he asked when he started his job at Hugo Boss was whether the company had a retirement plan. The company said no. In fact, the company actually did have a 401(k) and the warehouse workers were shut out because their low incomes and savings rates would drag down the tax breaks of higher-income employees.

In 2006, the company agreed to let the employees' union, Unite Here, set up a separate 401(k) for the warehouse and help run it. In exchange, the company would provide small matching contributions to their plans. The arrangement enabled the warehouse workers to have a 401(k) and receive company contributions, without affecting the Cleveland employees at all.

Many companies have these separate-but-unequal arrangements, with different 401(k)s for lower-paid and higher-income employees, who often get bigger company contributions. IRS rule 401(a)(5) says "a classification shall not be considered discriminatory merely because it is limited to salaries or clerical employees." In plain English, a company can have a lousy plan covering clericals and a terrific plan for the professionals. "Cadillac plans versus ghetto plans" is what one lawyer called them.*

There's another benefit to excluding low-paid workers from the retirement plans, or segregating them to less generous plans: It makes it easier for plans that executives participate in to pass another required discrimination test, called the "benefits" test. To prove it is nondiscriminatory, the plan must pay the low-paid participants, as a group, at least 70 percent of what the higher-paid get.

GERRYMANDERING

This is where the real creativity comes in. The tests don't require employers to compare the benefits of individuals; they can compare *ratios* of the benefits received by groups of highly paid with those of groups of lower-paid employees. Benefits consultants developed software that enabled them to gerrymander employees into hypothetical

---

* Eli Gottesdiener, referring to the PricewaterhouseCooper's plan in court documents.

groups. One might have only highly compensated employees, or HCEs, to use the technical lingo. Another might have only lower-paid employees. Still another group might include only executives and low-paid seasonal workers hired during the holiday.

The goal is to reduce the gap—albeit artificially—between the high-paid and low-paid in each group. To make the benefits of the low-paid, as a group, appear bigger, companies like CenturyTel count Social Security as part of employees' pensions. Employers might also contribute a small amount to the savings plans of low-paid workers—which makes their percentage of benefits look higher. This helps the plan pass the test, and doesn't cost the company anything, because the temp workers won't stick around long enough to vest and forfeit the employer's contribution.

This works with pensions as well. In 1999, for example, Royal & Sun Alliance Co., with the assistance of PricewaterhouseCoopers, amended its pension to award a small increase to one hundred employees. One employee got a pension increase of an additional $1.92 a month in retirement. This enabled the company to pass the discrimination tests and award eight officers and directors significantly more. The largest payment went to John Winterbauer, the sixty-year-old vice president of human resources, who got an additional $5,300 a month for life, paid out in a lump sum of $792,963.

PricewaterhouseCoopers, which pioneered many of these techniques, has used them on its own workforce. The accounting and benefits consulting giant provides its partners' contributions to the 401(k) with a 200 percent matching contribution—putting in $2 for every $1 the partners contribute—but only 25 percent for lower-paid workers.

The plan passes the discrimination test in part because new employees joining the plan receive a 200 percent matching contribution in the first month of participation, which is always in December, which is also when the company tests the plan for discrimination. This practice has the effect of making the contributions to the lower-paid, as a group, appear higher, which helps the plan pass the test.

YOUNG AND VESTLESS

Another clever way to pass the discrimination tests is by providing matching contributions. A common scenario is that an employer will chip in fifty cents for every dollar an employee contributes to his 401(k), up to 6 percent of pay. An employee making $50,000 who contributes 6 percent of pay ($3,000) to his 401(k) will get a matching contribution from his employer of $1,500.

Employers say they provide matching contributions to encourage lower-paid and younger employees to participate. That's true, but a bit disingenuous. If that were the whole story, the contributions would be the employees' to keep. In reality, lower-paid workers commonly forfeit the employer contribution, because of lengthy vesting requirements, which used to be as long as ten years but now are three years for savings plans and three to five years for pensions.

A company with high turnover can afford to provide a more generous match, since ultimately it won't pay it all out. Employers use the forfeited matching contributions to make future contributions, which reduces their costs. A 2 percent match will cost only 1 to 1.5 percent, because of forfeitures.

When employees forfeit the employer contributions, they also forfeit the earnings on those amounts. This means that the employer not only gets its contribution back; it also receives tax-free earnings on the money.

The vesting period can be stretched out in other ways. Some plans have required employees to be employed on the fifth anniversary of the day they were hired in order to vest, or on the last day of the fifth year. Wal-Mart employees must work for 1,000 hours in a consecutive twelve-month period to be eligible to participate in the profit-sharing plan. In 2009, 79,339 employees forfeited some of their benefit when they left.

The company then redistributed the money to the remaining

employees "based on eligible wages," meaning that some company contributions originally destined to aid lower-paid employees ended up benefiting longer-service, higher-paid employees.

Employers are perennially seeking to loosen the discrimination rules even further. They scored a big coup with Automatic Enrollment, a provision in the Pension Protection Act that became effective in 2007. This was touted as a way to improve participation. The theory is that poor participation rates are the result of worker apathy and that if they are automatically enrolled, it would solve that problem. It's hard to see how it will help improve savings rates: Employees can drop out at any time, and they aren't forced to contribute. At Wal-Mart, 8 percent of the employees who are considered participants in the retirement plan have nothing in their accounts.

What the new rules do, however, is give employers a free pass from the discrimination rules: As long as a plan merely offers automatic enrollment, employers don't have to worry about passing discrimination tests.

CHAPTER 9

Project Sunshine: A HUMAN RESOURCES PLOT TO DISSOLVE RETIREE BENEFITS

AT AGE NINETY-TWO, John Wesley Galloway had beaten the actuarial odds for someone who'd spent a lifetime in hard labor in an iron foundry. For thirty years, he'd churned out parts for Kelsey-Hayes, the Rockford, Illinois, unit of a Midwestern farm equipment maker. Galloway had also beaten even more impressive odds: He'd survived more than two decades with his retiree health coverage largely intact, despite the relentless efforts of his former employer—and the current owner of the retiree portfolio he's part of—to take it away. The company and its successors had used almost every trick in the book: legal maneuvers, illegal maneuvers, restructuring games, and deceit. Despite myriad attempts to whittle down the coverage for Galloway and his wife, Pansy, it was still intact.

But in 2006, and again in 2008, the plan administrator came up with a new trip wire. It sent Galloway a letter telling him that his health coverage would be canceled unless he could prove he wasn't dead. If the company didn't receive a notarized affidavit attesting to his continued presence on earth, the company, TRW, would cancel this coverage. Galloway had heard about IRS audits, but not death audits. This is just one of the many cost-saving maneuvers consultants have dreamed up in recent years to help their clients reduce the cost of their retiree health plans. Over the past twenty years, Galloway had just about seen it all. And there was more to come.

Galloway had never worked for TRW but, like millions of other retirees, including the Western Electric and AT&T employees who ended up with Lucent and the McDonnell Douglas retirees who ended up at Boeing, he was part of a portfolio of retirees that had passed through several owners' hands. Not surprisingly, none of the owners felt like paying the retirees' benefits, but they couldn't cut the pension plans, which are protected by law. Yet the law protecting retiree health benefits wasn't as ironclad as they thought. So this was where employers directed their legal firepower.

The quest to end Galloway's retiree health coverage actually began at another company, Massey Ferguson, which bought the company he worked for, Kelsey-Hayes. Massey Ferguson isn't a household name outside the Farm Belt, but for most of a century it was an almost iconic fixture in the Midwest. Founded in 1847 by a storied Canadian family whose descendants include the actor Raymond Massey, the company thrived until the agricultural recession in the 1970s dried up demand for its combines and tractors. The struggling company subsequently passed through many hands, all eager to extract a profit, at whatever cost. Conrad Black, the controversial Canadian businessman, gained control of the company in the late 1970s and added it to the portfolio of mining, media, and other businesses owned by holding company Argus Corp. The company didn't thrive, and Black resigned as chairman of Massey Ferguson in 1979 and moved on to become a media baron and a prison inmate after being convicted of mail fraud and obstruction of justice.*

Black may have been gone, but he was replaced by a new chief executive cut from the same cloth: Victor A. Rice, a pugnacious Brit

---

* Convicted in 2007, Black was freed on bail in 2010 while part of his case was on appeal. In June 2011, a federal judge ordered him back to prison for thirteen months.

who claimed to be the son of a chimney sweep. In 1986, Rice changed the name of the company from Massey Ferguson to Varity (after his initials), bought a couple of companies, including Kelsey-Hayes, the one Galloway worked for, and began looking for ways to boost profits. The retirees were an obvious resource.

Soon after ascending the throne, Rice demanded a status report on retiree costs. The managers at the company's Buffalo, New York, head-quarters gave their boss what they assumed was good news. The pension was overfunded, and retiree health costs were "low." But Rice wanted to cut retiree benefits anyway, even for the most elderly. A memo summariz-ing his "Philosophy & Objectives" made this clear. "The Company is not committed to maintenance of a retiree's standard of living."

Varity's managers sprang into action, but nothing they suggested was dramatic enough to satisfy Rice. He told them to be a little more creative, and he didn't let up. Under increased pressure to deliver a plan that would generate big savings, human resources manager Jill Well-man produced this snappish memo: "You have asked that I be inventive in coming up with a solution," she wrote to her superiors a week before Christmas in 1986. "As far as I can determine there is only one solution" to save the company the most money, she concluded. "That would be the death of all existing retirees." This happy outcome was, alas, many years in the future.

So Wellman's memo went on to detail "more practical" but "not necessarily legal" solutions to help her employer meet its cost-cutting goals. One option: Establish "an offshore company responsible for the retirees but not accountable under United States law and have it go bankrupt and thus terminate the plans." Another: Simply terminate the benefits, wait for the retirees to sue, and then drag out the litigation until the retirees gave up or died.

But Paul Pittman, a benefits and compensation manager, was wor-ried that Wellman's suggestion about provoking a lawsuit was risky. The company had promised the benefits to both salaried and union retirees. Varity's lawyers prepared a "litigation risk" report, which noted that the company had promised the benefits. "Worse yet," the report had said, "there is language in many of the contracts, booklets, and general descriptive material that implies a lifetime commitment. We would never succeed in court."

Indeed, Wellman herself had drafted a form letter she called a "death letter," which for years she sent out to widows of retirees, promising health coverage for life. A letter to one Flossie Pietila reassured her: "Mrs. Pietila, our health and dental benefits will continue for the rest of your life at no cost to you."

Pittman suggested lying to the retirees. In his memo, he called this the "pleading" strategy. The company should tell retirees "that the burden of medical expenses amongst US retirees is unbearably high and would ultimately cause Varity Corporation to cease trading in the US," Pittman suggested, "and that this would necessitate not only a loss of medical benefits, but also possibly the loss of some pension rights as well." Although this wasn't true, if the retirees believed it, they might agree to benefit reductions.

The company could also tell the employees and retirees that the pension plan was in bad shape, creating another burden on the company, Pittman suggested. He thought retirees would see through the maneuver, since it was widely known in the company that the pension plan was healthy, and even if Varity were to go under, he wrote, "the demise of Varity would not necessarily mean the loss of a pension."

In short, he didn't feel the company had much bargaining power with its retirees, but he was hoping it could fool the United Auto Workers, the main representative for Varity's wage earners. "We could convince the union that unless we can reduce our retiree and employees costs we will be unable to continue to operate . . . thus creating significant hardship for their members," he wrote in the memo.

If the union didn't agree, it would be tough to cut their benefits, because they were backed up by negotiated contracts that companies couldn't unilaterally change. So Pittman suggested a strategy he called "Creeping Take Aways." Using this approach, Varity "would progressively introduce minor reductions and usage controls rules into the medical benefits plan." These were "designed to be insufficient to warrant retirees incurring the legal cost and trouble to have the benefits reinstated." A few years later, Varity could take an ax to the benefits, provoking the union to sue. In court, the company would say that because the union hadn't objected to the earlier cuts, it tacitly agreed that the company had the right to cut their medical coverage unilaterally.

If that argument didn't sway the judge, no problem. "There have been a number of companies that have [reduced benefits] knowing that they would lose in court if challenged," he wrote. The company could simply drag out the case for years.

"The strategy works as follows: the employer implements a major reduction to employee benefits . . . retirees come together, pool resources or approach their union to fund their case and take the company to court. Financial pressure is applied to retirees during the potentially extended period leading up to the court hearing by forcing them to incur their own medical expenses, in addition to funding the legal proceedings. The next step is for the company, at a carefully chosen moment, to suggest to retirees that they agree to reinstatement of the plan, but at a much reduced level." The longer Varity could drag out the case, Pittman noted, the better the odds that cash-strapped employees would settle for much less than they were due. Fundamentally, the company had nothing to lose.

PROJECT SUNSHINE

The human resources managers then came up with a surefire way to cut most or all of a unit's retiree health benefits. "Organized liquidation," Pittman dubbed it. "This action involves the transferring of all retiree medical liability into a separate or subsidiary company that is then put into receivership," Pittman wrote. The retirees would sue, of course, but "if made to look realistic, the collapse of [the unit] could be part of a strategy leading to a negotiated reduction" of benefits. When the "financial pressure on retirees is greatest but before we appear to be losing [the] case," the company could "agree to reinstatement at a reduced level."

Rice and his executive team thought that was a great idea. Later that year, they organized a new corporate subsidiary, which they named Massey Combines. The bottom had fallen out of the agriculture industry, and demand for the tractors and combines had dried up. So the Varity executives loaded up this subsidiary with its money-losing farm equipment lines, plus millions of dollars in corporate debt, including benefit liabilities for four thousand retirees.

Varity executives then set about convincing active employees to transfer to the new entity, labeling the internal sales program "Project Sunshine." With meetings, videos, and brochures, executives sought to persuade employees that the spin-off had a "bright future" and that, if they switched over to the new unit, their benefits would remain unchanged. Ultimately, fifteen hundred workers took the bait.

The new firm had a negative net worth of $46 million on its first day of business, and two years later it collapsed. The retirees' medical coverage disappeared overnight. To celebrate, Victor Rice invited his business managers to his hotel suite in Chicago and boasted, over cognac and cigars, that he had "loaded all his losers in one wagon."

Even as it pursued Project Sunshine, Varity had begun implementing the less dramatic suggestions presented by its human resource managers, including a series of creeping take-aways. In 1987, Varity stopped reimbursing retirees for Medicare Part B premiums; in 1989, it moved retirees into a managed-care health plan and raised their health care co-payments and deductibles.

The "pleading" strategy had also met with some success. A union bargaining unit at a facility in Racine, Wisconsin, had agreed to accept reduced benefits.

But Rice wanted more. A big motive now was FAS 106, the new accounting rule that required employers to put the liability for its retiree health benefits on its books. Varity wanted to reduce its liability by 40 percent and turned to Towers Perrin for advice. The consulting firm said it would hook them up with one of their experts who had "success-fully negotiated rather dramatic decreases in postretirement welfare benefits." The consultant projected he could cut 63 percent from the company's estimated $344 million retiree liability by using his benefits-reduction model, which he called "Strawman."

Accounting smoke and mirrors could take care of some of the cost reductions. The company could change some of the key assumptions it used to estimate its obligations. For one, it could assume that fewer employees and retirees were married, so the liability for spousal and survivor benefits would be lower. Towers Perrin also suggested the company could use "liberalized" turnover assumptions. For example, they could assume that job turnover would be higher, so employees wouldn't build up significant benefits.

At the same time, it could lower mortality assumptions and assume that the people who remained would work until age seventy, which would make it look as if the company had fewer years of retirement to pay for. The consultant must have known that this latter point, for one, wasn't true. His research showed that virtually no one at Varity worked past sixty-five.

Though these moves would lower the liabilities the company would publicly disclose, "the real reduction," Towers Perrin concluded, "can come only if the benefits are reduced." To facilitate Varity's decision-making process, the consulting firm's actuaries prepared charts showing which units had the highest potential retiree costs.

Rice wanted quick results, and laid down the law in a memo to managers. "The reported FAS 106 liability will be closely reviewed by analysts and it will affect the stock price and debt ratings." Cutting benefits to reduce the costs that "will result from FAS 106 ABSOLUTE TOP PRIORITY."

In December, Rice gathered the president, the CFO, the vice president for HR, and the company's benefits chief and reiterated his goals: "We must reduce the liabilities, and take aggressive actions that would be reviewed favorably within the financial community." His statement of objectives was accompanied by a checklist.

- 40% MAY be all we can get now . . .
- Continue to aggressively push legal counsel on risk analysis.
- I don't believe in "show stoppers," and won't accept them. Give me a course of action. Keep on schedule.
- I am concerned we will run out of time. If you or the business units need more resources, get them. Let's not be penny wise and pound-foolish.

Not long after, the company's legal advisers prepared a "Litigation Risk assessment" listing dozens of manufacturing plants and facilities operated by the company, with estimates for retiree medical liabilities at each. Each was assigned a litigation risk number, with five having the highest risk ("virtually unavoidable commitments" with "almost certain loss" in litigation) and 1 having the lowest. Varity would go after the weakest units first. Varity sent managers a memo summing it up: "We are not averse to assuming acceptable levels of risk [of lawsuits]. . . . No approach is too aggressive to consider."

A few months later, in April 1993, Varity announced it would make steep cuts to the health benefits, effective January 1, 1994. Under the new accounting rules, the move allowed Varity to report reduced expense—as good as income from selling tractors.

As the company predicted, retirees sued. Hourly and salaried workers brought five suits altogether. A federal judge in one of the cases in Michigan cited "a veritable mountain of evidence" that Varity had promised lifetime medical coverage to the 3,300 retirees of Varity's Kelsey-Hayes unit and ordered the company to restore the benefits, which it did in 2000. Cases at two other units were settled in 1997 and 1998.

But, as Varity human resources managers had predicted, the process dragged out for years, and though most of the retirees prevailed, it was too late for the many retirees who had died in the interim.

The Massey Combines employees, who had been loaded into the unit that went bankrupt, sued Varity, and the court heard the testimony about how Rice had boasted, over cognac and cigars, that he'd dumped all his losers into the doomed unit. This didn't go over well with the Des Moines jury. They handed a victory to the Massey Combines employees and awarded them $38 million in punitive damages.

But no punitive damages are allowed under federal benefits law, so the judge threw out the award but ordered Varity to reinstate the retirees into Varity's health care plan. (The only thing a plaintiff can win in a federal benefits case is the benefit he should have been paid. If he's dead, there's nothing to award, even out-of-pocket costs the retirees had incurred.) Varity appealed, and the former employees fought their case all the way to the U.S. Supreme Court. In 1996—a full decade after Pittman and Wellman had begun sketching out Varity's plan—the Court, in *Varity Corp.* v. *Howe,* found that Varity had deceived the employees and thus violated its fiduciary duty. It ordered that the benefits be reinstated. But this victory was Pyrrhic; the employees were still out of a job, and some had died in the meantime.

Victor Rice, meanwhile, turned from breaking up retiree benefits to breaking up the company. In 1996, he sold Massey Ferguson's farm machinery business assets to AGCO and merged its auto-parts businesses with a British auto-parts maker, renaming it LucasVarity. The combination languished, and Rice started shopping the company almost as soon as he assumed the corner office. TRW bought the firm in 1999, and Rice collected $50 million in severance. TRW, an aerospace and automotive company, enrolled the portfolios of Varity retirees in its existing retiree medical plans. Things were fine—until 2006.

CREEPING REDUX

John Galloway, the retired foundry worker, had so far survived all these benefit shenanigans with his coverage largely intact. That was thanks in large part to the dogged efforts of Roger McClow, a lawyer in Detroit who had represented groups of retirees from different units of the company since 1993. At the same time the Varity employees were taking their case to the Supreme Court, McClow was juggling a handful of cases, representing both salaried and union retirees from the other units, including Massey Ferguson and Kelsey-Hayes.

It was during the tedious discovery phase for two of those suits that McClow unearthed the trove of Varity memos quoted above. When he requested records pertinent to the case, attorneys for the company responded with a "documents dump," the passive-aggressive move in which an opposing party responds to an adversary's information request by trying to bury it in paperwork. McClow and an assistant spent days shoveling through decades-old payroll records, benefits booklets, and the other detritus of the human resources departments from various units, some defunct.

Against great odds, the colorful documents had survived the company shredders. When the company had shuttered an operation in Buffalo, a former Massey Combines officer who was transferred to Kelsey-Hayes brought his Massey Ferguson documents with him to Romulus, Michigan, where they gathered dust in the orphaned files of a long-gone human resources manager until they were rounded up to add bulk to the documents dump.

McClow obtained another batch of strategy memos when he subpoenaed Towers Perrin. On the final day of shoveling through a roomful of printouts of actuarial projections, he found the suggestions for ways to cut the retiree benefits and "Litigation Risk" analyses. These kinds of unflattering strategy memos come to light so rarely that when Massey Ferguson found out that McClow had obtained them, a lawyer for the company accused him of stealing the documents, then filed a motion for a protective order to get them back. The judge denied the request.

Ironically, the documents never played a role in any court case, even the famous *Varity Corp.* v. *Howe* case that went before the Supreme Court, nor did McClow need them for the case he was handling, in which he succeeded in getting the company to restore 80 percent to 100 percent of the retirees' benefits. He thought the matter was settled.

For several years, nothing happened. Then, in 2006, TRW resurrected the game book of its predecessor and began a series of creeping take-aways. It conducted its first "death audit," sending letters to retirees, telling them they had to prove they were alive or lose their coverage. Death audits seem to serve a legitimate purpose; after all, companies audit health plans to ensure that ineligible family members aren't included. With retiree health plans, a cynical person might think death audits exist primarily to generate fees for benefits consulting firms. After all, if a retiree dies, he isn't running up prescription drug costs, and few eighty-year-olds have dependent children.

Panicked retirees called McClow, who contacted TRW and got the company to back off. After all, the settlement provided for lifetime benefits. It didn't have any provision about requiring the retirees to prove they were still alive.

Months later, the retirees were notified that they had been dropped from Medicare. Why? Because TRW had automatically enrolled them in a Medicare Advantage plan. These are health plans run by private insurers, who receive a government subsidy to provide the equivalent of Medicare. The benefits differ slightly—Medicare Advantage plans might provide low-cost benefits, such as gym memberships and discounts on hearing aids, but as a trade-off the plans limit the retirees' choice of hospitals and doctors. TRW called it a "better" plan, and it was—for TRW. The plan saved the company $95,000 a month.

McClow, who looks like a cross between Sean Connery and the

Archbishop of Canterbury and has the slightly exasperated air of a middle-school teacher dealing with unruly teens, took the company to court. He pointed out that the settlement didn't allow the company to change the plan. TRW filed a motion to say it hadn't changed the plan—it had only changed the administrator. The magistrate agreed.

McClow filed an appeal, and in December 2009, a federal judge vacated the magistrate's decision because, under federal law, people must be given the choice to remain on Medicare. TRW then filed a motion for reconsideration. This lingered on the judge's docket for eight months, until McClow filed a motion to get the judge to make a decision.

Finally, in November 2010, the retirees' prior coverage was restored. Still, TRW and its lawyers came out ahead: The several hundred thousand dollars it paid in legal fees was more than offset by the $1.7 million in savings it enjoyed while the retirees were on the Medicare Advantage Plan.*

A few years earlier, in 2008, TRW had initiated a different cost-savings tack when it eliminated coverage for certain categories of drugs. John Galloway learned that TRW was no longer paying for a prescription drug that his wife, Pansy, takes for acid reflux when, instead of a co-pay of $3, he got a bill for $103. According to TRW, the drug wasn't medically necessary; Tums would do just as well. Maybe for healthy people, but not for someone confined to a bed in a nursing home. McClow filed a motion for an injunction; the settlement hadn't agreed to allow TRW to establish its own formulary.

---

* Less fortunate were the retirees who ended up at auto-parts maker Hayes Lemmerz. To dump the retirees, the company initially explored the idea of suing them in court and asking a judge to agree that an earlier settlement McClow had negotiated, in which the company had agreed to provide a certain level of lifetime coverage, was ambiguous. The company filed for Chapter 11 in 2009 and shed most of its retiree obligation. When it emerged from bankruptcy, it was obliged to pay only $1,000 a year per post-sixty-five retiree.

In October 2010, TRW began trying another cost-savings tack: It sent the dwindling number of retirees yet another death audit. The "Life Verification Declaration" required the retirees to provide a notarized affidavit, the first page of their federal income tax returns, and a marriage license if they had coverage for a spouse. To acquire the needed documentation, the verification form advised retirees to contact the county clerks in the locations of the marriages and births and the local Social Security Administration. And for all those Web-savvy octogenarians, it provided "Helpful Web sites," such as Michigan.gov.

Retirees were instructed to return all the required documents by November 29. "If you do not, TRW will automatically terminate coverage for you and your dependants as of December 31, 2010." It also warned them about the "Possible Consequences of Insurance Fraud," which would include having to reimburse TRW for the cost of services the ineligible person receives. "Research has shown that ineligible members left on a healthcare plan can contribute thousands of dollars to raising healthcare costs that impact everyone," the letter said.

Audits of regular health plans might save company money by turning up ineligible dependents, such as grown children or ex-spouses. But with retiree health coverage, the only way a person can become ineligible is by dying. If that's the case, his name turns up within two months on the Social Security death register, which benefits administrators parse monthly to make sure they discontinue sending pension checks and drop the deceased retiree from its plan.

McClow considered the death audit to be a cynical trick to strip retirees of their coverage: "The real savings comes from terminating the retirees who do not respond," which, in fact, one-third of the retirees failed to do. McClow asked TRW for a list of the one hundred or so Kelsey-Hayes retirees it was prepared to drop because it hadn't received their affidavits. One by one, McClow looked up each retiree's name in the Social Security death index. All but one was alive. The trick was to locate the rest and get them to turn in their paperwork.

He began by calling those he had numbers for, sometimes letting the phone ring twenty times to give them time to totter to the phone. "By the end of the conversation, some of them couldn't remember what I was calling about. 'What was it you wanted?' they'd say." Equipped with printouts from MapQuest, McClow went door to door in some of the desolate neighborhoods of Detroit, where some of the retirees were too nervous to come to the door. In one case, he was able to get a neighbor to persuade one elderly woman to let McClow pass the papers through the bars on her door.

Some were in nursing homes or had moved in with their families. Several others died while McClow was on the hunt. As of March 2011, McClow had located all the missing retirees. Their coverage was safe. Until the next audit.

CHAPTER 10

Twilight Zone: HOW EMPLOYERS USE PENSION LAW TO THWART RETIREES

UNTIL RECENTLY, someone pausing at the Wal-Mart in Delmont, Pennsylvania, might have been greeted by Ed Peksa, who had retired years before from GenCorp, the former General Tire and Rubber Co., whose well-known jingle goes, "Sooner or later, you'll own General."

Peksa, a former marine, hadn't planned on working at Wal-Mart in retirement, or traveling. But he ended up doing both. He needed the greeter job because he was no longer receiving the $320-a-month pension he'd earned after working a quarter-century in the tennis ball department at GenCorp. His former employer was keeping it all to pay for Peksa's share of his retiree health coverage. The coverage had been company-paid when he retired, but the company had unilaterally begun charging very steep premiums. Peksa couldn't drop the coverage, because he needed it to help cover his wife's prescription drugs, so he began working thirty hours a week at Wal-Mart. He thought the job was pretty decent, since he got an hour for lunch and two fifteen-minute breaks a day.

He also ended up traveling to court, over and over, as the retirees tried to reverse the company's decision. Though he didn't know it, he was living out a process that the Varity human resources managers had so candidly discussed behind closed doors years ago: Companies had little to lose by unilaterally cutting benefits they had promised retirees in written contracts. The retirees might pass the hat and try to raise funds to file a suit, but even if they got that far, it would be easy for an employer to drag out a case until the employees died. And whatever the outcome, the company saves money in the meantime.

Such was the legal odyssey of the GenCorp retirees. In January 2000, the company, by then a manufacturer of aerospace products, began charging 2,063 hourly retirees health care premiums, despite a labor contract that promised them free coverage for life. John Van Dyke, a retired millwright, thought fighting back in court was the answer. "I was sure that once the judge saw the contract, it would be over," he said. "How long could it take?"

Longer than many of them would be around. Frank Palumbo was one of the oldest. Born in 1914, he went to work for the General Tire and Rubber Co. when he was sixteen years old. In 1934, at age nineteen, he participated in the first sit-down strike to organize the rubber workers at the Akron, Ohio, plant. Always active in the union, he worked at the company for forty-four years until he retired in 1975, with a promise of lifetime medical coverage.

By the early 1990s, most of the retirees, like him, were on Medicare, so their company-paid benefits covered only prescription drugs and Medicare premiums and deductibles. Not a huge amount for the company, but critical for the retirees, most of whom had pensions in the low three digits.

In the mid-1990s, the company used a trick the Varity managers hadn't thought of: It sent the retirees enrollment forms giving them a choice between remaining in their no-cost plan or switching to one with significant cost sharing.

Elderly but not demented, Palumbo and the other retirees of course chose to remain in their current plan. But perhaps with their failing eyesight, they didn't notice, at the bottom of the form, a sentence in microscopic print. It said that the retiree acknowledged that the "benefits elected . . . replace benefits under the prior GenCorp/URN retiree medical plans."

About five years after Palumbo returned the form, his January pension check arrived. It was smaller. A mistake? No. The company said it was beginning to deduct some of their pensions to help pay for their health coverage. The retirees pointed out that the contract said the company would provide lifetime coverage. GenCorp didn't dispute that, but said "lifetime" didn't mean "at no cost."

Their union couldn't help them because, when it negotiated a contract in 1994, the United Rubber Workers had agreed not to represent retirees in any future lawsuit in exchange for delaying an increase in benefits. Some unions have less noble reasons for not backing retirees. When negotiating compensation for current workers, some are tempted to toss the retirees, who don't vote, overboard. Without a union to back them in court, the retirees face almost impossible odds. There are few attorneys who handle ERISA cases for plaintiffs. One reason is that an individual employee or retiree can't afford the fees, and class actions can be hard to bring for a variety of reasons. Courts have interpreted ERISA as disallowing any punitive or pain-and-suffering damages, so there are no potential damages of this sort that attorneys can use to finance cases. All a plaintiff can win is restoration of the disputed benefit, if he's still alive. The plaintiff's attorney takes a risk, too: Thanks to the way in which courts have interpreted ERISA's attorneys' fee provision, it's up to a judge to decide whether the plaintiff's lawyer will be reimbursed for any of his time and expense.

Still, the retirees who had worked at the Jeannette plant passed a hat and chipped in: $100 per couple. Mabel Kramer, a widow, chipped in $50. She'd begun working at the company in 1944, making gas masks for World War II soldiers. She was no longer receiving her pension of $179 a month, based on her husband's thirty-four years with the company, because GenCorp deducted every cent to use for her health coverage, for which it was charging her $284 a month. She had to pay the company the remaining $105 from her $810 Social Security check.

The $12,000 the retirees collected would cover only a fraction of the cost of mounting a suit, but the retirees found a lawyer who was willing to take the case anyway: William Payne, a Pittsburgh attorney who had represented retirees over the years in more than sixty cases. One of the first cases he worked on, soon after getting out of law school in the late 1970s, was the now infamous Continental Can case, in which company managers had used a secret program with the code name "BELL," which is a reverse acronym for "Let's Limit Employee Benefits." The can company used the system to identify older workers who were about to lock in bigger pensions and targeted those plants for closing. The case was a rare win for workers. It has been mostly downhill since. Payne has spent the rest of his career watching ERISA protections get eroded in the courts.

Payne and his law partner, John Stember, met the retirees at Dick's Diner, a popular fuel stop just off the highway between Pittsburgh and Jeannette, and over coffee and cheesesteaks he cautioned them that the case could take a long time. The retirees were undaunted. Three, John Van Dyke, Stanley Wotus, and Ed Peksa, all veterans who had served in the Pacific during or after World War II, volunteered to be plaintiffs. Nor were Payne and Stember daunted by the cardboard boxes the retirees hauled with them, filled with decades-old documents they'd dredged out of basements, closets, and garages. They filed suit in October, and the first meeting with the judge was scheduled the following May. In the seventeen months since GenCorp had started charging them for health coverage, the retirees' costs had doubled.

ROAD TRIP

The first court conference was in Akron, Ohio, 110 miles away. Van Dyke, who had the best eyesight, drove the other guys in the predawn darkness to rendezvous with Payne, who drove them the rest of the way in the minivan he usually used to take his sons to hockey practice. They had to pull over numerous times. Van Dyke had had part of his stomach removed following a bout of cancer in the 1990s and needed small, frequent meals. Others had prostate problems, and Wotus was taking several medications for blood pressure and heart problems. Peksa, who misjudged the insulin shots he was taking for his diabetes, at one point passed out in the backseat, prompting a quick pit stop at a gas station mini-mart for orange juice.

Despite their various pit stops, the retirees made it to the 9 A.M. court session on time. There, the eager retirees cited labor contracts promising lifetime coverage. But GenCorp, in court documents, maintained that "lifetime" didn't mean "at no cost." This kind of semantic game had become common. Another popular one was to say that "lifetime" referred not to the life of the retiree but to the life of the contract.

GenCorp argued that the retirees had knowingly released the company from its obligation to pay, and pointed to the enrollment forms retirees had filled out years earlier, saying coverage was "replaced." In short, the retirees, not GenCorp, were trying to renege on a written agreement, company lawyers maintained.

The judge could have decided the case on the merits or sent it to trial. Instead, he insisted that the parties work it out. But when neither side budged, the judge scheduled a mediation meeting in Cleveland—a year later. A year passed. GenCorp then insisted that the retirees should include people from other locations, so several retirees traveled from Kentucky and Ohio, booking senior-discount rooms at the Holiday Inn. Kenneth Bottolfs, then in his eighties, came the farthest. His three-connecting-flight trip from Waco, Texas, took eight hours.

When neither side backed down in this second mediation hearing, the judge ordered a third meeting. Eight months later, the retirees traveled to this third meeting, minus Wotus, who'd had a stroke. This meeting failed, too, so the judge finally ordered depositions and document production to proceed. This meant the retirees had to travel to Cleveland to be deposed by GenCorp lawyers. The May 2003 sessions took several hours each. The retirees whiled away their waits playing cards and trading war stories about their times at Okinawa and Iwo Jima.

END OF THE ROAD

The following August, the retirees' lawyers filed to have the suit certified as a class action. Without this, even if the named plaintiffs won, no others would get their benefits restored. GenCorp opposed this. It said that the plaintiffs were too befuddled to represent the class. As was clear from their depositions, some had forgotten what they were thinking when they signed enrollment forms. One didn't remember what was in Gen-Corp's slide presentation explaining the benefit options eight years earlier.

GenCorp also accused the retirees of destroying evidence. The reason: They'd commingled their paperwork when they pooled their brochures in a cardboard box while searching for a lawyer. That constituted "spoliation," GenCorp said, adding that it would "seek appropriate remedies at a later date." Remedies in these situations can include charging retirees for a company's legal fees.

Finally, GenCorp said the retirees should be denied class status because they were too dispersed, so that different legal standards governing different parts of the country would apply, and because the named plaintiffs were too sick to adequately represent everybody. The plaintiffs were, in fact, sick. Shortly after, in October 2003, Robert Berger, age sixty-nine, died. Polumbo died the next month, at eighty-nine. His widow, Mary Elizabeth, eighty-eight, volunteered to take his place. In December, the judge sided with GenCorp and denied the retirees' request to be certified as a class.

The retirees had discovered another harsh reality: If he is so inclined, a judge can keep a case from ever reaching a trial. Judge Dan Polster had badgered the parties to settle and the retirees had to travel, time and again, to court hundreds of miles away, in some cases to attend incremental hearings that took only a short time.

The retirees figured that by denying the class action, the judge was just trying to get them to give up. But after this setback, the retirees rallied and signed up an additional 294 plaintiffs. They filed another suit in July 2004, in time to beat a statute of limitations that the company said was about to expire. The next month, the judge dismissed that case, telling the roughly four hundred retirees, mostly in their eighties, that each would have to file an individual case and pay the $150 filing fee for each one.

The retirees called the judge's bluff. Payne and Stember filed four hundred individual suits, paying $60,000 in filing fees, rather than the $350 it would have cost if the judge hadn't insisted on separate individual cases. They had to act fast: "They were dropping like flies," Payne says. He told the judge that the average age of the retirees was eighty-two.

The judge's reaction: He said he would grant each of the 342 retirees a trial. One at a time. Hearing one case individually, each month, minus vacation and holidays, would take years, and few of the retirees, whose average age was 82, would live long enough to see it be resolved.

The retirees were backed into a corner. They couldn't appeal because an appeal can't be made until a final judgment and there's no final judgment until the end of a trial. They agreed to settle, and would pay a portion of their coverage. They did not, of course, get reimbursed for what they'd spent for the coverage over the prior six years.

The terms of the late 2005 settlement are confidential, but securities filings make one thing very clear: GenCorp accomplished exactly what the Varity HR managers had predicted would happen in these situations: It saved money. From 2000 to 2008, the company's liabilities for retiree health care fell almost 70 percent, to $76 million, thanks to the number of retiree dropouts and deaths. And even with the settlement, the plan's costs have continued to fall steadily. Every year after 2005, the retiree health plan actually contributed a total of $8.4 million to GenCorp's quarterly earnings. Regardless of whether a company wins or loses its case, it always wins the game.

PREEMPTIVE STRIKE

As companies grew increasingly eager to cannibalize their retiree benefits over the past decade, they realized just how important it is to get their cases heard by the right court.

The first legal hurdle for many was that, like Varity, they had promised the benefits, often in writing. Ironically, one of their most powerful tools was federal pension law, which had been enacted in 1974 to protect employees and retirees. The ERISA law was intended to thwart employers who promised retiree benefits and then refused to pay them. Until then, pension and benefits agreements fell under state contract and trust laws. ERISA was supposed to be an improvement, because it overrode a patchwork of state laws.

The problem was that the law was written for pensions, so it had rules about funding and vesting. If someone had a vested right to a pension, the company couldn't just decide not to pay it. But ERISA didn't explicitly mention vesting of medical pensions. So employers argued that retiree health benefits weren't vested but were merely the equivalent of a gratuity.

Until the early 1970s, all retiree benefits—pensions and medical coverage—fell loosely under state contract laws. If there was a dispute about benefits, the courts would examine the plan documents and handouts given to employees to see whether pensions and retiree health coverage were promised benefits, which must be paid, or, indeed, as employers later insisted, the equivalent of tips.

Employers attacked the problem of written promises by introducing ambiguity into the equation. They began inserting clauses, or sometimes a single sentence, into the technical documents that described the rules and workings of the benefits plans. These reservation-of-rights clauses state that the employer has reserved the right to change the benefits.

General Motors, which figures so prominently in discussions about troubled pension plans, has played a big, largely unsung role in the dismantling of retiree health benefits, for both union and salaried employees, across all industries. In the 1980s, GM promised lifetime health coverage as an incentive to get employees to retire. A total of 84,000 salaried employees ultimately took the bait.

When GM later cut the benefits, retirees sued for breach of contract, pointing to the written promises: "Your basic health care coverage will be provided at GM's expense for your lifetime." You'd think a six-year-old could decipher that. A contract, after all, is a contract. Without contracts, the U.S. economy would fall apart. Think how this would play out in a small claims court. Judge Judy would ask the plaintiffs, "Do you have a written agreement?" She'd then ask GM to explain why it reneged on the deal. "Your honor," GM would say, "Sure, we promised, in writing, to pay for health coverage, but costs have gone up, and now we don't want to pay." Judge Judy would say, "I'm not interested in your problems. You're an idiot. Judgment for the plaintiff." Not so under ERISA.

A lower court ruled for the retirees. GM appealed, and the Sixth Circuit Court of Appeals in Cincinnati ruled in 1998 that it didn't matter what the company had told people verbally, and it didn't matter that the company gave prospective retirees brochures that advised them that health coverage would be provided "at GM's expense for your lifetime."

What mattered, the appeals court said, in *Sprague* v. *General Motors,* was that GM had added an escape clause to the summary of the plan documents (SPD) it gave the first group of retirees. The clause, included in the documents that few employees read, and even fewer understand, stated that GM "reserved the right" to make changes to the plan. "We see no ambiguity in a summary plan description that tells participants both that the terms of the current plan entitle them to health insurance at no cost throughout retirement and that the terms of the current plan are sub-ject to change," the court said.

But wait—there wasn't any reservation-of-rights clause in the SPD that GM gave this group of retirees. Score one for the retirees? You'd think so. But with the elastic logic so common in ERISA decisions, the court of appeals concluded that this was a summary plan description; "as such, it was a summary, so wouldn't include everything, including such things as reservation of rights clauses."

Further, the court concluded that an employer didn't even need to write down a reservation-of-rights clause. So, even if the documents didn't include such a clause, the court must infer that the company intended to reserve the right to cut benefits.

As for the retirees, just because the company promised orally and in writing that their benefits were to be paid by GM, the court could not infer that GM intended to pay the benefits. "GM never told the early retirees that their health care benefits would be fully paid up or vested upon retirement. What GM told many of them, rather, was that their coverage was to be paid by GM for their lifetimes." In other words, because GM didn't use the word "vested," the benefits weren't.

"Interpretive gymnastics," scoffed one of the dissenting judges. The three dissenting judges said the majority's ruling gave employers a green light to lie to employees by luring them into early retirement with promises of health coverage, then canceling the benefits once the people had made an irrevocable decision to retire. "When General Motors was flush with cash and health care costs were low, it was easy to promise employees and retirees lifetime health care. . . . Rather than pay off those perhaps ill-considered promises, it is easier for the current regime to say those promises were never made. There is the tricky little matter of the paper trail of written assurances of lifetime health care, but General Motors, with the *en banc* majority's assistance, has managed to escape the ramifications of its now-regretted largesse."

For years, union retirees generally had greater security because their benefits were protected by negotiated contracts, which fall under the federal Labor–Management Relations Act, as well as ERISA. When employers tried to cut health benefits for union retirees—pointing to reservation-of-rights clauses—the courts generally concluded that the contracts, not the companies' unilaterally created plan descriptions were what mattered.

But after the GM ruling, employers began to argue that the benefits for union retirees should be governed by the same pro-employer inference that was applied in that ruling. To enhance their chances of success, some companies started to use a strategy outlined by the Varity managers: creeping take-aways. This involves taking small steps—increase premiums a small amount, or perhaps start charging premiums in the future. The retirees and unions ignore them. Then, a few years later, the company cuts benefits in a big way, saying that the retirees' prior lack of legal action signaled tacit agreement that the company could change the plan.

Another ploy companies have used in an effort to increase the chances of appearing before a sympathetic judge is to sue retirees preemptively as they cut the benefits.

Chuck Yarter, a retired miner living in the Sonoran Desert outside Marana, Arizona, learned that he was being sued in 2003 when he got a phone call from a process server who was lost. Yarter gave the guy directions to his stucco home, which sits at the end of an unnamed dirt road, with a distant view of the open-pit Silver Bell copper mine, where Yarter had been a mechanic on ore crushers.

Yarter waited in his yard, curious. He'd never been sued in his life. The approaching trail of dust told him the car was arriving. When the process server pulled up, Yarter's dog wouldn't let him out of the car, so after exchanging a few pleasantries, he handed the papers through the car window before trundling away through the saguaro and mesquite.

The papers told Yarter that his former employer, Asarco, was suing him and other retirees in federal court in Phoenix. Asarco, an integrated copper producer that was once known as American Smelting and Refining Co., said it was asking the court to agree that it had the right to cut the union retirees' benefits.

Asarco, a unit of Grupo Mexico SA, didn't dispute that it had a contract with the retirees to provide health care until they were eligible for Medicare. But it said the agreements had expired when the labor contracts had, sometime back in the 1990s. The company then sent a letter to its 901 union retirees and dependents, explaining that falling copper prices and rising health care costs left it no choice but to reduce their health coverage. "The continuing low copper price has caused Asarco severe financial distress. . . . As a result, Asarco is no longer in a position to continue to provide health plan benefits at the current levels."

The retirees were in a slightly better position than the GenCorp retirees: Some could pile into a van and drive to Mexico for their prescription drugs; others, however, dropped out of the plan as prices spiraled and went on public programs. Yarter appreciated the irony: Not only did his health care costs rise but, as a taxpayer, he would ultimately be picking up the tab for others.

Gonzalo Frias, a retiree-defendant who was a shovel operator at the Ray Mine in Kearny, Arizona, had been president of the local United Steelworkers union when the contracts were negotiated, and said it was ludicrous to think the workers would have agreed to lower wages in exchange for health coverage until sixty-five if the agreement meant the company could pull the plug at any time. The Steelworkers supported the retirees in the lawsuit. "'Unforeseen circumstances' do not justify a breach of contractual obligations . . . to persons living on fixed income who can ill afford to pay the costs the company has shifted upon them," they told the court. It added that the "alleged 'severe financial distress' has not prevented the company from paying its top management quite handsomely."

Like the GenCorp retirees, the Asarco retirees ultimately settled, in 2007, agreeing to pay some of the benefits, with the amounts remaining unchanged for six years. It was a reprieve of sorts. They felt lucky to get that: The company, facing a number of environmental lawsuits, filed for bankruptcy in 2005 and emerged in 2010.

CIRCUIT BREAKER

In early 2002, Rexam, a maker of cans for beverages, including Diet Coke, made a tiny increase in retirees' share of the cost of prescription drugs. For more than a year, retirees complained to the company that it had no right to change the negotiated agreements, which stated that "Company-paid major medical coverage will be provided for all retirees." Successive contracts noted that the parties had agreed that "the Company will continue to pay the entire cost." But the changes weren't a big enough deal for the retirees to take legal action.

The company was also planning to make more major cuts in benefits. But rather than wait for the retirees to sue, it sued the retirees. Under legal rules, the first party to file generally gets to have its case heard in the location where it files the suit. So, suing the retirees first enhances a company's chances to get the case heard in a circuit with pro-business judges.

In "declaratory judgment" suits, such as Rexam's, the company asks a judge to rule that the company has the right to change the retiree health plans. Rexam pointed to a line in a booklet it gave retirees. It stated that the company "reserves the right to amend, modify or discontinue the plan in the future in conformity with applicable legislation."

The retirees said the clause meant that if government legislation or regulations changed, then the plan might have to be modified accordingly. It didn't give the company a right to unilaterally change the agreement. They pointed to another sentence stating that the right to modify the benefits "was subject to any applicable collective bargaining agreement." In any case, the union wouldn't go to the trouble of negotiating benefits for retirees if they assumed the employer could subsequently cancel the benefits at will. This was an inference in favor of union retirees.

Rexam filed in Minneapolis, within a conservative circuit. There was little logic to this from a geographic standpoint. Minnesota was home to only 100 of the 3,600 retirees, and the company—known as American National Can before Rexam bought it in 2000—is based in Chicago and has offices in Charlotte, North Carolina. It's a subsidiary of Britain's Rexam PLC.

The retirees, supported by the United Steelworkers of America, countersued in Toledo, Ohio, asking that the case be dismissed or transferred there. They said that Rexam had made a preemptive legal strike in order to choose the jurisdiction.

The judge in Minneapolis rejected all the retirees' arguments. She ruled that the case would remain there, because the company had 110 employees there. She said the retirees threatened to sue and hadn't sued quickly enough, so couldn't claim that Rexam was suing as a preemptive strike—there was nothing to preempt. She also made a nonlegal observation: She cited a $79 million liability for the benefits on Rexam's balance sheet and said the company was harmed "because it cannot lower the liability unless it reduces the retirees' benefits."

Still, she found in a later decision that the language was ambiguous, rejecting the company's motion for judgment on the papers alone, and she allowed the suit to move forward to a trial by jury, a move that may have led to a favorable settlement for the retirees. But the case was then assigned to Judge Patrick Schiltz, a former law clerk for Supreme Court Justice Antonin Scalia. Schiltz didn't think the language in the contract was ambiguous and, rather than go to trial, where a jury would hear the facts, he invited Rexam to move for reconsideration, meaning it could file another motion asking the judge to decide the case on the papers alone. Rexam was happy to oblige. Schiltz concluded that the language in the documents was unambiguous for approximately 80 percent of the retirees, and clearly gave the company the right to unilaterally change the benefits that it had a contractual agreement to provide.

Occasionally, a judge will refuse to hear a case in the jurisdiction where it is originally filed and send it to another circuit. But this doesn't occur often. Crown Cork & Seal, a Philadelphia-based packaging company that makes wrappers for such things as Mars bars and bottles of beer, sued its union retirees in U.S. district court in Chicago, but the judge wasn't convinced that was where the case belonged.

"From day one, it seemed to me that Illinois was an unlikely home for this litigation," Judge Milton Shadur told Crown's lawyers, according to a transcript of a meeting he held in his chambers in August 2003 to determine whether the case should remain in Chicago or move to Cincinnati, where the retirees had countersued.

"I am not faulting you for this, but it's pretty obvious why you chose the Seventh Circuit as your forum," he said. "Because it's very unfriendly to the idea of retiree benefits being vested at all." He added that he was inclined to send the case to Pittsburgh. "You know, they [the retirees' attorneys] want Ohio, because I think they view the Sixth Circuit on this subject of retirees as more favorable, but I am not going to give them that."

"They shopped more than we did, Judge," said James Rydzel, a lawyer with Jones Day, in Cleveland, representing Crown.

"Well, I am not sure about that," the judge responded. He subsequently sent the case to Pittsburgh, where a number of the company's retirees lived. The Crown retirees were initially hopeful because the case was assigned to a judge with a proworker reputation. However, the judge recused himself because his mother had worked in a factory at Continental Can, a predecessor company, and was potentially a member of the class. The next judge sent the case to Cincinnati, where it ultimately went to arbitration.

It may be routine for litigants to try to pick a favorable jurisdiction. If two parties sue each other, the courts generally hear the case that's filed first. But a court can dismiss or transfer a case if it believes a company is "forum shopping" or suing retirees as a preemptive strike to deprive them of their rights, as "natural plaintiffs," to sue in the court they would choose.

ACF Industries, a railroad-car maker headquartered in St. Charles, Missouri, took the additional step of provoking a retiree and then filing suit, claiming that the company was suing to protect itself. The company didn't dispute that the contract promised health coverage at "$100 per month for life," but said this referred only to the major medical coverage, not explicitly to the hospital/surgical portion.

And it maintained that St. Louis was the proper venue for the suit because "a substantial part of the activities and events giving rise to these claims occurred in this district." Most of its 678 retirees and dependents lived four hundred miles away, in West Virginia, in the Fourth Circuit, which had ruled in favor of retirees in a similar case.

ACF, controlled by CEO Carl Icahn through an investment vehicle in New York, prepared its suit and had its legal guns lined up when its human resources vice president called up a retiree in Barboursville, West Virginia. Basil Chapman, a retired union representative, was sitting on his porch with his dog, Bo, enjoying a mild Friday in December, when he got the call. The executive told him that ACF was going to start charging the union retirees for their benefits. Chapman had been the chair of the union's bargaining committee and had helped negotiate contracts in which the trade-off for lower salary increases was lifetime health coverage that would cost retirees a flat $100 a month.

"We have a contract. You can't do that," Chapman replied. "We will file in federal court against you bastards, I'll guarantee you that." That, in any case, was what ACF claimed, in court papers, Chapman had said, when it sued him the following Monday in federal district court in St. Louis. In its complaint, the company said Chapman had threatened them, and it was taking the step to protect itself from a lawsuit it anticipated from the retirees. "Defendant Chapman has already informed ACF that he plans to file a lawsuit concerning the amendments of the plan," the complaint said.

The day after ACF sued the retirees, it sent them a letter, blaming a slump in the railcar-building-and-leasing industry, "particularly the covered hopper car producers. Because of this we are forced to make changes in our group insurance coverage." And, by the way, it said, the plan documents gave the company the right to modify or revoke the benefits at any time.

Retirees were told to complete a form so that payments could be deducted from their pension checks; if they failed to return the form within two weeks, the company would terminate their benefits. Chapman worried that some of the less literate retirees "in the hollows" might not understand the letter or respond to it, and spent hours on the phone making sure they turned it in.

The Steelworkers union countersued in federal court in Huntington, West Virginia, to dismiss ACF's complaint, contending that ACF had gone through "the charade of telephoning retiree Chapman about the cuts, just so it could provoke a predictable negative reaction and then use the reaction to immediately sue."

The retirees' suit also complained that ACF was suing not because it had been harassed but as a preemptive strike "to beat its own retirees to the courthouse," and chose St. Louis because "ACF apparently believes that the Eighth Circuit is more favorable to employers in retiree medical benefits cases, and apparently feels that its chances are improved if it makes the retirees litigate hundreds of miles from their homes."

In 2004, the court in St. Louis said that ACF's move had "resulted in a proverbial race to the courthouse in order to deprive defendants of their choice of forum" and moved the case to federal court in Huntington, West Virginia. ACF may have lost its chosen venue, but it won the case anyway. The retirees appealed, and the case settled, with retirees paying more for their coverage than before.

CHAPTER 11

In Denial: INCENTIVES TO WITHHOLD BENEFITS

AFTER FORTY-TWO YEARS working in a coal mine, Elmer Daugherty could barely breathe. Doctors told him he had pneumoconiosis, commonly called black lung disease, a disabling, incurable ailment that has killed ten thousand miners over the past decade. His employer, Constellation Energy, provides disability and workers' compensation for those injured or sickened on the job. It also provides black lung disease coverage, a benefit mandated by Congress.

Daugherty applied for black lung benefits in 2001, but the company denied his claim. Over the next three years, Daugherty was examined by nine different pulmonologists, underwent a battery of painful tests, and had more than thirty X-rays. Even though most of the doctors agreed he had black lung caused by his years in a coal mine, the company continued to deny his claim. He died in 2005.

Daugherty's struggle to be awarded black lung benefits wasn't unusual. Industry-wide, only fifteen claims in one hundred are paid. Providing benefits wouldn't have put a dent in Constellation's finances: Black lung is such a common outcome of working in coal mines that the federal government requires coal companies to pay into a central fund, run by the Labor Department, to finance the benefits.

But black lung coverage has something else is common with pensions: it's a "postretirement obligation," and under accounting rules is treated like other retiree liabilities, including retiree health care, long term disability, executive supplemental pensions, and deferred compensation. Coal producers must estimate the amounts they will likely pay over their afflicted miner's lives, as short as they may be, and record that obligation on their financial statements.

These accounting rules, which reward employers for cutting retiree benefits, also provide them with an incentive to prevent workers and retirees from collecting benefits in the first place. Denying claims doesn't just save coal companies money, it also helps the bottom line.

Consider the black lung obligations at Console Energy, one of the largest coal producers in the country. The $185 million "coal workers' pneumoconiosis" obligation is calculated using assumptions including the incidence of disability, medical costs, mortality, death benefits, and interest rates.

But because the company has been so successful in denying claims, it has a pool of actuarial gains to draw on each year to offset the expense of its black lung obligation. As the company puts it in its financial disclosures: The gains are the result of "lower approval rates for filed claims than our assumptions originally reflected." In 2010, Console recognized $21.6 million in gains; as far as accounting rules go, gains from denying benefits to dying miners are no different from profits from selling coal and methane gas.

In an effort to get the coal industry to shoulder more of the costs for its afflicted workers, the Patient Protection and Affordable Care Act of 2010 created new rules to make it harder for coal companies to deny claims. For one thing, the new law established the legal presumption that miners suffering from totally disabling black lung disease who have worked at least fifteen years in coal mines, have, in fact, contracted the disease on the job, not from smoking, living with a smoker, or some other means. And rather than a miner's having to prove he contracted the disease by breathing coal dust, under the new law, a coal company that wants to deny benefits has to prove that a miner doesn't have black lung disease or didn't contract it from breathing coal dust. Coal companies are also required to continue paying benefits to dependent survivors, even if the miners with black lung disease die from something else, such as lung cancer.

Console Energy estimated that the impact of the new law increased its black lung liability by $45.7 million. But thanks to the flexibility built into benefits accounting, this didn't hurt earnings. As the company explains, somewhat obliquely, in its financial disclosures, "In conjunction with the law change, Console Energy conducted an extensive experience study regarding the rate of claim incidence. Based on historical company data and industry data, with emphasis on recent history, certain assumptions were revised," it says. "Most notably, the expected number of claims, prior to the law change, was reduced to more appropriately reflect Console Energy's historical experience . . . This resulted in a decrease in the liability of $47.7 million."

In other words, the company retrofitted its assumptions, which not only kept its black lung obligation from increasing but actually reduced it by $2 million. Combined with gains it took from denying benefits to dying miners in the past, the company reported *income* of $3.5 million for its black lung benefits program in 2010.

Only in the alternative universe of postretirement benefits accounting can a company profit from its black lung benefits plan. And Console Energy will likely continue to do so. The company disclosure is basically telling the world that while the company may be required to pay benefits to more old-timers, it will find ways to more aggressively deny them to everyone else.

Massey Energy, another giant coal producer, didn't go through the same actuarial acrobatics. It reported a $98 million obligation for "traumatic workers' compensation" benefits, which is what the company estimates it will pay for black lung, crushed limbs, and other traumatic injuries one might expect to find in mines that have racked up thousands of safety violations.

As for its black lung benefits, it estimated that the new law would increase its obligation by only $11.3 million, pushing its total black lung obligation to $77 million. "We do not believe the impact of these changes will significantly impact our financial position," its filings said. The total amount Massey Energy paid out to miners for their black lung benefits in 2010 was just $2.4 million.

To put this into perspective, compare it with what the company spent for a single Massey retiree, chief executive Don Blankenship, who stepped down in December 2010. During his eighteen years as CEO, Blankenship aggressively promoted "mountaintop removal," the practice of blowing off the tops of mountains to uncover seams of coal, and was at the helm when one of the company's slurry ponds spilled 300 million gallons of toxic sludge into nearby streams, an event the EPA calls the worst man-made environmental catastrophe in the Southeast.

Though healthy for shareholders, the company's practices haven't been healthy for miners—or their families and neighbors, who have complained that poisoned groundwater has caused a litany of illnesses. Fatal mine accidents have been common, including the worst mining accident in forty years: the explosion at the Upper Big Branch mine in 2010, which killed twenty-nine miners. After the tragedy, shareholders sued Blankenship and the board of directors for mismanagement, and the Justice Department launched a criminal investigation into the Big Branch disaster.

In the wake of all this, Blankenship decided to retire, a decision for which the board awarded him $12 million in cash. He'll also collect a pension worth at least $5.6 million, and $27.2 million in deferred compensation, which was on top of $10.4 million in pay. He can remain, rent-free, in a company-owned home in Sprigg, West Virginia, a property well protected by steel fences and security cameras. He'll retain his company office, plus a full-time secretary. And he gets to keep a 1965 blue Chevrolet truck.

Blankenship will likely be healthier than most of his neighbors. *Rolling Stone* reported that Massey Energy constructed a pipeline to bring potable water from Matewan to Blankenship's home. Corporate filings show that should he get sick, the company will pay 100 percent of the health coverage for him and his family.

The total payout for all this in 2010? More than $55 million.

The total the company paid its retired coal miners in 2010 for black lung, traumatic workers' compensation, and other retiree benefits: $37 million.

HOLDING THE LINE

Profits may motivate many employers to hold the line on awarding pensions, retiree health care, or disability. Pension law helps them tackle retirees who push back.

Victor Washington, a former San Francisco 49ers running back, spent most of his life fighting the NFL for disability benefits. His battle illustrates how federal benefits law, ERISA, though intended to protect workers, has become a legal shield for employers, enabling them to deny benefits with no penalty—and even finance their legal defense using pension assets.

Football was Washington's ticket out of the rougher towns of northern New Jersey, where he'd spent part of his teen years in an orphanage in Elizabeth. A college scholarship eventually led to the 49ers, who picked him in the 1970 NFL draft. He was the team's rookie of the year in 1971–72 and went to the Pro Bowl at the end of the season. The five-foot-eleven, 195-pound Washington later played for the Houston Oilers and Buffalo Bills. Playing as a running back, defensive back, and wide receiver, he took the field against the likes of Joe Namath, Terry Bradshaw, and O.J. Simpson. At his peak, he was earning about $50,000 a year. When he racked up injuries to a shoulder (in 1973), back (1974), and elbow (1976), he says teams gave him painkillers and Valium so he could keep playing. "I took every play like it was my last play—that's the only way to play," Washington says.

Washington left the game the same way most players do: He was too injured to play. Knee trouble sidelined him for good in 1976. He'd lasted longer than most: Players on average leave after 3.2 years, often after multiple injuries. Players from the 1960s to the 1980s are a particularly busted-up bunch, having played on artificial turf that was little more than a carpet over poured concrete, in flimsy helmets and protective gear that provided little protection to someone who was rammed in the head by opposing players using the kinds of maneuvers that have since been banned. Concussions were regarded as badges of honor and, to keep players in the game, doctors doped them up with amphetamines and painkillers and looked the other way when players bulked up on steroids, oblivious to the long-term effects.

When Washington left pro football, he was thirty years old and had no other marketable skills. His marriage unraveled, and he moved in with his grandmother in New Jersey. He enrolled in business courses at a community college, but, in pain and depressed, he couldn't concentrate or sit still. It would take more than two decades for the league to acknowledge that concussions cause brain damage. Seven years after leaving the game, Washington, who didn't have health coverage and couldn't afford physical therapy, applied for football disability benefits and went through the gauntlet of doctors the league hires to evaluate players' claims. Orthopedists hired by the NFL plan enumerated his ailments, which included arthritis, degenerative joint disease, and an inability to fully extend one knee. A Rutgers University professor of psychiatry hired by the NFL concluded that depression and difficulty with concentration, "combined with his physical injury and significant pain (both knee and back) indeed render him disabled by his football related injuries."

One would think that awarding the benefits would be a simple call. But league officials, though agreeing that Washington had a disability, deemed that it wasn't football-related, so his benefit would be $750 a month instead of $4,000.* Washington appealed, and after more medical reviews, league doctors again concluded that Washington was disabled totally by football injuries. The determination went to the trustees for a vote, and they deadlocked: Three trustees representing players agreed his disability was caused by football; team-owner trustees said that Washington's problems were the result of a crummy child-hood, a failed marriage, and money troubles. It was all in his head—but not the result of a concussion. In 1986, three years after Washington first applied for benefits, the decision went to an arbitrator, who noted that the plan defined a football-related disability as being the result of "a football injury." Focusing on the word "a," the arbitrator said this meant a former player had to have a *single* injury to be eligible for football-related disability benefits. Because Washington had several injuries, he was out of luck.

TIME OUT

Based on this creative interpretation, the NFL plan denied the claims of many other former players that were pending at the time. If Washington's claim had been brought before a state court, it would have come under state insurance laws regarding unfair claims denials, where a judge may have concluded that the arbitrator's decision was "arbitrary and capricious," a legal standard referring to a decision that has no reasonable basis.

But employees benefits cases fall under ERISA, which "preempts," or overrides, state laws, including insurance laws about fairness. Where does that leave plaintiffs? In a black hole.

When Congress created ERISA in 1974, it assumed that the law

---

* The football disability benefit increased to $5,585 in December 1994, $6,835 in April 1997, and $7,667 in April 2000.

would apply to pension plans, so it granted trustees of a pension plan broad "discretion" to make decisions, such as how to invest money and how to determine who is eligible for benefits. When it comes to pensions, this can be a straightforward decision: If the rules say that a person who works five years is eligible for a pension, then he's eligible.

But in 1987, the Supreme Court ruled that ERISA covers not only pensions but other benefits, such as medical and disability plans. Suddenly, trustees were deciding what constitutes a disability. But few players have disabilities as clear-cut as those of wide receiver Darryl Stingley, who was paralyzed during a preseason game in 1978. The more common injuries cited in disability claims—cervical-spine injuries, osteoarthritis, and knee, hip, and other joint injuries—can't be as easily measured. Debilitating problems may not show up for years and can be exacerbated by the use of painkillers and steroids, along with substance abuse.

And when it comes to depression or head injuries, determinations can be especially subjective. For years, the NFL steadfastly maintained that there was little credible research linking football with developing health problems, such as arthritis, heart disease, or cognitive impairment, in later life. This was like the tobacco industry insisting that smoking doesn't cause lung damage.

Though Congress didn't intend trustees to have so much power to decide who gets benefits, employers have blocked and tackled every effort to create rules similar to those existing in state courts. The well-publicized medical-claims denial cases in the 1990s weren't really about rogue behavior by HMOs; rather, they were merely examples of what employers and insurers could do when unfettered by state insurance laws. Benefits provided in the workplace are all shielded by ERISA, which is why the employer-plan market has been so lucrative for insurers. Disability, long-term care, life insurance—if it's provided in the workplace, even if the employee pays 100 percent of the cost, it falls under ERISA, and has no state-law protections for unfair denials or for compensatory or punitive damages.

Ironically, the very people who decided that benefits would fall under ERISA are themselves exempt from that federal law: Congress. All government employees are exempt from ERISA, which means that judges, lawmakers, police, and municipal meter readers have access to state courts to ensure their benefits, while their neighbors who are employed by private businesses do not.*

Vic Washington could have created a league of his own out of all the players the NFL denied paying disability to. Scores of other players from the 1960s to the 1980s faced similar long fights with the league over disability. Although most NFL players suffer injuries of one sort or another during their careers, only ninety of the more than seven thousand former pro players covered by the NFL disability plan were receiving football disability benefits at the time Washington was pursuing his claim in the courts.† And the total amount the league was paying in disability benefits was a mere $1.2 million a month, or just $14.5 million for the year. Of that, about $8 million came from the league's more than $5.2 billion in annual revenue, and the rest was paid from the players' pension plan, the Bert Bell/Pete Rozelle NFL Player Retirement Plan.

The NFL has maintained that the generosity of the benefits attracts unqualified applicants, which is why it has to aggressively hold the line to protect the plan. "The trustees have to make some tough calls," said a key league attorney, Douglas Ell. He maintained that many former players are too quick to blame football for causing their problems and that the league wants to avoid awarding benefits to someone "sitting in his den drinking beer and feeling sad and thinking football made him crazy. The trustees are fiduciaries, and can't just say, 'This guy was in the Hall of Fame' . . . and pay him extra money he doesn't qualify for."

---

* Employees of religious organizations are also exempt from ERISA.

† Only about half of former pro players are eligible for coverage under the plan, because they had fewer than three credited seasons, which is the minimum required.

Certainly, players from the 1970s and 1980s didn't have the gargantuan pay packages that today's stars negotiate and have therefore had an incentive to apply for football disability benefits, but that doesn't mean they're all mooches. "Injuries may not put you in a wheelchair for the rest of your life, but you still have injuries," said Randy Beisler, who was a guard and defensive end with the Philadelphia Eagles, San Francisco 49ers, and Kansas City Chiefs until a broken neck put him out of the game in 1978. Although NFL doctors concluded in the 1990s that he was 80 percent disabled, he gave up seeking benefits after his claim dragged on for five years.

NO FOUL, NO PENALTY

Another hurdle for employees and retirees: ERISA doesn't say anything about punitive damages; there are no damages for wrongful death, financial loss, or pain and suffering. With no penalties for egregious conduct, employers have little disincentive to aggressively deny claims. The worst that can happen is that the plans can later be ordered to provide the benefit.

Basically, under federal benefits law, if you mug an old man and steal his wallet, the worst that can happen is that you'll have to give the wallet back. If the old guy dies from his injuries, you won't have to do even that.

Mike Webster had been a center on the offensive line for the Pittsburgh Steelers from 1974 to 1988, then played two more seasons for the Kansas City Chiefs. He played 177 consecutive games—the fifth highest in league history—and the games took a toll. Webster suffered multiple concussions in his career, and when he retired in 1991 he was so cognitively impaired that he was unable to hold a job. According to court papers, he earned $10,000 in 1992, and $1,000 in 1993, from signing football cards and making appearances. In the 1994–95 season, the Chiefs hired him as a "conditioning coach," mostly because team officials felt sorry for him. Webster had been homeless at various points in the 1990s and slept in his car, train stations, and the Chiefs' equipment room.

In 1998, Webster applied for disability benefits, and a series of doctors, including a neurologist, a psychiatrist, and a psychologist, concluded that he was totally and permanently disabled; one noted that he suffered from a "traumatic or punch drunk encephalopathy, caused by multiple head blows received while playing in the NFL." And they all concluded that his disability arose when he was an active player, in 1991.

The NFL plan trustees, however, pointed to a medical report by a neurologist Webster had visited in 1996, who made no mention of a head injury. On this basis, the trustees concluded that there was doubt about the onset of Webster's disability, and awarded him "degenerative" benefits rather than "active" benefits, making him ineligible for payments retroactive to 1991.

Webster appealed. His case dragged on. He died in 2002, at age fifty, while his appeal was pending. In 2003, the plan denied his appeal. The administrator of Webster's estate then sued the NFL plan. In March 2005, a federal court said the plan had "abused its discretion," because even if the trustees had found a "scintilla" of evidence to support their contention that Webster wasn't disabled until 1996, that wasn't enough to ignore the mountain of evidence presented by its own doctors. The court awarded Webster's estate the value of the benefits he should have been paid.

RESUME PLAY

Vic Washington thought he had one more chance to qualify for disability benefits when the NFL and the players' union adopted a new disability plan with more flexible rules in 1993. But the NFL trustees denied his claim, providing no explanation. When Washington appealed again, the league plan hired private investigators to question his neighbors, friends, minister, and ex-wife, seeking evidence that his injuries were exaggerated and that he'd held a paid job. It scrutinized his income tax returns for evidence he'd held a job. He had not.

Washington had moved to Phoenix, where he'd played once in a college game, against Arizona State University; his mother was in a nearby nursing home. He joined the local Black Republican group and was a volunteer minister in a local Baptist church.

Finally, in 1998, the NFL plan offered Washington $400,000 to settle his longstanding disability dispute, and he accepted it, taking advice from a former player turned attorney, who was unfamiliar with ERISA law and didn't know that the NFL had just lost a critical Court of Appeals case in the Eighth Circuit in Minneapolis. A judge had ruled in favor of an ex-player who, like Washington, was denied football disability benefits because he had more than a single injury. "To require that a disability result from a single, identifiable football injury when the relevant plan language speaks of 'a football injury while an active player' is to place undue and inappropriate emphasis on the word 'a.'" The judge concluded that the NFL's decision to deny benefits was "arbitrary and capricious."

When Washington later learned of the earlier case, he felt like he'd been duped into taking the settlement, and sued the league, asking a court to set aside his settlement on the ground that the NFL had breached a fiduciary duty by not telling him of the other decision five years earlier.

A STRONG DEFENSE

Washington was up against a tough team. To tackle players who file disability claims, the NFL has long relied on Groom Law Group, a Washington, D.C., law firm whose ranks include former officials from the Labor Department, the Treasury, and other agencies.

Groom's star player in these football disputes is Douglas Ell, who has handled—and won—most of the NFL's disability suits since 1994. Like other lawyers who defend plans, he said the trustees are only doing what the plan required to protect resources for everyone. "A lot of people say, 'The evil NFL denies disability benefits,' but that's not the issue," said Ell. "It's whether the person met the terms of the plan." There's a reason the law gives the trustees the power to overrule the league's own doctors. Without the legal protections ERISA provides employers, he said, they'd have to lower the benefits they pay, because they'd be paying ineligible claims. "The people running the plans shouldn't be second-guessed by judges. We want to pay the player, not the lawyers."

With Ell heading the NFL's defense, the league has enjoyed an impressive winning streak in the courtroom. Of more than twenty lawsuits filed by retired players in the decade before Washington filed his suit, all but four were initially decided in favor of the NFL plan, and of those four, two were reversed on appeal.

Taking on the NFL, Washington faced a well-funded foe, as do most employees or retirees who challenge a pension decision: ERISA allows plan administrators to use pension assets to pay for fees associated with running the plans; these include fees to record keepers, investment managers, consultants, and . . . lawyers. Thus, the defense pockets are very deep. The NFL paid Groom Law Group $2.9 million from its pension assets in 2008, and roughly $25 million over the prior decade, though not all of that was for defense work. Former players, who may have little or no income other than Social Security disability benefits, usually crash into a wall when they try to find an attorney to represent them.

Like most people who initially flail about looking for legal help with their pensions, the players contact lawyers they pull from the Yellow Pages or Internet ads, oftentimes personal injury lawyers unfamiliar with the boggling quirks of the federal law—as evidenced by the fact that they often file the claims in state court, where they have a brief life.

Most people can't afford hourly fees for an attorney, so they seek out lawyers who take cases on a contingency-fee basis. But few attorneys represent employees and retirees in ERISA cases because the most a plaintiff can recover is the benefit, not other damages that can finance the case. Yet another quirk of ERISA: The attorneys, if successful, are awarded fees only at the court's discretion. Plaintiffs face a financial risk as well: If they lose, they could be required to pay the other side's costs. Delvin Williams, a former 49ers and Miami Dolphins running back, successfully sued the NFL for seven years' worth of back benefits, but the NFL appealed, and the Ninth Circuit not only reversed his victory but also ordered him to reimburse the NFL plan $75,000 for legal fees. The league's plan deducts $625 a month from his disability checks. His debt will be paid off in 2012.

Washington had been fortunate enough to find an attorney willing to take his case on a contingency basis, and initially, it seemed as though he would prevail. In March 2005, a federal judge in Phoenix ruled that the NFL plan had breached a duty to Washington by not disclosing relevant facts. The judge ordered the NFL plan to reconsider Washington's claim for football-related disability payments.

The league stalled, at one point saying they were suspending processing his claim until Washington sent twenty years' worth of income tax returns. The league then appealed, and in 2007 the U.S. Ninth Circuit Court of Appeals reversed the lower court's ruling and handed a victory to the NFL. Victor Washington's long game in the courts was finally over.

Washington refused to believe it. He continued to mail copies of his records and appeals to lawmakers, the media, and anyone he thought would listen. He died of heart and renal failure in a Pennsylvania hospice on New Year's Eve 2008. He was sixty-two. Elapsed time: twenty-eight years.

PENSION PARTISAN

Another quirk in ERISA ensures that most employees and retirees who dispute a benefits decision are knocked off the field before the game even starts. Before they can take a case to court, they must follow a lengthy claims-and-appeals procedure that can take months or years, trying to obtain critical documents and attempting to meet tricky deadlines.

And they must deal with the benefits clerks. Anyone who has waited on hold to talk to a benefits plan administrator at a call center in Bangalore knows what a Kafkaesque process this can be.

If anyone was up for the challenge, it was Fred Loewy. He had worked in a lab at Motorola Inc. near Phoenix, Arizona, for more than thirty-five years, analyzing systems failures in guided missiles and nuclear power plants. As a teenager in France, he had joined the partisans and fought the Nazis. So Loewy was not daunted by complex calculations or uneven battles.

But he had never tried to fight a benefits administrator. His battle began the day after he retired in 1998. Loewy (pronounced *Low-ey*) noticed that his pension had been calculated incorrectly. It wasn't a big deal—under $100 a month, reducing his pension to $1,100.

Loewy wrote a polite letter to the pension administrator, asking the staff to review their math and recalculate his pension. Instead of an answer, the next month the administrator sent him a check for $111, with no explanation. Loewy wrote again. A month later he received a check for $222, again with no explanation. This was just the beginning of a long, unhappy relationship. But before Loewy could pursue the matter further, his wife died unexpectedly, and he put aside his pension dispute while he dealt with family matters and medical claims.

He resumed his pension pursuit in December 2001, when he mailed a certified letter to the pension administrator asking it to explain how it was calculating his pension and to send copies of the pension documents they used, which are rights under ERISA.

After a month went by with no response, Loewy phoned the administrative offices and was told his letter hadn't arrived. He sent a certified letter a second time, and again got no answer. In February 2002, he called again, and was again told that his letter hadn't arrived. In March, not having heard back, he sent his letter a fourth time, and, in April, a fifth time. Finally, an administrator wrote back saying they had received his letter. In May, the administrator sent Loewy a copy of the pension-plan rules from

1998, the year Loewy retired, but didn't include an explanation of how it calculated his pension.

Loewy already had a copy of the pension rules booklet from 1998. What he really wanted was an explanation of how his benefit was being calculated. So in June he wrote to Motorola's Appeals Center, complaining that his requests for a review of his pension calculation had been "consistently ignored." They ignored him.

After five more months of phone calls and letters, Motorola mailed Loewy a copy of the 1998 plan rules, which it had already sent in June. Loewy persisted. In January 2003, he began addressing his monthly letters to Noemi Lopez, an administrator in the Scottsdale office with whom he had been corresponding. His letter was returned, unclaimed, after three delivery attempts.

In March, after another round of unanswered letters and phone calls, Loewy reached Lopez on the phone. She said she hadn't received his letter. He re-sent it. At the end of March, when he called again, Lopez said she had received his letter, and would write back regarding his pension calculation. She didn't.

A month later, at the end of April, Lopez called Loewy and said she'd received an actuary's report regarding his benefits calculation and would write him within three or four days. She never wrote back.

Plan participants have a legal right to review pension documents at the company's offices, a point noted in a booklet Motorola had distributed to employees. Inspired by this, the diminutive Loewy, clad in a three-piece, drove twenty miles from his Glendale home to Motorola's offices in Scottsdale and asked to see the pension documents and speak to Lopez. The receptionist told him he couldn't see any documents, and that Lopez was leaving the building for a meeting.

Loewy's efforts were not completely in vain. The company finally responded. Shortly after his visit to the Scottsdale office, he got a letter from Frederic Singerman, a lawyer at Seyfarth Shaw, a large law firm in Washington, D.C., which represented Motorola, saying it was too late for Loewy to file a claim. Loewy had never seen a reference to a statute of limitations, so he wrote back, asking the lawyer to provide more details about the time frame for filing an appeal.

Two weeks later, Singerman replied, stating that the appeal period had expired in 1998 after Loewy first contacted the company. He added that Loewy was free to sue, but that it was too late. "Legal action on your part is no longer timely."

The letter added that Lopez would send the plan documents for 1995 to 1998, but that Loewy's continued efforts would be in vain. "If you are aware of other documents relevant to your claim, you will need to specify them. However, we cannot permit you to use the Plan's offices to browse Plan records without limit in hopes of finding something 'useful,' and we are not aware of additional documentation that would serve to perfect your claim."

The letter stated that Lopez "has been very cooperative and patient in explaining how your benefits were calculated and why the calculation amount was correct." That month, Lopez was promoted to project manager and second vice president at Hewitt Associates, an outside administrator based in Lincolnshire, Illinois, to whom Motorola had outsourced the pension administration earlier in the year.

By this point, most retirees would have given up. But Loewy was tougher than he looked. His father, Elias, had run a radio shop in Alsace, France, until 1940, when his family was interned. An old business partner of his father's, who was in charge of the local police, helped them obtain false identity papers, and the family fled to the mountains in the south, near Montpelier. A teacher whose fiancé had been killed in the First World War taught them how to pass as Catholics. Fred, then sixteen, used his chemistry skills to make shoe polish and soap, which he traded for tobacco that he swapped for food. He also helped his father harvest chestnuts and fix radios and sewing machines. In May 1943, Fred and his older brother, Max, joined an underground partisan group, Saint-Germain-de-Calberte. Fred repaired the ragtag weapons the unit cobbled together and fought in numerous skirmishes against the Germans. In August 1944, Max was killed.

After the war, Fred, his sister, and his parents resettled in the United States. Elias's health was shattered, so they looked for someplace warm. They knew little about Phoenix, but they'd heard it needed a radio repair shop. Loewy worked in the family business until 1962, when he got a job at Motorola. He enjoyed his job as senior staff reliability engineer so much that he delayed retiring until he was almost seventy-three.

LEGAL AID

Although Motorola's lawyer said it was futile to sue, Loewy hired a lawyer anyway. He found a good ally. There are relatively few experts on pension law who represent plaintiffs; most represent employers. One of those who did happened to practice in Phoenix. Susan Martin is not only willing to take on boggling, protracted cases against deep-pocketed adversaries, but she has a soft spot for long-shot cases involving little guys being shoved around by large Washington law firms. And she'd never had a client as organized as Loewy, who showed up with every document, letter, records of phone calls, post office receipts, and Post-it notes going back to 1998, organized chronologically.

Martin is a tenacious fighter in her own right. And having raised three teenagers, she has little patience for companies that flout the rules. Martin ascertained that the pertinent pension plan rules were contained in a 1978 pension document and asked Motorola to produce it. No response. She requested it again. No response. Martin filed a motion to compel the company to produce the document. Motorola finally complied—a year after she'd requested it. An actuary who then reviewed the pension rules determined that Motorola had failed to pay Loewy the correct amount for eight years. It owed him a total of $181,500.

Motorola didn't agree with that conclusion. So Loewy, having "exhausted all his administrative remedies," as they say in ERISA, was finally free to sue. The complaint, filed in federal court in Phoenix, was a class action because, as it turned out, Motorola had miscalculated the benefits of roughly five hundred other retirees who, like Loewy, had worked past age sixty-five.

In court, Motorola maintained that it had calculated Loewy's pension correctly. Its reasoning: Just because the method it used wasn't in the rule book, the plan didn't actually have language *forbidding* the method, and thus it was allowed.

It also said it had cooperated exhaustively with Loewy, and that its benefits administrator, Hewitt, had spent 196 hours responding to Loewy's lawyer's document requests. In a sworn affidavit, Lopez said she had "repeatedly explained the benefits calculation and gave him plan documents."

As his claim wended through the court, Loewy spent his time organizing and translating his records from the war years, including a eulogy that a Protestant clergyman gave in 1944 at his brother's funeral: "Max found death in this uneven battle," the cleric said. He fell against an adversary that had outclassed him "in number and strength of weapons."

Sifting through old photographs of his days with the partisans, he came to a picture of Max in his school uniform before the war, and he shook his head. "I'm eighty. My days are numbered. I only hope to live long enough to see this suit completed."

He got his wish. The judge didn't buy Motorola's arguments, and the company agreed to settle. If Motorola had recalculated Loewy's pension in the first place, when he had asked for it, it would have been out a total of about $9,300. Having picked a fight with the wrong guy, Motorola now had to pay more than $11 million to more than one thousand retirees. The payments went out in 2006. Loewy died a few months later.

CHAPTER 12

Epitaph: THE GAMES CONTINUE

JUST DAYS AFTER the massive health care overhaul became law on March 23, 2010, large companies announced that health care reform was already costing them billions of dollars. Caterpillar was the first, announcing a $240 million hit, followed by Deere & Co., ($220 million), Verizon ($970 million), and AT&T, with the largest charge of all, $1 billion.

These statements were red meat to Fox News, where pundits concluded that this was evidence that "Obamacare" was already on its way to bankrupting the country. Former Arkansas governor Mike Huckabee, speaking on *Fox Business Happy Hour,* was troubled by the impact on Americans as a whole. "Whether it's your phone bill or the cost of a tractor, the only way the companies can survive is they're going to have to up their cost, cut their benefits, lay off employees."

Administration officials went on the defensive, frantically trying to explain that the "charges" were merely accounting effects having to do with the *retiree* health coverage, not employee health coverage, and had something to do with Medicare subsidies. But they might as well have been speaking Sanskrit to the nimble-fingered reporters rushing to get the Really Big Numbers online and into print. In the initial press frenzy, no one reported that none of the companies taking these massive charges was on the hook for a cent. The $1 billion charge that AT&T was taking? It represented the loss of a deduction for something that was costing the company nothing in the first place.

This mini-drama was just the latest example of employers crying wolf about the cost of retirement benefits, or, in this case, employer-subsidized prescription drug coverage. But it illustrates how employers continue to use the public's ignorance of accounting and the way retiree benefits work to bamboozle analysts, employees, retirees, unions, Congress, and the courts.

This Medicare charade was just the latest inning of a game that started in late 2003, when Congress was poised to add prescription drugs to the things Medicare covered. Large employers recognized an opportunity: Many were providing prescription drug coverage to retirees as part of their retiree health benefits. Their basic message to lawmakers was "Why should we continue to provide prescription drug coverage if Medicare is going to start covering it?"

Employers threatened to dump millions of retirees onto the government program unless the government sweetened the deal for them. The companies were bluffing. For one thing, they had already largely dropped prescription drug coverage for salaried retirees or had shifted much of the cost to them. And they couldn't unilaterally cancel coverage for union retirees covered by collectively bargained contracts. But lawmakers didn't know employers were making an empty threat. In any case, providing a subsidy to employers was a safe political move: They would appear to be helping retirees, being pro-business, *and* saving taxpayers money.

So lawmakers awarded employers a generous subsidy. Beginning in 2006, the companies would receive a subsidy of 28 percent of what they paid, up to $1,330 per retiree, per year, to help pay for prescription drug coverage.

That sounds straightforward, but there were windfalls within windfalls. Not only was the subsidy tax-free, but employers could deduct the government handout. In other words, they could treat the free government money as if it were coming out of company coffers, and deduct every cent. Employers did the happy dance.

Even better: The legislation said that employers would receive a subsidy of 28 percent of the *cost of the coverage,* but it didn't say the *employer's* cost. Thanks to the lack of one critical word, companies maintained they could receive the subsidy based on what the *retirees* spent. This created a situation in which, even if the retirees paid for 100 percent of the prescription drugs themselves, their former employer would get a tax-free subsidy of 28 percent of what they paid, and then deduct that amount. This combination made it possible for some employers to restructure their programs so that 100 percent of the prescription drugs was paid for by the government and the retirees.

It isn't clear whether this boondoggle was the result of a drafting error—after all, these bills tend to be nailed down in the dead of night, after a lot of horse trading among various interested parties. Or, more likely, it was the result of the stealthy fingers of lawyers and lobbyists for employers. Regardless of how it got there, this unintended benefit for employers went unnoticed until after the Medicare drug law was passed.

When the Treasury discovered it in early 2004, it complained about this gravy train, which was, as tax loopholes go, pretty impressive. The federal Centers for Medicare & Medicaid Services, among others, criticized the deduction as a windfall. From the first, it was tops on the list of execrable giveaways that some in the Treasury had their knives out for, though they didn't get a chance to take a stab at rescinding it until late in 2009.

At that point, the Obama administration was scrambling to identify dubious tax breaks it could eliminate to help offset the cost of the new health care program. The Medicare subsidy deduction was a prime candidate. Employers launched their lobbyists to try to save what some critics were calling double deduction. Echoing the threat they'd made in 2003, employers said that unless they were allowed to keep the deduction, they wouldn't be able to afford to continue to provide the prescription drug coverage and would drop it altogether. This time, the argument didn't work. The deduction would end, but not right away. Employers still had four more years to deduct the free money they received to subsidize benefits that the retirees, in many cases, were paying for.

But when health reform passed, employers correctly assumed that almost no one knew this backstory, or how the accounting worked, and were able to make some political hay.

AT&T announced that, because of health reform, it was taking a $1 billion hit. As predicted, shareholders, analysts, lawmakers, and the media assumed this meant that AT&T's health care bills would rise by $1 billion. AT&T didn't disabuse the public of this misperception.

What was really happening was that AT&T had to reverse part of the gain it had taken after the subsidy was granted in 2003. When it was awarded the subsidy, it estimated how much it would receive in government subsidies over the years, including the value of the deduction, which is recorded as a "deferred tax asset" (which simply means that when a company knows it will pay pensions, deferred comp, or other retiree benefits in the future, and deducts the amounts, it reports the value of those future deductions as an asset).

AT&T estimated how much it would receive in subsidies over the lives of its retirees and reduced its obligation by $1.6 billion in 2003.

Like many other companies, AT&T went ahead and cut prescription drug coverage for salaried retirees anyway. Less than a month after the Medicare Prescription Drug Act was passed, AT&T announced steep increases in deductibles and co-pays for prescription drugs, which shaved its costs by $440 million in 2004 alone.

Fast-forward to 2010: Because it would no longer be able to deduct the subsidy after 2013, AT&T had to reverse the value of the deduction it had recorded as a deferred tax asset. Although AT&T could continue to deduct the subsidy until 2013, accounting rules required it to recognize the change right away.

Under the alchemy that is retiree benefit accounting, AT&T, which in 2003 had estimated that the total value of the subsidy would be $1.6 billion, was now saying that losing the ability to deduct the subsidy—which it would still receive, tax-free—would erase $1 billion in deferred tax assets. Other companies reported surprisingly high charges but wouldn't say how they calculated the amounts.

Towers Watson released a "study" concluding that the loss of the deduction would cost corporate America $14 billion in profits, though it, too, was thin on details about how it summoned up that figure. The irony was that if anyone had an incentive to inflate the figure, it was the administration, since a bigger figure would make it look like it was raising more revenue to pay for healthcare reform. Its estimate: $4.5 billion.

Henry Waxman, chairman of the House Energy and Commerce Committee, was suspicious of the figures, and called for a hearing of the Subcommittee on Oversight and Investigations. He invited the CEOs of Caterpillar, Verizon, Deere, and AT&T to disclose the assumptions they used to generate their giant accounting charges.

This provided fresh fodder to critics of health care reform. "Waxman Convenes the First Death Panel" was the eye-catching headline of an online editorial on the *Wall Street Journal* Web site. "Dems Threaten Companies for Revealing Obamacare Costs" was a flash line on Fox Nation. "Are they going to pressure these big companies into not really telling the truth about the economic effects of health care on their organizations?" asked Gretchen Carlson, co-host of *Fox & Friends*. The more animated online critics regressed to fifth-grade, calling Waxman a variety of names, including Nazi, Czar, and hobbit.

Though Representative Waxman's doubts had to do with the size of the charges, not the timing, the companies, in an effective public relations move, accused the White House of playing political games with the accounting. A *Wall Street Journal* editorial pointed out (correctly) that "accounting rules require that corporations immediately restate their earnings to reflect the present value of their long-term health liabilities, including a higher tax burden." Then it pointed out (incorrectly) that the administration was trying to force companies to commit accounting fraud. "Should these companies have played chicken with the Securities and Exchange Commission to avoid this politically inconvenient reality? Democrats don't like what their bill is doing in the real world, so they now want to intimidate CEOs into keeping quiet."

Meanwhile, *Wall Street Journal* reporters, who some believe were put on earth so that they and the *Wall Street Journal* editorial writers would cancel each other out, explained—take a deep breath—that the companies were merely taking noncash charges to reflect the loss of a deduction for the projected amount of tax-free money the companies expected to receive in the future, to pay drug benefits that retirees were paying for anyway.

That less-than-snappy message was what Commerce Secretary Gary Locke tried futilely to explain to reporters seeking a sound bite. In the wake of the backlash, Waxman postponed his hearing indefinitely. But the American Benefits Council, which represents three hundred large employers and has for years diligently worked to help eviscerate retiree health benefits, hosted a media briefing "to set the record straight" and urged the White House and Congress to repeal the change. The "new tax," it said, would discourage companies from hiring new workers and lead to hardship for retirees. "The fact of the matter is, one-and-a-half to two million retirees will not be able to keep the coverage they like," concluded James Klein, the spokesman.

AT&T, which had again slashed retiree health coverage in 2009 and 2010, said it was considering dumping its prescription drug coverage altogether. That prospect cheered shareholders; following the announcement, AT&T shares closed nine cents higher.

TROUBLEMAKERS

The false alarm about the impact of health reform on retiree health benefits is just one of the latest ways employers have used the opaque retiree accounting rules to dupe a gullible public. When it comes to retiree benefits, stirring people into a frenzy about supposed problems has always been an effective way to distract them from real problems and disguise the purpose of the proposed solutions.

Employers blame the growing ratio of retirees for some of their woes. Yet as we've seen, a growing number of retirees leads to falling pension obligations. Once employees retire, their pensions stop growing, and the liability for their pension declines with each dollar paid out. If the retirees take their pensions as a one-time lump sum, the obligation for their pensions falls to zero, and liabilities are further reduced when the lump sums are worth less than the monthly pension, as is common. Lump sums also shift longevity risk to retirees, as well as investment risk, interest rate risk, and inflation risk.

"Spiraling retiree health obligations" are another often overblown peril. The reality is that many employers face little exposure to the risk of rising health care costs because they've capped the amounts they will pay. As retirees shoulder a greater share of the costs, the healthier ones get cheaper coverage elsewhere, and the sicker ones remain in the plans, driving up costs. The spiraling costs are passed on to the retirees, forcing more to drop coverage. The drop-outs and benefit cuts further reduce the obligations and generate gains. And, as counterintuitive as it seems, as retirees age, the cost for their health coverage falls. When retirees reach sixty-five, most of the costs are picked up by Medicare, and employers receive a taxpayer subsidy to pay for much of the remaining prescription drug costs.

Paying for the benefits isn't always as onerous as employers make it sound. Utilities are subsidized by ratepayers, and military contractors are subsidized by taxpayers. Salaried employees often subsidize union retirees, whose benefits are contractually bargained for and thus can't be unilaterally cut by employers. (But don't blame the unions: Employers often promise to maintain their benefits in lieu of salary increases, a deal that saves the companies money.) As in the cases of Lucent and others, many employers have the ability to tap their pensions to pay the benefits.

What's having a bigger impact on earnings at many companies is the cost for their executive deferred-compensation plans, which affect income the same way unfunded retiree health plans do: They're unfunded obligations and, without income from assets to offset their expense, they hit earnings hard. Unlike retiree health obligations, these executive obligations are steadily growing, and aren't subject to the same steady hatchet employers have taken to their retiree health plans.

The growing burden employers don't want to talk about is for their executive liabilities, which are growing steadily behind the scenes and at some companies now exceed the obligations for the rank-and-file pensions. And for all the beefing people are doing about public pensions, they don't realize that executive liabilities are the equivalent of having a public pension plan buried in the balance sheet: The liabilities can spike in the final years, are hidden, understated, growing, and underfunded (actually, they're completely unfunded, which makes them a bigger burden).

SELF-INFLICTED

Employers that freeze pensions blame their "volatility" and their unpredictable impact on their balance sheets. But if pension plans are volatile, employers should blame no one but themselves. In the 1990s, a lot of them stopped managing pension plans as long-term investment portfolios and began treating them like casinos. Pension managers shifted more of the assets into stocks to take advantage of the accounting rules that let investment income flow, indirectly, into company profits and lift earnings.

These accounting rules further encouraged risk by letting companies use hypothetical, or assumed, rates of return for the assets in the pension plans, rather than the actual returns, when calculating the pension plan's impact on company earnings. Consequently, any investment, regardless of quality or risk—leases in overbuilt strip malls, timber rights, dodgy bonds, cash, or the company's own stock—can provide a guaranteed "return" of

8 percent to 10 percent, or whatever assumed rate of return the employer adopts. On paper, anyway.

These rules give pension managers a false sense of security because they delay the impact of the investment losses. With no immediate consequences for bad investment decisions in the pension plans, it's not surprising that the percentage of equities in pension plans doubled, from 35 percent of assets in the early 1990s to more than 60 percent by 1999, a level that remains today.

Companies should have learned their lesson when the tech bubble burst in 2000, ushering in a grinding three-year bear market. Pension plans lost billions, but many companies could draw on their stockpiled credits to delay the impact on earnings. These stockpiles were quickly depleted, which led to a frenzy of pension freezes.

Thanks to double-digit returns during the ensuing mortgage bubble, combined with gains from pension cuts, the plans were collectively fully funded by 2007. But pension managers had no margin for error. The percentage of plan assets in stock still exceeded 60 percent, and when the subprime crisis arrived in late 2008 and 2009, it erased as much as one-third of the assets in pension plans.

By then, employers had already consumed the huge cushions of surplus and had used up the stockpile of credits. Their solution: Many that hadn't already done so froze their plans.

This ability to cut pensions when the plans had investment losses effectively shifted the investment risk to employees and retirees. It's a trend that has upended the risk-reward trade-off in retirement plans: In 401(k)s, employees bear the investment risk but also keep all the upside. In pensions, employers are supposed to bear the investment risk and keep the upside. Not anymore.

The real problem with pensions isn't "volatility." It's that the accounting rules enable employers to gamble with retirees' money and then shift the risk to them. And if the plans collapse altogether, companies can shift the risk to the PBGC.

Having shot off their own toes, employers are now seeking "funding relief," which would enable companies with weak pension plans to delay putting money into them: Forcing them to contribute to their pensions, they say, will divert precious cash they need to avoid layoffs, hire new workers, and create more jobs.

Their argument, some version of which has been around since the dawn of ERISA funding rules sounds plausible to many lawmakers on both sides of the aisle. But companies seeking funding relief fail to acknowledge that most of their current woes are self-inflicted. They took on too much risk but failed to fund when the party inevitably wound down. They withdrew too much money—and in many cases paid their executives too much compensation—instead of contributing to the pension plans for retirees. Their pleas for funding relief are little different from the banks asking for bailouts after their own risky lending practices and financial shenanigans brought the economy to its knees.

Companies in financial trouble, and with chronically deficit-riddled pensions—notably automakers and steelmakers—are the ones pushing most aggressively for funding relief, though they're the very companies that shouldn't get it. Likewise, financially troubled companies with *well-funded* plans don't need relief, either: What's really needed is laws that make it tougher for companies to terminate their pensions to capture the surplus money.

Healthy companies with well-funded pensions certainly don't need "relief." Many are sitting on record amounts of cash and are happy to contribute billions to their plans. The contributions are deductible and grow tax-free, while the expected investment returns provide a guaranteed lift to profits. Because remember: If the investments were outside the pension plan, the only way to get income from them would be to sell them, pay taxes on the gains, and report what's left as income. Add to these tax benefits the variety of ways employers can tap the assets and the pension plan looks like a pretty nice place to park money. And, as the ERISA Advisory Council demonstrated in their meeting in 1999, the surplus is never really locked up.

What these healthy companies with healthy pensions really want is the ability to stuff even more money into their pension plans, which they're prevented from doing. Congress enacted the full funding limit in 1987 to prevent employers from using their pension plans as tax shelters. It prohibits employer contributions if assets exceed 150 percent of the current liability. Employers have lobbied to undo this regulation ever since.

Bottom line: When it comes to funding rules, employers don't want to be forced to contribute, yet they also want to be able to contribute as much as they'd like. They argue that these freedoms would enhance retirement security. We've seen how well the current laws work. These "solutions" would only lead to more of the same.

Another reality check: Analysts' reports on the state of pension funding, which employers, lawmakers, and the media routinely cite, overstate the amount of underfunding. The funding figures come from SEC filings, which include the value of executive pensions and foreign pensions. These are typically unfunded, which brings down the funding percentages, thus making the supposed "underfunding" of employee pension plans in the United States appear worse than it is.

BAD PLAN

As employers phase out pensions, 401(k)s are becoming the dominant way to save. But 401(k)s won't save the day. Many excellent books have been written about the inadequacies of these plans. They've already proven to be failures for young and lower-paid workers, who don't participate, contribute too little, and then spend whatever they have saved when they change jobs.

Even middle-class workers who diligently save are unlikely to accumulate enough to support them in retirement. The plans may be loaded with employer stock that employees are locked into, and the accounts are collections of investing accidents that are even less likely to survive the inevitable market meltdowns. At the end of the day, 401(k)s have been a boon primarily for high-income employees, who can afford to save, and who simply move existing assets into tax-sheltered retirement plans.

These deficits have been well documented. They aren't the only ones. Like pensions, 401(k)s have a hidden history, and a darker side. That's why the "solutions" to improve 401(k)s won't work.

For one thing, despite the 401(k) plan's image as a democratic savings plan for the masses, it was never intended to be a savings vehicle for the rank-and-file. Employers first set up 401(k)s in the early 1980s so managers could defer their bonuses. The IRS stepped in, saying that taxpayers shouldn't be subsidizing a discriminatory system. To keep the tax breaks, the plans had to cover a broad group of the rank-and-file.

If the IRS had said "all employees," or "all employees whose last names begin with the letters P through Z," there would be no question about who could or could not participate in the 401(k). But, as we've seen, employers took advantage of loopholes in the discrimination rules to exclude millions of low-paid workers, provide them with less generous contributions, and make it hard to join the plan and build benefits. In short, many companies have continued to manage 401(k)s for the benefit of the highly paid.

With this in mind, consider the employers' proposals to increase participation among the lower-paid. One is "automatic enrollment," enacted in the 2006 Pension Protection Act, which was sold as a way to include participation among the low-paid, because employees are automatically signed up unless they opt out. As long as employers merely *offer* automatic enrollment (even if low-paid employees opt out) and contribute 3 percent to their accounts, the plans don't have to pass discrimination tests.

In the abstract, automatic enrollment sounds great. But plug in some real numbers and the picture isn't so rosy. For a nurse's aide making

$20,000 a year, the 3 percent contribution will cost the employer just $600. That won't exactly break the bank. But employers are now lobbying for "relief" from the mandated 3 percent contribution, citing hard times. They still want to have the safe harbor from the discrimination rules, though.

They also continue to lobby for a repeal of the contribution limits, currently $16,500 a year for an employee, saying that this would increase retirement savings. It would—for the highly compensated employees who are already saving. Employers would also benefit, because more of a highly paid employee's savings would be in the 401(k) rather than the unfunded deferred-comp plan.

But how would allowing the highest-paid employees to save more—including those with far more lucrative deferred-compensation plans—improve savings rates for the low-paid? Employers' answer: By giving executives more of a stake in the small-fry 401(k), they're more likely to maintain it, not eliminate it altogether.

Not likely. Employers enjoy too many benefits from 401(k) plans.

ESOPs FABLES

We saw in Chapter 1 how many 401(k)s were created to enable companies to capture surplus money from pensions they terminated: By setting aside 25 percent of the surplus in a replacement plan, like a 401(k), they could pay only a 20 percent tax on the rest of the money, and keep it.

Companies then began using employee stock ownership plan (ESOP) assets to fund their contributions to 401(k)s, an arrangement called a KSOP. Since the early 1990s, more than a thousand companies, including Marriott, McKesson, Bank of America, Verizon, Sears, McDonald's, Parker Hannifin, Procter & Gamble, Abbott Labs, and Ford, have quietly adopted this new hybrid structure.

One way this works: An employer that wants to build a factory might borrow $100 million from a bank, use it to buy $100 million of its own shares, and contribute the shares to an ESOP. The ESOP repays the bank, and the employer contributes an equal amount to the ESOP. The employer than taps the shares to contribute to employees' 401(k) accounts.* By funneling loan money through ESOPs, employers can deduct both the principal and interest on their loan repayments, reducing borrowing costs by as much as 40 percent. KSOPs provide employers with an additional tax break: They can deduct the dividends on the company stock they contribute to 401(k)s, a move worth tens of millions of dollars a year to large companies. KSOPs demonstrate the dual purpose retirement plans often have: They enable employers to get low-cost loans while inexpensively funding their retirement plans.

There's nothing inherently wrong with a company trying to maximize its tax savings, but it isn't always a win-win situation for employees. Like the hybrid pensions companies were adopting in the 1990s, these hybrid 401(k)s provide benefits to the employers, sometimes at the expense of employees.

More than 10 percent of the total assets in 401(k)s is invested in employers' own stock, and at some companies the percentage of employer stock in 401(k)s is even higher, which leaves employees dangerously exposed to the fate of their company and industry. If a money manager put that much of a pension plan's assets into a single stock, he'd be fired for idiocy and sued for violating fiduciary standards. But retirement savings plans—where the employees bear all the risk—are exempt from "diversification rules" that make it illegal to invest more than 10 percent of a pension plan's assets in the employer's own securities. This lack of diversification led to some spectacular debacles, including the $1.2 billion employees at Enron lost when the tech bubble burst.

---

* These are called "leveraged" ESOPs, to distinguish them from ESOPs used by owners of small, privately held companies to buy out the owners' shares.

RISK DIFFERENTIAL

The miracle of the 401(k) was again put to the test in 2008. During the worst market meltdown since the dawn of 401(k)s, fifty million workers lost a total of at least $1 trillion in their 401(k)s when the market cratered in 2008.

Jacqueline D'Andrea, of Henderson, Nevada, was among them. She lost more than 60 percent of the 401(k) savings she'd built over a decade as a manager at Wal-Mart. Her account had grown to almost $20,000 by the beginning of 2008. By the end of the year it had fallen to $6,000. When she lost her job in May 2009, D'Andrea, forty-eight, cashed out her account to pay for living expenses until her unemployment check kicked in. She's learned her lesson, she says: If she ever has a job again that offers a 401(k), she'll steer clear. "It's too risky," she says. Other Wal-Mart employees did better, but, overall, the 1.2 million employees in the retailer's 401(k) retirement plan lost 18 percent as the market plunged. Even the employee discount isn't going to make up for that.

The outcome was different in the corner office. Chief executive H. Lee Scott Jr.'s supplemental retirement savings plan had a guaranteed return of 6.6 percent, which added $2.3 million to his account during the investment storm, bringing the total to $46.7 million.

Employees are expected to bear all the investment risk in their 401(k)s, but when it comes to the executive equivalent of 401(k)s, their deferred-comp plans, that isn't always the case. The same year that employees were losing upward of 40 percent of their savings, one-quarter of top executives at major U.S. companies had *gains* in their supplemental executive retirement savings plans that year, thanks to the guaranteed returns many receive.

Comcast, the giant cable operator, provides top executives with a guaranteed 12 percent return on their supplemental savings. This produced $7.4 million in gains for executive vice president Stephen Burke in 2008, boosting his deferred-compensation account to $71 million. The

72,000 Comcast workers lost 28 percent of their savings, a total of $649 million. The average account size by the end of the year: $24,000.

"When the market went down, executives in fixed plans were happier than hogs," said a benefits consultant in Sacramento who works with employers.

One would think that at the other 75 percent of companies, which don't offer guaranteed returns for top management, the executives would face the same risk as the employees. Typically, they're given investment selections that mirror the mutual funds available in the employee 401(k) plans.

But they don't necessarily face the same risk. Even when given the same investment selections as employees, some executives managed to pick only winning funds.

Don Blankenship, CEO of Massey Energy, the controversial coal company, could have elected to allocate his supplemental savings among eight investment options, including small capitalization, international, and index mutual funds. Most of these funds were down 40 percent or more in 2008. But Blankenship's account had earnings of $909,939 that year because he apparently allocated his $27 million in savings to the only fund among the eight that had a positive return, Invesco Stable Value Trust, which was up 3.4 percent. Massey employees, who had the same fund selections as the executives, lost a total of $44 million, or 25 percent of their savings.

Top officers at Cummins Inc. also had a choice of investment options: the return on the S&P 500 Index, the Lehman Aggregate Bond Index, or 10-Year Treasury Bill + 2%. All the top executives selected only winning investment options, and had a total of $1.4 million in gains on their accounts. Meanwhile, the employees of the Indiana-based engine maker lost 12 percent on their 401(k) retirement accounts. A spokesman had an explanation for this investment success: "These are more senior people who can be expected to make more conservative investment choices than a 25 year-old in the 401(k)."

Employees who saw their retirement savings slaughtered then had another setback: Hundreds of companies stopped contributing to the 401(k) accounts at all. United Parcel Service was one of the larger ones: It suspended contribution to its 60,000 employees' 401(k) plans in 2009. The move saved the global package delivery company $190 million that year. The company blamed the "challenging worldwide economic environment" for its decision.

But the company's cost cutting didn't extend to stock awards for highly paid managers and executives: It paid a few thousand of them more than $450 million in stock awards that year, an increase of almost 10 percent over the year before. "The Compensation Committee believes that the retirement, deferred-compensation and/or savings plans offered at UPS are important for the long-term economic well-being of our employees, and are important elements of attracting and retaining the key talent necessary to compete," noted the March 2009 proxy.

UPS is part of a broader trend that hasn't been highlighted in annual reports, analyst surveys, or benefits consultants' reports to the media: Even as they limit or suspend contributions to 401(k)s, employers have been awarding a growing amount of stock compensation to their upper ranks. This isn't just stock options, whose ultimate value can be a crapshoot. Most of this is in the form of restricted shares, which have an actual, defined cash value to the recipient.

Comcast's expense for stock awards and options was $208 million in 2008, up 27 percent from the year before. The expense for the 401(k) plan: $178 million.

Honeywell employees also took a one-two blow to their 401(k)s. The 178,000 employees in the "Savings and Ownership Plan" (a KSOP) lost 29 percent of their savings. Senior managers at the engineering-and-aerospace conglomerate, however, enjoyed guaranteed returns ranging from 6.3 percent to 10 percent. The next year, in 2009, Honeywell cut its 401(k) match in half and said it wouldn't increase it "until there is greater certainty in the economy." By 2010, the expense for the 401(k) plans had fallen to $105 million from $220 million in 2008. Stock compensation expense, meanwhile, grew 28 percent over the same period, to $164 million.

Regardless of whether companies are suspending contributions, dozens are spending more on stock awards than they are for 401(k)s: Kraft Foods, State Street Bank, Dell, Marriott, and International Paper, just to name a few.

The trend hasn't been studied, but it might be worth a look. Employer contributions to 401(k) plans and awards of restricted stock have a lot in common. Both are forms of deferred compensation—i.e., pay for services rendered today that employees don't receive until later. Both are subject to vesting rules, meaning that employees and executives can forfeit the company contributions if they don't stay long enough to lock them in. Employees don't pay income taxes on contributions to 401(k)s until they withdraw the money, nor do they owe income taxes on restricted shares until they cash them in.

The chief difference, as we've seen, is that savings plans for employees don't create a liability; deferred comp and restricted shares do. So, as companies shift more of their retirement resources from employees to executives, they're also adding to their retirement obligations.

HELPLESS

The architects of today's retirement mess—consultants and financial firms—have also played a non-starring role in the public pension debacle. The difference was that, while they helped private employers hide pension cuts and exaggerate their pension woes, they also helped public employers quietly boost benefits and hide the growing liabilities.

They not only helped private companies drain assets from pension plans, but also helped public employers avoid contributing in the first place, enabling legislators and politicians to conjure up cash for popular projects, without raising taxes, and look like community heroes.

And while they were helping private employers to load their

retirement plans with stock, some consultants and financial firms duped many public pension managers into investing in complex and risky derivatives whose value later exploded, just like the subprime loans with low teaser rates that predatory lenders conned millions of homeowners into.

In the private sector, current and future retirees are bearing the brunt of the retirement heist; in the public sector, the carnage is being borne by the employees and by the communities around them.

The scapegoat game continues. Corporate employers are still blaming aging workers, retiree "legacy costs," and "spiraling" retiree health care costs for their financial woes—not their own actions that squandered billions of dollars in pension assets, their thinly masked desire to convert benefits earned by and promised to retirees into profits for executives and shareholders, and their willingness to sacrifice retiree plans, and the well-being of retirees, for short-term gains.

In the public plan sector, the scapegoats are the public employees and retirees, who are beginning to have the haunted look of victims of the Salem witch hunts. The real culprits are the self-serving politicians and officials who passed the funding buck to future generations, the consulting firms that helped them do this, and the investment banks that conned local governments into investing taxpayer-funded pensions in risky, abusive investments.

The reforms employers are pushing today are the same reforms the ERISA Advisory Council proposed when it met in 1999 to discuss the "problem" of companies having too much surplus in their pension plans: Allow employers greater latitude to use pension money to pay retiree health and layoff benefits, ease funding rules, lift funding ceilings, and lift the benefits limits in 401(k)s and pension plans. The latter recommendation would facilitate discrimination in retirement plans and enable employers to shift billions of dollars of executive liabilities into their regular pension plans. More quietly, employers and insurers are looking to ease restrictions on buying life insurance on workers, which they supposedly use to pay for retiree health benefits but actually use to finance deferred compensation.

Though characterized as reforms that would improve retirement security, employers propose them with a veiled threat. They remind lawmakers and regulators—as they have for the past thirty years—that it's a voluntary system, and they don't have to have pension or retirement plans at all. If they don't get their way, they might just pull the plug on their plans altogether. This often causes lawmakers to fall in line. (And besides, who isn't for retirement security?)

But this threat is the equivalent of a five-year-old threatening to hold his breath until he turns blue. The fact is, employers can't fold their benefits tents at will: The pensions people have earned are legally earned delayed compensation, protected by law. (Though they can be cut or frozen going forward.) Retiree health benefits for unions are protected by negotiated contracts. Employers have put pretty much everything else—future pension accruals, retiree health for salaried retirees—on the chopping block already. Or can at any moment.

And, of course, the "pull-the-plug" threat is a bit less effective when companies have already frozen their pensions. The only move left is to terminate the plans. But they aren't going to do this, either. Not yet. Unless the pension is woefully underfunded and a candidate for dumping in bankruptcy, a frozen pension plan is more valuable alive than dead.

Apart from all their other benefits for employers, frozen pension plans can function as shadow plans for executive liabilities. The investment returns offset the cost of the executive obligations, and the frozen plans often contain QSERPs, the mini–executive pensions that employers carve out within the regular pensions by taking advantage of loopholes in the discrimination rules.

The assets in pension plans have largely recovered from the market crisis losses, and, as interest rates finally begin to rise from their historic lows, liabilities will fall. The surpluses will build again and be available for a variety of corporate purposes. And unless employers withdraw the money, when the surplus is substantial enough, companies may pull the plug on their pensions and use the termination loophole to capture much of the surplus money. At that point, the only pensions left will be for the executives.

This is the hidden history of the retirement crisis—a story that hasn't made it to Fox News, the Huffington Post, or even Comedy Central. This retirement heist has produced a transfer of benefits earned by three generations of post–World War II middle-class workers to a comparatively small cohort of company executives, shareholders, and the financial industry that orchestrated the plunder.

If employers continue to control the retirement system and manage it for their own benefit, then within our lifetimes, "retirement" will inevitably revert to what it was in the 1930s and before. Society—and taxpayers—will be paying for services to support the millions of elderly, formerly middle-class Americans.

ACKNOWLEDGMENTS

IN THE LATE 1990S, I went to Washington to talk to pension experts about why companies were adopting new kinds of pension plans.

My first stop was a leading law firm where the hallways were paved with lush Oriental carpets. There, two $600-an-hour lawyers explained that companies were changing their pensions to make them better for a more mobile workforce and to improve retirement security. They're still saying this.

My next stop was the Pension Rights Center, with its battered furniture and shabby wall-to-wall. I brought a tray of lattes as a joke, because Fidelity Investments was sponsoring a campaign saying that skipping the daily Starbucks beverage would put someone on the road to retirement riches.

Karen Ferguson, the director of the center since its inception in the 1970s, had rounded up her minuscule staff and a few retiree advocates. They all got the joke but wouldn't touch the lattes because there weren't enough to go around. Someone finally rounded up some mugs and the lattes were divvied up. It was a small thing, but it distilled the spirit of the place, which under the guidance of Ferguson has done so much to improve the retirement security of Americans.

Ferguson has always generously shared her knowledge of the legislative horse trading, history, policy, tax rules, and players with every reporter who knocks on her door. Though eternally outgunned by employer groups, insurers, and the investment industry, Ferguson retains unshakable diplomacy and grace and is always a fountain of sources and legislative updates.

Norm Stein, a law professor at Drexel University, provided valuable input over the years. David Certner, an AARP policy expert, has been a valued source on legislation affecting retiree benefits. The attorneys Susan Martin, Bill Payne, and Roger McClow, who have helped thousands of retirees regain the pensions and health benefits they had earned, were amazingly generous with their time.

Many employees and retirees, some now deceased, shared their stories. Ed Beltram, with the National Retiree Legislative Network, spent many hours prospecting for retirees to interview.

I have benefitted greatly from the expertise and guidance of Joelle Delbourgo, my agent, and from the patience and professionalism of Brooke Carey and the staff at Portfolio. Nancy Cardwell provided valuable structural advice, collegues Sara Silver and Vanessa O'Connell read sections of the manuscript and were mensches, and my pet sitter, Diane Woodle, made it possible for me to spend nights and weekends at the office without worrying about the mental health and well-being of my geriatric Jack Russell, Cody.

Many of the stories in this book first appeared in some form in *The Wall Street Journal,* to which I owe the greatest debt. Every editor I worked with embraced the paper's high standards for both accuracy and fairness, including its "no surprises" policy, which requires reporters to fully apprise companies and individuals of the content about them in stories before they run.

Dan Hertzberg, the deputy managing editor of *The Wall Street Journal* for many years, was an early supporter of these stories, which "looked out for the little guy."

Dan Kelly, *The Wall Street Journal*'s only part-time Iowa farmer and full-time editor, scrutinized most of my page-one stories, which benefitted immeasurably from his intellectual nimbleness, ability to locate flaws in reasoning, and skills as a devil's advocate. ("You say here, 'They ate kittens for dinner.' What's wrong with that? Is there a law against it? Did you get their side?") If the facts and analyses got past Dan, the paper knew it had little to fear.

This book owes a huge debt to Theo Francis, who teamed with me on many of these stories, including our investigation of "dead peasant" insurance and executive compensation. Theo did groundbreaking work in mapping out and measuring the size of CEOs' deferred compensation, thanks to his unmatched ability to drill into proxy filings to extract well-hidden tidbits. A journalist of catholic interests, he actually found postretirement benefits accounting interesting.

My colleague Tom McGinty joint-ventured on several projects, which could not have been done without his data-mining mastery. I feel dumb just being around him. Thanks also to Elyse Tanouye, my one-time bureau chief, who provided unstinting support and pretends to be interested when I talk about my dog.

Dedicated to the memory of Jersey Gilbert, husband and friend. *Je had gelijk in het einde.*

NOTES

A NOTE ON SOURCES

UNLESS OTHERWISE INDICATED, all financial figures are derived from Securities and Exchange Commission and Internal Revenue Service filings. The pension figures come primarily from the pension footnotes in annual reports (Form 10-K), which include annual data on assets, liabilities, costs, assumptions, and other pertinent figures.

Form 5500, which companies file with the IRS, was the source of some of the liability figures and participant information for qualified (i.e., employee) pension plans.

Executive pensions and deferred-compensation figures and facts come from annual proxy statements (Schedule 14A). Liability figures for deferred compensation at individual companies are extrapolated from deferred tax assets in the 10-Ks and (for banks) from reports filed with the Federal Financial Institutions Examination Council (FFIEC). Liability figures for executive pension liabilities at individual companies come from, or are extrapolated from, pension data in the 10-Ks. Estimates of total executive pay obligations at U.S. companies are derived from Social Security payroll data and were confirmed.

Data for 401(k) plans at individual companies come from Form 11-Ks.

To simplify matters, I have omitted specific citations of pages and dates, but figures for a specific year come from filings made the following calendar year. For example, a figure about GE's pension obligation in 2009 will be found in the 10-K filed in 2010, just as details about the size of pensions for GE's top officers in 2010 come from the proxy filed in 2011.

I used Morningstar Document Research (formerly 10-K Wizard) for the securities filings; the IRS 5500s were obtained from the Department of Labor. A free, though somewhat limited, database of 5500s, for both pensions and 401(k) plans, is available at freeerisa.com.

As noted below, other generally nonpublic figures and facts come from court documents.

Unless indicated, comments from individuals are from interviews with the author.

CHAPTER 1: SIPHON

10 **"Rigid and irrational legal restrictions":** ERISA Advisory Council, "Report of the Working Group Studying Exploring the Possibility of Using Surplus Pension Assets to Secure Retiree Health Benefits," November 10, 1999, http://www.dol.gov/ebsa/publications/gulotta.htm.

11 **"We believe making excess pension assets":** Ibid.

14 **"This restructuring reflects":** PR Newswire, "Verizon Communications Announces Restructuring of Management Retirement Benefits," news release, December 6, 2005, http://goliath.ecnext.com/coms2/gi_0199-5008432/Verizon-Communications-Announces-Restructuring-of.html.

15 **Mark Zellers:** "Hardship Testimonies," gathered by the National Retiree Legislative Network.

16 **which are called "420 transfers":** IRS.gov.

16 **In the deal, it transferred thirty thousand employees:** Ellen E. Schultz, "Raw Deals: Companies Quietly Use Mergers, Spinoffs to Cut Worker Benefits," *The Wall Street Journal,* December 27, 2000.

17 **GE countersued the U.S. government:** Ibid.

18 **Don't put it in writing:** "Consulting in Mergers & Acquisitions," Conference on Consulting Actuaries, annual meeting, Colorado Springs, Colorado, 1996.

19 **Royal & Sun Alliance, a global London-based insurer:** *Gromala* v. *Royal & Sun Alliance,* No. 01-72196 (U.S. Court of Appeals, Sixth Circuit, 2004).

19 **got an additional $5,270 a month for life:** Ibid.

19 **Fruehauf Trailer Corp. used a trickier maneuver:** *Fruehauf Trailer Corp., Debtor Pension Transfer Corp.* v. *Beneficiaries Under the Third Amendment to Fruehauf Trailer Corporation Retirement Plan No. 003,* No. 05-1374 (U.S. Court of Appeals, Fourth Circuit, 2006).

20 **by cutting the benefits of more than 46,000 long-tenured employees:** *Engers* v. *AT&T Management Pension Plan,* No. C.A. 98-3660 (District of New Jersey, 2005).

20 **provided ASA managers with 200 percent to 400 percent:** Ibid.

20 **more than twice the amount needed to cover the pensions:** Ibid.

22 **Florida real estate developer:** Footnoted.org, March 2, 2011.

23 **Occidental Petroleum terminated its pension in 1983:** "Non-Traditional Pension Plan Terminations," Record of the Society of Actuaries, 1983, Vol. 9, No. 4.

23 **Ronald Perelman, who took over Revlon:** Ellen E. Schultz, "Pension Terminations: 80s Replay," *The Wall Street Journal,* June 15, 1999.

23 **Congress slapped a 50 percent excise tax:** Omnibus Budget Reconciliation Act of 1990.

25 **"the future of the airline is at stake":** Ellen E. Schultz, Theo Francis, and Susan Carey, "Two Airlines Press Workers for Deeper Cost Cuts—US Airways' Termination of Pilots' Pensions Could Set Example for Industry," *The Wall Street Journal,* March 18, 2003. Quote reported by Susan Carey.

25 **Few challenged the "terminate or liquidate" statement:** Ellen E. Schultz and Theo Francis, "Most Workers Are in Dark on Health of Their Pensions—US Airways Killed a Plan That Pilots Had No Inkling Was in Financial Danger," *The Wall Street Journal,* July 1, 2003.

26 **Without the information, the pilots:** Author interview with James Kenney, the pilots' actuary. See also U.S. Airways Group, Inc., United States Bankruptcy Court, Eastern District of Va., Alexandria Div., Case No. 02-83984-SSM, Ch. 11.

26 **Denis Waldron, a retired pilot in Waleska, Georgia:** "Hardship Testimonies."

27 **The maximum in 2011: $54,000:** Pension Benefit Guaranty Corp., Maximum Monthly Guarantee Tables.

27 **Don Tibbs, of Gainesville, Georgia:** "Hardship Testimonies."

CHAPTER 2: HEIST

29 **In 1997, Cigna executives held a number of meetings:** *Amara* v. *Cigna,* Defendants' Response to Plaintiff's Proposed Findings of Fact, No. 3:01-CV-2361 (MRK) (District of Connecticut, 2006).

31 **In September 1997, consulting firm Mercer signed:** *Amara* v. *Cigna.*

31 **"We've been able to avoid bad press":** Exhibits, *Amara* v. *Cigna.*

32 **The law "doesn't require you to say":** "Introduction to Cash Balance/Pension Equity plans," Meeting of the Society of Actuaries, New York, 1998.

33 **"Jan, you would be sick if you knew":** *Amara* v. *Cigna.*

34 **"immediately reduce pension costs about 25 percent to 40 percent":** A Kwasha Lipton partner, benefits conference in 1984.

34 **Bank of America was the first company to test-drive:** Bank of America's senior vice president of compensation and benefits, 1993 Conference Board meeting.

34 **"One feature which might come in handy":** Robert S. Byrne, partner, Kwasha Lipton, letter to a client, 1989.

35 **Amara's opening balance was $91,124:** *Amara* v. *Cigna.*

36 **Gerald Smit, a longtime AT&T employee:** *Engers* v. *AT&T.*

36 **"masquerading as a defined contribution":** Eric Lofgren, "The Better Alternative Defined Benefit or Defined Contribution Plans," Record of the Society of Actuaries, 1986, Vol. 12, No. 1.

38 **Jim Bruggeman was forty-nine:** Ellen E. Schultz and Elizabeth MacDonald, "Retirement Wrinkle: Employers Win Big with a Pension Shift; Employees Often Lose," *The Wall Street Journal,* December 4, 1998.

38 **Steven Langlie had spent three decades:** Ellen E. Schultz, "Problems with Pensions: What You Don't Know About the Cash-Balance Retirement Plans Can Hurt You," *The Wall Street Journal,* November 8, 1999.

39 **the giant accounting firm, made a big miscalculation:** Schultz and MacDonald, "Retirement Wrinkle."

41 **"The plan took me months to understand":** Donald Sauvigne, IBM's head of retirement benefits, 1995 actuaries' conference in Vancouver.

42 **Watson Wyatt had been marketing its "pension equity plan":** "Workforce Management: Strategic Retirement Design," *Watson Wyatt Insider* newsletter, October 1998.

42 **"It is not until they are ready to retire":** Watson Wyatt actuary, "Introduction to Cash Balance/Pension Equity Plans," Society of Actuaries, New York, October 1998.

42 **"but they are really happy":** Meeting of the Society of Actuaries, October, 1998.

42 **One service was the firm's "Aging Diagnostic":** *Watson Wyatt Insider* newsletter, October 1998.

44 **Finlay was exactly the kind of employee:** Ellen E. Schultz, "Pension Cuts 101: Companies Find Host of Subtle Ways to Pare Retirement Payouts," *The Wall Street Journal,* July 27, 2000.

47 **"it masks a lot of the changes":** William Torrie, PricewaterhouseCoopers, "Plan Design Issues: The Corporate Perspective," New York Annual Meeting, Society of Actuaries, Vol. 24, No. 3, New York, October 1998.

47–48 **"If you decide your plan's too rich":** Norman Clausen, principal, Kwasha Lipton, Society of Actuaries meeting, Colorado Springs, June 1996.

48 **Single Payment Optimizer Tool (SPOT):** Watson Wyatt client material.

49 **"Choosey Employees Choose Lump Sums!":** *Watson Wyatt Insider* newsletter, 1998.

49 **lump sums . . . shift longevity risk:** Author's analysis. The Social Security Administration has details about life expectancy at http://www.ssa.gov/history/lifeexpect.html; the Wharton School has a life expectancy calculator at http://gosset.wharton.upenn.edu/mortality/perl/CalcForm.html.

50 **General Motors, for instance, doesn't allow:** Theo Francis, "Pension Tension: Figuring Out When to Lump It," *Wall Street Journal,* March 15, 2007.

50 **about one-third of blue-collar workers:** Bureau of Labor Statistics, 2010.

50 **The Marine Engineers' Beneficial Association:** Theo Francis, "Pension Tension."

51 **Mary Fletcher, a marketing services trainer:** Author interview.

52 **During oral arguments before the Supreme Court:** *Amara* v. *Cigna,* November 30, 2010.

CHAPTER 3: PROFIT CENTER

55 **Their primary tools included the new accounting rules:** Financial Accounting Standards Board, "Employers' Accounting for Pensions," Statement of Financial Accounting Standards No. 87, 1985.

57 **"You could have real economic wealth transfers":** Julia D'Souza, John Jacob, and Barbara Lougee, "Why Do Firms Convert to Cash Balance Pension Plans? An Empirical Investigation," American Accounting Association, Annual Meeting, 2003.

58 **companies with the most pension income:** Ellen E. Schultz, "Joy of Overfunding: Companies Reap a Gain of Fat Pension Plans," *The Wall Street Journal,* June 15, 1999.

58 **Patricia McConnell, a senior managing director at Bear Stearns:** Robert McGough and Ellen E. Schultz, "How Pension Surpluses Lift Profits," *The Wall Street Journal,* September 20, 1999.

60 **Researchers at Harvard:** Daniel Bergstresser, Mihir Desai, and Joshua Rauh, "Earnings Manipulation, Pension Assumptions and Managerial Investment Decisions," *Quarterly Journal of Economics,* February 2006.

62 **The panelists put on a skit:** "Consulting in Mergers & Acquisitions" panel, Conference on Consulting Actuaries, Colorado Springs, 1996.

63 **Warren Buffett, chairman of Berkshire Hathaway:** Warren E. Buffet, "Who Really Cooks the Books?" editorial, *The New York Times,* July 24, 2002.

CHAPTER 4: HEALTH SCARE

65 **"Health care costs continue to skyrocket":** John McDonnell, CEO, McDonnell Douglas, letter to retirees, October 7, 1992.

67 **A sample from late 1991:** "Automakers Face Massive Charges," Associated Press, November 12, 1991; "Rude Awakening on Health Costs," *The Los Angeles Times,* November 13, 1991; Lee Burton and R. J. Brennan, "New Medical-Benefits Accounting Rules Seen Wounding Profits, Hurting Shares," *The Wall Street Journal,* April 22, 1992.

67 **"The Street views FAS 106 obligations":** Ethan Kra, then the chief retirement actuary at William M. Mercer, "Basics of Funding Retiree Medical," Proceedings of the Conference of Consulting Actuaries, 1996.

68 **McDonnell Douglas's pump-and-dump maneuver:** Company filings; Ellen E. Schultz, "This Won't Hurt: Companies Transform Retiree-Medical Plans into Source of Profits," *The Wall Street Journal,* October 25, 2000.

69 **"they created a piggy bank of earnings improvers":** Jack Ciesielski, "Why SFAS Is Not a Dead Issue," Vol. 3, No. 3, *The Analyst's Accounting Observer,* March 23, 1994.

70 **R.R. Donnelley, a printing company based in Chicago:** Ibid.

71 **his largest client, a Big Six accounting firm, fired him:** Jeffrey Petertil, "Ignore the Retiree Health Benefits Rule," *The Wall Street Journal,* February 21, 1992.

71 **Defense contractors and public utilities had an additional incentive:** Schultz, "This Won't Hurt."

72 **Shaklee had to take a minimum-wage midnight-shift job:** Author interview.

72 **"Just as in war, there are no winners":** Unisys Corp. Retiree Medicare Benefits Erisa Litigation, No. MDL 969, U.S. District Court, E.D., Penn., Aug. 13, 1996.

74 **Liz Rossman, Sears's vice president for benefits:** Author interview.

75 **Robert Eggleston, an IBM retiree in Lake Dallas:** Author interview.

75 **Xerox split its active and retired employees into two pools:** Company confirmed.

76 **Eugene Nathenson, a retired controller:** Author interview.

77 **William Falk, who oversaw the retiree medical consulting practice:** Conference of Consulting Actuaries, October 1998.

77 **Companies could also adopt "more aggressive assumptions":** Enrolled Actuaries meeting, Washington, D.C., March 1998.

78 **The flexibility built into the accounting rules:** For a detailed examination, see Julia D'Souza et al., "Accounting Flexibility and Income Management: The Case of OPEB Recognition," Johnson School of Management, Cornell University, 1999.

CHAPTER 5: PORTFOLIO MANAGEMENT

80 **"I guess I'm going to have to die before then":** Author interview with Margaret Jelly.

81 **Ackerman had flown corporate jets:** Author interview.

83 **Justin Freeborn, a legal-aid lawyer:** Author interview.

84 **found a note from the retired executive, with a personal:** Author interview with Audrey Ackerman.

85 **Fidelity . . . concluded that 316 retirees had mistakenly been paid:** Author interview with BP official.

85 **Craven, a widower with macular degeneration:** Author interview.

91 **Schacht made a presentation to a group:** Interviews with Lucent retirees, Henry Schacht.

92 **Howard O'Neil, who was ninety at the time:** Author interview.

93 **Parano . . . sued Lucent in small claims court:** Author interview with Joseph Parano, California; *Joseph and Susan Parano* v. *AT & T Corp.*, Case No. SCS 114017 and 114097, Small Claims Court, San Mateo, 2004.

94 **Connie Sharpe, a widow in Las Cruces, New Mexico:** Author interview.

96 **Walt Ehmer . . . chief executive of Lucent Technologies Denmark:** Author interview.

97 **Schacht later defended the bonuses:** Author interview.

CHAPTER 6: WEALTH TRANSFER

104 **GM has often claimed that its U.S. pension plans:** Ellen E. Schultz and Theo Francis, "Hidden Burden: As Workers' Pensions Wither, Those for Executives Flourish—Companies Run Up Big IOUs," *The Wall Street Journal,* June 23, 2006.

104 **board of directors of Mercantile Stores met:** Transcripts of Mercantile board meetings.

108 **total retirement payout was more than $130 million:** estimate of total by Theo Francis, Footnoted.org.

113 **executives were receiving more than one-third of all pay:** This and other details in this section are based on the author's calculations and analysis, which were confirmed by Stephen Goss, chief actuary of the Social Security Administration.

114 **"The most important contributor to higher profit margins over the past five years":** Steven Greenhouse and David Leonhardt, "Real Wages Fail to Match a Rise in Productivity," *The New York Times,* August 28, 2006. Thanks to colleague Tom McGinty for pointing this out.

CHAPTER 7: DEATH BENEFITS

116 **Just before Christmas 2008, Irma Johnson:** *Irma Johnson* v. *Amegy Bank,* No. 4:2009cv01424 (Southern District of Texas, 2009).

117 **"dead peasants insurance":** The memos were exhibits in a lawsuit in which the United States Court of Appeals for the Eleventh Circuit held that Winn-Dixie's COLI policies were a sham transaction for federal income tax purposes. *Winn-Dixie Stores, Inc.* v. *Commissioner of Internal Revenue,* No. 00-11828 (U.S. Court of Appeals, Eleventh Circuit, 2001).

121 **"Without these suicides, NCC would be running at 33%":** Exhibits provided by Mike Myers, of McClanahan, Myers, and Espey, a Houston law firm that has handled numerous COLI cases.

121 **To keep track of when employees and retirees die:** Ellen E. Schultz and Theo Francis, "Companies Tap Pension Plans to Fund Executive Benefits—Little-Known Move Uses Tax Break Meant for Rank and File," *The Wall Street Journal,* August 4, 2008.

122 **His mother died in 1998 at age sixty-two. Her family received a $21,000 benefit:** Author interview with John Reynolds.

123 **a brown envelope was left on the desk of Ken Kies:** Ellen E. Schultz and Theo Francis, "Death Benefit: How Corporations Built Finance Tool Out of Life Insurance," *The Wall Street Journal,* December 20, 2002.

124 **Ways and Means chairman Bill Archer, who had criticized janitors insurance:** Clark/Bardes Inc. proxy statement.

127 **The mass death of heavily insured executives:** Society of Actuaries meeting, Washington, D.C., 2003.

128 **The twenty-year-old was working at a Stop N Go:** Schultz and Francis, "Death Benefit."

130 **Banks took out billions of dollars' worth of this life insurance:** Bank "call reports" filed with the Federal Financial Institutions Examination Council.

131 **Insurance regulators, who often accommodate the wishes of the industry:** Disclosure information based on interviews with regulators and industry representatives.

CHAPTER 8: UNFAIR SHARES

135 **The company's effective guaranteed return on the contribution in the first year:** Schultz and Francis, "Companies Tap Pension Plans"; calculation by Theo Francis.

141 **Lorenzo Walker, one of the warehouse workers at Hugo Boss:** Author interview.

143 **One employee got a pension increase:** *Gromala* v. *Royal & Sun Alliance.*

CHAPTER 9: PROJECT SUNSHINE

148 **"The Company is not committed to maintenance of a retiree's standard of living":** Internal company memos, Ellen E. Schultz, "Retirees Found Varity Untruthful," *The Wall Street Journal,* November 6, 2000.

148 **"death of all existing retirees":** Company memo.

CHAPTER 10: TWILIGHT ZONE

160 **He thought the job was pretty decent:** Author interviews with GenCorp retirees, including Ed Peksa, Kenneth Bottolfs, Mabel Kramer, and John Van Dyke; court records in *Wotus* v. *Gencorp,* 5:00 cv 2604 (N.D. Ohio).

170 **Asarco, was suing him and other retirees in federal court:** *Asarco* v. *United Steelworkers of America,* 03-CV-1297-PHX-FJM, 2005 U.S. Dist. Lexis 20873 (D. Ariz. 2005); Author interview with Edward C. Yarter et al.

172 **Rexam, a maker of cans for beverages:** *Rexam, Inc.* v. *United Steelworkers of America,* No. 03-2998, 31 E.B.C. 2562 (D. Minn. 2003), later proceedings, 2005 WL 2318957 (D. Minn. 2005).

174 **"They shopped more than we did, Judge":** *Crown Cork & Seal* v. *United Steelworkers of America,* 03-CV-1381, 32 E.B.C 1950, 2004 U.S. Dist. Lexis 760 (W. D. Pa. 2004), related to *Lawhorn* v. *Crown,* No. 1:03-CV-461 (S.D. Ohio 2003).

175 **"We will file in federal court against you bastards":** *ACF Industries* v. *Chapman,* 4:03CV1765 HEA, reported decision at 2004 U.S. Dist. Lexis 27245 (E.D. Mo. 2004), related to *Chapman* v. *ACF Indus.,* 3:04-0062, 430 F. Supp. 2d 570 (D. W. Va. 2006).

CHAPTER 11: IN DENIAL

177 **but the company denied his claim:** Brief of Amici Curiae, National Black Lung Association and Appalachian Citizens' Law Center, Inc., *Lawyer Disciplinary Board* v. *Douglas A. Smoot,* Supreme Court of Appeals of West Virginia, No. 34724.

180 **protected by steel fences:** Ken Ward Jr., "The Dark Lord of Coal Country," *Rolling Stone,* November 30, 2010.

180 **And he gets to keep a 1965 blue Chevrolet truck:** Compensation details from the company proxy statement.

182 **"I took every play like it was my last play":** Author interview.

183 **Focusing on the word "a," the arbitrator said:** *Victor A. Washington* v. *Bert Bell/Pete Rozelle NFL Player Retirement Plan, et al.,* Nos. 05-16366, 05-16533, 05-16845 (U.S. Court of Appeals, Ninth Circuit, 2007).

185 **only ninety . . . former pro players covered by the NFL disability plan:** Ellen E. Schultz, "A Hobbled Star Battles the NFL: Doctors Say Football Left Victor Washington 'Totally Disabled.' Two Decades Later, the League Still Disagrees," *The Wall Street Journal,* December 3, 2005.

186 **"Injuries may not put you in a wheelchair for the rest of your life":** Author interview with Randy Beisler.

186 **Mike Webster had been a center on the offensive line:** *Sunny Jani, as Administrator of the Estate of Michael L. Webster, deceased,* v. *Bert Bell/Pete Rozelle NFL Player Retirement Plan, et al.,* No. 1:04-cv-01606-WDQ U.S. District Court for the District of Maryland, 2005.

188 **Douglas Ell, who has handled—and won:** Author interview with Douglas Ell.

189 **The NFL paid Groom Law Group $2.9 million:** IRS Form 5500.

190 **Delvin Williams, a former 49ers and Miami Dolphins running back:** Author interview with Delvin Williams.

191 **As a teenager in France, he had joined the partisans:** Author interview with Loewy.

191 **Instead of an answer, the next month the administrator sent:** *Fred Loewy et al.* v. *Motorola, Inc. Pension Plan et al.,* No. CV 03-2284 (District of Arizona, 2004).

CHAPTER 12: EPITAPH

198 **happy dance:** Homage to Gail Collins.

198 **companies maintained they could receive the subsidy:** Ellen E. Schultz and Theo Francis, "U.S. Drug Subsidy Benefits Employers," *The Wall Street Journal,* January 4, 2004.

204 **shift the risk to the PBGC:** For a detailed look at the most prominent instances of companies passing the buck to the PBGC, see Fran Hawthorn, *Pension Dumping: The Reasons, the Wreckage, the Stakes for Wall Street* (New York: Bloomberg, 2008), and articles by Mary Williams Walsh of *The New York Times,* who has also provided extensive coverage of the fate of pension plans in bankruptcies, particularly at automakers and airlines.

206 **Many excellent books have been written:** Among them: Teresa Ghilarducci, *When I'm Sixty-four: The Plot Against Pensions and the Plan to Save Them* (Princeton: Princeton University Press, 2008); Karen Ferguson and Kate Blackwell, *Pensions in Crisis: Why the System Is Failing America and How You Can Protect Your Future* (New York: Arcade Publishing, 1995). This lucid and readable book focuses on pensions, but it has an excellent discussion of the problems with 401(k)s and other defined contribution plans, and it clearly explains "discrimination" rules. Recent reports on 401(k)s include *The Failure of the 401(k),* a report by Robert Hiltonsmith, a policy analyst at Demos, November 2010: http://www.demos.org/pubs/thefailureofthe401(k).pdf. See also *Private Pensions: Some Key Features Lead to an Uneven Distribution of Benefits,* GAO-11-333, March 2011, http://www.gao.gov/new.items/d11333.pdf. The Congressional Research Service has done a number of studies on 401(k)s, including *401(k) Plans and Retirement Savings: Issues for Congress,* July 2009. Its reports can be found on the CRS Web site: http://www.pensionrights .org/report-topic-areas/defined-contribution-plans-such-401ks-and-iras.

209 **reducing borrowing costs by as much as 40 percent:** Analysis by Theo Francis; Ellen E. Schultz and Theo Francis, "Companies' Hot Tax Break: 401(k)s—Why Firms Stuff Plans with Stock," *The Wall Street Journal*, February 11, 2002.

210 **fifty million workers lost a total of at least $1 trillion in their 401(k)s:** Center on Retirement Research, Boston College.

210 **D'Andrea, forty-eight, cashed out her account:** Author interview.

210 **one-quarter of top executives at major U.S. companies had *gains*:** Analysis by Tom McGinty, based on Compustat data; Ellen E. Schultz and Tom McGinty, "Executives Enjoy 'Sure Thing' Retirement Plans, *The Wall Street Journal,* December 16, 2009.

211 **"executives in fixed plans were happier than hogs":** Bob Nienaber, director, benefitRFP, Sacramento, California, telephone conversation with author.

214 **In the public plan sector:** For a history and analysis of how public plans can become seriously underfunded, see Roger Lowenstein, *While America Aged: How Pension Debts Ruined General Motors, Stopped the NYC Subways, Bankrupted San Diego, and Loom as the Next Financial Crisis* (New York: Penguin Press, 2008). See also Mary Williams Walsh's extensive coverage of public pensions in *The New York Times.*

INDEX